EVERYDAY
SlowCooker
& ONE DISH RECIPES

For other *Taste of Home* books and products, visit **ShopTasteofHome.com**.

EDITORIAL
EDITOR-IN-CHIEF Catherine Cassidy
CREATIVE DIRECTOR Howard Greenberg
EDITORIAL OPERATIONS DIRECTOR Kerri Balliet

MANAGING EDITOR/PRINT & DIGITAL BOOKS Mark Hagen
ASSOCIATE CREATIVE DIRECTOR Edwin Robles Jr.

EDITOR Christine Rukavena
ART DIRECTORS Maggie Conners, Raeann Sundholm
LAYOUT DESIGNER Courtney Lovetere
EDITORIAL PRODUCTION MANAGER Dena Ahlers
COPY CHIEF Deb Warlaumont Mulvey
COPY EDITORS Dulcie Shoener, Joanne Weintraub
CONTENT OPERATIONS ASSISTANT Shannon Stroud
EDITORIAL SERVICES ADMINISTRATOR Marie Brannon

FOOD EDITORS James Schend; Peggy Woodward, RD
RECIPE EDITORS Mary King; Jenni Sharp, RD; Irene Yeh

TEST KITCHEN & FOOD STYLING MANAGER Sarah Thompson
TEST COOKS Nicholas Iverson (lead),
Matthew Hass, Lauren Knoelke
FOOD STYLISTS Kathryn Conrad (lead),
Shannon Roum, Leah Rekau
PREP COOKS Megumi Garcia, Melissa Hansen,
Bethany Van Jacobson, Sara Wirtz

PHOTOGRAPHY DIRECTOR Stephanie Marchese
PHOTOGRAPHERS Dan Roberts, Jim Wieland
PHOTOGRAPHER/SET STYLIST Grace Natoli Sheldon
SET STYLISTS Stacey Genaw, Melissa Haberman,
Dee Dee Jacq, Nancy Seaman
PHOTO STUDIO ASSISTANT Ester Robards
CONTRIBUTORS Mark Derse (photographer),
Nancy Seaman (set stylist)

EDITORIAL BUSINESS MANAGER Kristy Martin
EDITORIAL BUSINESS ASSOCIATE Samantha Lea Stoeger

EDITOR, *TASTE OF HOME* Jeanne Ambrose
ASSOCIATE CREATIVE DIRECTOR, *TASTE OF HOME* Erin Burns
ART DIRECTOR, *TASTE OF HOME* Kristin Bowker

BUSINESS
VICE PRESIDENT, GROUP PUBLISHER Kirsten Marchioli
PUBLISHER, *TASTE OF HOME* Donna Lindskog
**GENERAL MANAGER, TASTE OF HOME
COOKING SCHOOL** Erin Puariea
**EXECUTIVE PRODUCER, TASTE OF HOME ONLINE
COOKING SCHOOL** Karen Berner

THE READER'S DIGEST ASSOCIATION, INC.
PRESIDENT AND CHIEF EXECUTIVE OFFICER Bonnie Kintzer
VICE PRESIDENT, CHIEF OPERATING OFFICER, NORTH AMERICA
Howard Halligan
CHIEF REVENUE OFFICER Richard Sutton
CHIEF MARKETING OFFICER Leslie Dukker Doty
VICE PRESIDENT, CONTENT MARKETING & OPERATIONS
Diane Dragan
SENIOR VICE PRESIDENT, GLOBAL HR & COMMUNICATIONS
Phyllis E. Gebhardt, SPHR
VICE PRESIDENT, BRAND MARKETING Beth Gorry
VICE PRESIDENT, CHIEF TECHNOLOGY OFFICER
Aneel Tejwaney
VICE PRESIDENT, CONSUMER MARKETING PLANNING
Jim Woods

COVER PHOTOGRAPHY
PHOTOGRAPHY Mark Derse
FOOD STYLIST Leah Rekau
SET STYLING Nancy Seaman

© 2015 RDA Enthusiast Brands, LLC
1610 N. 2nd St., Suite 102, Milwaukee WI 53212-3906

INTERNATIONAL STANDARD BOOK NUMBER:
978-1-61765-394-0
INTERNATIONAL STANDARD SERIAL NUMBER:
1944-6382
COMPONENT NUMBER:
119400033H00

PRINTED IN CHINA
1 3 5 7 9 10 8 6 4 2

PICTURED ON THE FRONT COVER:
Peachy Baby Back Ribs, page 48;
Oven Fish and Chips, page 227;
Pink Grapefruit Cheesecake, page 86;
Caribbean Chipotle Pork Sliders, page 84.

PICTURED ON THE BACK COVER:
Apricot Pork Roast with Vegetables, page 54;
Smoked Salmon Quesadillas with
Creamy Chipotle Sauce, page 154;
Chicken Cordon Bleu Pasta, page 192.

Table of Contents

Slow Cooker

Stovetop Suppers

Oven Entrees

Bonus Chapter:

Slow Cooking 101

The original slow cooker, introduced in 1971 by Rival, was called the Crock-Pot. It's still so successful that the term "slow cooker" and the name Crock-Pot are often used interchangeably—but Crock-Pot is a brand of the beloved slow cooker appliance.

Most slow cookers have two or more settings. Food cooks faster on the high setting, but the low setting is ideal for all-day cooking or working with less tender cuts of meat. Slow cooker recipes in this book refer to cooking on either high or low settings. The warm setting keeps food hot and tasty until it's ready to serve.

In general, one hour of cooking on high equals roughly two hours of cooking on low. Read on for more useful tips and soon you'll be slow-cooker savvy.

Advantages of Slow Cooking

CONVENIENCE. Slow cookers provide people with the ease of safely preparing meals while away from home. The appliances are readily available and budget-friendly.

HEALTH. As people have sought out more nutritious food choices to improve their health, slow cooking has gained popularity. Low-temperature cooking retains more vitamins in foods, and leaner cuts of meat become tender in the slow cooker without added fats. Lower-sodium and lower-fat versions of many canned goods are available, which can help you create even lighter, healthier meals. And, for many busy folks, knowing that a healthy meal is waiting at home helps them avoid the temptation of the drive-thru after work.

FINANCIAL SAVINGS. A slow cooker uses very little electricity because of its low wattage. For instance, it would cost about a quarter to operate a slow cooker for a total of 10 hours. If you cook a pork roast for only 2 hours in an oven instead of using the slow cooker for 10 hours, it would cost you seven to 10 times as much (depending on whether the oven is gas or electric). Also, slow cookers do not heat up the kitchen as ovens do, which saves on summertime cooling costs.

Handy icons
throughout the book!

OVEN-FRIED CHICKEN DRUMSTICKS, PAGE 184

EAT SMART

Recipes are lower in calories, fat and sodium. Most include Diabetic Exchanges. More than 80 recipes offer classic down-home flavor while being better for you!

SWEET AND SPICY ASIAN MEATBALLS, PAGE 91

FREEZE IT

Freezer-friendly recipes include directions for freezing and future use. Stretch your kitchen time with more than 40 recipes that make it a breeze to plan future meals.

know when it's
DONE!

→ **145°F**

- Medium-rare beef and lamb roasts
- Fish

→ **160°F**

- Medium beef and lamb roasts
- Pork
- Egg dishes

→ **165°F**

- Ground chicken and turkey

→ **170°F**

- Well-done beef and lamb roasts
- Chicken and turkey that is whole or in pieces

Purchasing a Slow Cooker

Slow cookers range in price from $20 to more than $200 and are available in sizes from 1½ to 7 quarts. Decide on a price range that fits your budget and choose a size appropriate for your family (see chart below).

Most slow cooker inserts are ceramic, but some pricier models have aluminum inserts that let you brown meats in them before slow cooking. For convenience, look for inserts that are dishwasher-safe.

Slow cookers are available in round and oval shapes. If you plan to prepare roasts in the slow cooker, you may wish to consider an oval shape. If stews and soups are your forte, a round slow cooker is perfect for your cooking needs.

SLOW COOKER SIZES	
HOUSEHOLD SIZE	**SLOW COOKER CAPACITY**
1 to 2 people	2 to 3½ quarts
3 to 4 people	3½ to 4½ quarts
4 to 5 people	4½ to 5 quarts
6 or more people	5 to 7 quarts

Cooking Basics

- While slow cooker models vary, they usually have at least two settings, low (about 180°) and high (about 280°). Some models also have a keep-warm setting.

- The keep-warm setting is useful if you plan to use the slow cooker to serve hot foods while entertaining. Some slow cookers will automatically switch to a keep-warm setting after cooking. This provides added convenience and helps you avoid overcooking the food while you're away from home.

- A range in cooking time is provided to account for variables such as thickness of meat, fullness of the slow cooker and desired finished temperature of the food being cooked. As you grow familiar with your slow cooker, you'll be able to judge which end of the range to use.

- New slow cookers tend to heat up more quickly than older ones. If you have an older model and your recipe directs to cook on low, you may wish to cook on high for the first hour to ensure food safety.

- Old slow cookers can lose their efficiency and may not achieve proper cooking temperatures. To confirm safe cooking temperatures, review the steps of Slow Cooker Temperature Check on page 9.

- To learn more about specific models, check online or in reputable consumer magazines for product reviews.

Preparing Foods for the Slow Cooker

BEANS. Dried beans can be tricky to cook in a slow cooker. Minerals in the water and variations in voltage affect various type of beans in different ways. Always soak dried beans prior to cooking. Soak them overnight or place them in a Dutch oven and add enough water to cover by 2 inches. Bring to a boil and boil for 2 minutes. Remove from the heat, cover and let stand for 1 to 4 hours or until softened. Drain and rinse beans, discarding liquid. Sugar, salt and acidic ingredients such as vinegar interfere with the beans' ability to cook and become tender. Add these ingredients only after the beans are

fully cooked. Lentils and split peas do not need soaking.

COUSCOUS. Couscous is best cooked on the stovetop rather than in the slow cooker.

DAIRY. Milk-based products tend to break down during slow cooking. Items like milk, cream, sour cream or cream cheese are best added during the last hour of cooking. Cheeses don't generally hold up during the slow cooker's extended cooking time and should be added near the end of cooking. Condensed cream soups generally hold up well in the slow cooker..

FISH & SEAFOOD. Fish and seafood cook quickly and can break down if cooked too long. They are generally added to the slow cooker toward the end of the cooking time to keep them at optimal quality.

MEATS. Meat may be browned before adding to the slow cooker. While browning is not necessary, it adds to the flavor and appearance of the meat and allows you to drain off the fat. Cut roasts over 3 pounds in half before placing in the slow cooker to ensure even cooking. Trim off any excess fat. Fat retains heat, and large amounts of fat could raise the temperature of the cooking liquid, causing the meat to overcook.

OATS. Quick-cooking and old-fashioned oats are often interchangeable in recipes. However, old-fashioned oats hold up better in the slow cooker.

PASTA. If added to a slow cooker when dry, pasta tends to become very sticky. It's better to cook it according to the package directions and stir it into the slow cooker just

before serving. Small pastas such as orzo and ditalini may be cooked in the slow cooker, however. To keep them from becoming mushy, add during the last hour of cooking.

RICE. Converted rice is ideal for all-day cooking. If using instant rice, add it during the last 30 minutes of cooking.

VEGETABLES. Firm vegetables like potatoes and carrots tend to cook more slowly than meat. Cut these foods into uniform pieces and place on the bottom and around the sides of the slow cooker. Place the meat over the vegetables. During the last 15 to 60 minutes of cooking, add tender vegetables like peas and zucchini, or ones you'd prefer to be crisp-tender.

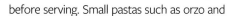

COOK TIMES

Conventional Oven
15 to 30 minutes

Slow Cooker
Low: 4 to 6 hours
High: 1½ to 2 hours

Conventional Oven
35 to 45 minutes

Slow Cooker
Low: 6 to 8 hours
High: 3 to 4 hours

Conventional Oven
50 minutes or more

Slow Cooker
Low: 8 to 10 hours
High: 4 to 6 hours

Thickening
Stews & Sauces

Quick-cooking tapioca can be used as a thickener for stews. Add it along with other ingredients at the beginning of cooking.

To thicken juices at the end of cooking, use flour or cornstarch. Mix flour or cornstarch with some cold water until smooth. Stir into the slow cooker. Cover and cook on high for 30 minutes or until the cooking juices are thickened.

Or, strain cooking juices and place in a saucepan. Mix flour or cornstarch with some cold water until smooth. Stir into juices. Bring to a boil; cook and stir for 2 minutes or until thickened.

Converting Recipes for the
Slow Cooker

Almost any recipe that bakes in the oven or simmers on the stovetop can be converted for the slow cooker. Here are some guidelines.

- Before converting recipes, check the manufacturer's guidelines for your particular slow cooker. Find a recipe that is similar to the one you want to convert and use it as a guide. Note the amount and size of meat and vegetables, heat setting, cooking time and amount of liquid.

- Since there is no evaporation, adjusting the amount of liquid in your recipe may be necessary. If a recipe calls for 6 to 8 cups of water, try starting with 5 cups. Conversely, recipes should include at least a little liquid. If a recipe does not include liquid, add ½ cup of water or broth.

- In general, 1 hour of simmering on the stove or baking at 350°F in the oven is equal to 8 to 10 hours on low or 4 to 6 hours on high in a slow cooker. Check the chart at top left.

- Cornstarch, flour and tapioca are often used to thicken stews and sauces in the slow cooker. See the information at left for more details.

Useful Handles for Lifting Food

Layered dishes or meat loaves are easier to get out of the slow cooker with foil handles. Here's how:

For a 3-qt. slow cooker, cut three 20x3-in. strips of heavy-duty foil (or 25x3-in. for larger slow cookers). Or cut 6-in.-wide strips from regular foil and fold in half lengthwise. Crisscross the strips so they resemble the spokes of a wheel.

Place the strips on the bottom and up the sides of the slow cooker insert. Let strips hang over the edge of the slow cooker. Coat strips with cooking spray.

Place food in the center of the strips and lower until the food rests on the bottom of the slow cooker.

After cooking, grasp the foil strips and carefully lift food up. Remove food from foil strips and serve.

Slow Cooker Temperature Check

To be considered safe, a slow cooker must be able to cook slowly enough that it can be left unattended, yet fast enough to keep the food at a proper temperature. Here's how to check your slow cooker:

1. Fill the slow cooker half to two-thirds full with room-temperature water.

2. Cover and heat on low for 8 hours.

3. Using a thermometer, check the temperature of the water quickly, since the temperature can drop once the lid is removed.

4. The temperature should be at least 185°. If it's too hot, a meal cooked for 8 hours would likely be overdone. If the temperature is below 185°, the slow cooker is not safe to use and should be discarded.

Power Outage Solutions

If the power goes out while you are using a slow cooker, the U.S. Department of Agriculture offers the following recommendations:

• Fully cooked foods are safe at room temperature for up to 2 hours. If the food has been sitting for 2 hours or longer, or for an unknown period of time, it should be discarded.

• If the food is not fully cooked and you're home when the power goes out, immediately finish cooking it with another method, such as with a gas stove or grill.

CLEANING TIPS

■ Removable inserts make cleanup a breeze. Be sure to cool the insert before rinsing or cleaning with water to avoid cracking or warping. Do not immerse the metal base in water. Clean it with a damp sponge.

■ If the insert is dishwasher-safe, place it in the dishwasher. Otherwise, wash it in warm soapy water. Avoid using abrasive cleansers, since they may scratch the surface.

■ To remove mineral stains on a ceramic insert, fill the cooker with hot water and 1 cup of white vinegar; cover. Turn the heat to high for 2 hours, then empty. When cool, wash the insert with hot soapy water and a cloth or sponge. Rinse well and dry with a towel.

■ To remove water marks from a highly glazed ceramic insert, rub the surface with canola oil and allow to stand for 2 hours before washing with hot soapy water.

CARIBBEAN CHIPOTLE
PORK SLIDERS, PAGE 84

"One of our favorite pulled pork recipes combines the heat of chipotle peppers with cool tropical coleslaw. The robust flavors make these sliders a big hit with guests."

—KADIJA BRIDGEWATER DEERFIELD BEACH, FL
about her recipe, Caribbean Chipotle Pork Sliders, on page 84

Slow Cooker

Beef & Ground Beef

17 18 25

Heartwarming, versatile and **stick-to-your-ribs** delicious...nothing satisfies like **comfort-food classics** made with **beef** in the slow cooker. From **roasts** and slow-simmered **stews** to family-pleasing **meatballs, burritos** and more, you'll discover **dozens of new favorites** within the pages of this chapter.

AUTUMN SLOW-COOKED BEEF STEW

Autumn Slow-Cooked Beef Stew

If any dish could taste like a holiday, it's this hearty stew made with beef, pears, walnuts and sweet dried apricots. We recommend a leafy salad and rolls to complete the meal.
—**AMY DODSON** DURANGO, CO

PREP: 35 MIN. • **COOK:** 6 HOURS
MAKES: 8 SERVINGS

- 2 **pounds boneless beef chuck roast, cubed**
- ½ **teaspoon garlic salt**
- ½ **teaspoon pepper**
- 2 **tablespoons olive oil**
- 2 **cups dry red wine or reduced-sodium beef broth**
- 1 **cup reduced-sodium beef broth**
- 4 **garlic cloves, minced**
- 1 **teaspoon rubbed sage**
- 1 **teaspoon dried thyme**
- ½ **teaspoon salt**
- 2½ **pounds small red potatoes (about 20)**
- 4 **medium carrots, cut into 1-inch pieces**
- 1 **large onion, halved and sliced**
- 2 **medium pears, quartered**
- 1 **cup walnut halves**
- 1 **cup dried apricots**
- 2 **tablespoons cornstarch**
- 3 **tablespoons cold water**

1. Sprinkle beef with garlic salt and pepper. In a large skillet, heat oil over medium-high heat. Brown beef in batches. Remove with a slotted spoon; transfer to a 6-qt. slow cooker.
2. In a large bowl, combine wine, broth, garlic, sage, thyme and salt; pour over beef. Top with potatoes, carrots, onion, pears, walnuts and apricots. Cook, covered, on low 6-8 hours or until meat is tender; skim fat.
3. In a small bowl, mix cornstarch and water until smooth; gradually stir into stew. Cook, covered, on high 20-30 minutes or until the sauce is thickened.
PER SERVING *1¾ cups equals 522 cal., 23 g fat (5 g sat. fat), 74 mg chol., 394 mg sodium, 51 g carb., 8 g fiber, 29 g pro.*

All-Day Meatballs

I pop these meatballs in the slow cooker before work, and they're done by dinner.
—**CATHY RYAN** RED WING, MN

PREP: 25 MIN. • **COOK:** 6 HOURS
MAKES: 6 SERVINGS

- 1 **cup milk**
- ¾ **cup quick-cooking oats**
- 3 **tablespoons finely chopped onion**
- 1½ **teaspoons salt**
- 1½ **pounds ground beef**
- 1 **cup ketchup**
- ½ **cup water**
- 3 **tablespoons cider vinegar**
- 2 **tablespoons sugar**

1. In a large bowl, combine the first four ingredients. Crumble beef over mixture and mix well. Shape into 1-in. balls. Place in a 5-qt. slow cooker.
2. In a small bowl, combine the ketchup, water, vinegar and sugar. Pour over meatballs. Cover and cook on low for 6-8 hours or until meat is no longer pink.

Taco Meat Loaf

Our children think there are three basic food groups—pizza, tacos and burgers! They like to doctor up slices of this meat loaf with their favorite taco toppings.
—**DIANE ESSINGER** FINDLAY, OH

PREP: 10 MIN. • **COOK:** 8 HOURS
MAKES: 8 SERVINGS

- 1 **egg, beaten**
- ½ **cup sour cream**
- ⅓ **cup salsa**
- 2 **to 4 tablespoons taco seasoning**
- 1 **cup crushed tortilla chips**
- ½ **cup shredded cheddar cheese**
- 2 **pounds lean ground beef (90% lean)**
  Optional toppings: sour cream, salsa, shredded cheddar cheese, shredded lettuce, sliced ripe olives

1. In a large bowl, combine the first six ingredients. Crumble beef over mixture and mix well. Pat into a 3-qt. slow cooker.
2. Cover slow cooker and cook on low for 8 hours or until no pink remains and a thermometer reads 160°. Serve with toppings if desired.

"This marvelous roast lets you forget about it while it's cooking (but the aroma will remind you). We serve it with brown rice or mashed potatoes."

—**DONNA ROBERTS** MANHATTAN, KS

SPRING HERB ROAST

Spring Herb Roast

PREP: 20 MIN. • **COOK:** 4 HOURS + STANDING
MAKES: 8 SERVINGS

- 2 **large onions, halved and sliced (about 3 cups)**
- ½ **pound sliced fresh mushrooms**
- 1 **beef rump roast or bottom round roast (3 to 4 pounds)**
- 2 **teaspoons salt**
- ½ **teaspoon pepper**
- 1 **tablespoon canola oil**
- 1½ **cups water**
- 2 **tablespoons tomato paste**
- 3 **garlic cloves, minced**
- ½ **teaspoon each dried basil, marjoram and thyme**
  Minced fresh parsley

1. Place onions and mushrooms in a 5- or 6-qt. slow cooker.
2. Sprinkle the roast with salt and pepper. In a large skillet, heat oil over medium-high heat, brown roast on all sides. Transfer to slow cooker.
3. In a small bowl, mix water, tomato paste, garlic, basil, marjoram and thyme; pour over roast. Cook, covered, on low 4-5 hours or until meat is tender (a thermometer should read at least 145°).
4. Remove roast from the slow cooker and tent with foil. Let stand for 15 minutes before slicing. Serve beef with onion mixture; sprinkle with parsley.
PER SERVING *5 ounces cooked beef with ¼ cup vegetable mixture equals 257 cal., 10 g fat (3 g sat. fat), 101 mg chol., 650 mg sodium, 6 g carb., 1 g fiber, 35 g pro.* **Diabetic Exchanges:** *5 lean meat, 1 vegetable, ½ fat.*

Slow-Cooked Swiss Steak

Everyone raves about how tender and rich this dish is. I make it about every two weeks during the winter! I modified my mom's Swiss steak to cook the recipe hands-free in the slow cooker.

—**KATHIE MORRIS** REDMOND, OR

PREP: 15 MIN. • **COOK:** 8 HOURS
MAKES: 6 SERVINGS

- ¾ **cup all-purpose flour**
- 1 **teaspoon pepper**
- ¼ **teaspoon salt**
- 2 to 2½ **pounds boneless beef top round steak**
- 1 to 2 **tablespoons butter**
- 1 **can (10¾ ounces) condensed cream of mushroom soup, undiluted**
- 1⅓ **cups water**
- 1 **cup sliced celery, optional**
- ½ **cup chopped onion**
- 1 to 3 **teaspoons beef bouillon granules**
- ½ **teaspoon minced garlic**

1. In a shallow bowl, combine the flour, pepper and salt. Cut steak into six serving-size pieces; dredge in the flour mixture.
2. In a large skillet, brown steak on both sides in butter. Transfer to a 3-qt. slow cooker. Combine the remaining ingredients; pour over steak. Cover and cook on low for 8-9 hours or until meat is tender.

SLOW-COOKED SWISS STEAK

Beef Brisket with Cranberry Gravy

With just a few minutes of hands-on work, this tender beef brisket simmers into a delectable entree. The meat and gravy are great for sandwiches and leftovers the next day.

—NOELLE LABRECQUE ROUND ROCK, TX

PREP: 15 MIN. • **COOK:** 5½ HOURS
MAKES: 12 SERVINGS

- 1 **medium onion, sliced**
- 1 **fresh beef brisket (3 pounds), halved**
- 1 **can (14 ounces) jellied cranberry sauce**
- ½ **cup thawed cranberry juice concentrate**
- 2 **tablespoons cornstarch**
- ¼ **cup cold water**

1. Place onion in a 5-qt. slow cooker; top with brisket. Combine cranberry sauce and juice concentrate; pour over beef. Cover and cook on low for 5½ to 6 hours or until meat is tender.
2. Remove brisket and keep warm. Strain cooking juices, discarding onion; skim fat. Place in a small saucepan and bring to a boil. Combine cornstarch and cold water until smooth; gradually stir into the pan. Cook and stir for 2 minutes or until thickened. Thinly slice brisket across the grain; serve with gravy.
NOTE *This is a fresh beef brisket, not corned beef.*
PER SERVING *3 ounces cooked beef with 3 tablespoons gravy equals 225 cal., 5 g fat (2 g sat. fat), 48 mg chol., 46 mg sodium, 21 g carb., 1 g fiber, 23 g pro.* **Diabetic Exchanges:** *3 lean meat, 1½ starch.*

SLOW COOKER LASAGNA

Slow Cooker Lasagna

Convenient no-cook lasagna noodles take the work out of a traditional favorite adapted for the slow cooker. We like our lasagna with Parmesan bread or garlic cheese toast.

—LISA MICHELETTI COLLIERVILLE, TN

PREP: 25 MIN. • **COOK:** 4 HOURS
MAKES: 6-8 SERVINGS

- 1 **pound ground beef**
- 1 **large onion, chopped**
- 2 **garlic cloves, minced**
- 1 **can (29 ounces) tomato sauce**
- 1 **cup water**
- 1 **can (6 ounces) tomato paste**
- 1 **teaspoon salt**
- 1 **teaspoon dried oregano**
- 1 **package (8 ounces) no-cook lasagna noodles**
- 4 **cups (16 ounces) shredded part-skim mozzarella cheese**
- 1½ **cups (12 ounces) 4% cottage cheese**
- ½ **cup grated Parmesan cheese**

1. In a skillet, cook beef and onion over medium heat until meat is no longer pink. Add garlic; cook 1 minute longer. Drain. Stir in the tomato sauce, water, tomato paste, salt and oregano.
2. Spread a fourth of the meat sauce in an ungreased 5-qt. slow cooker. Arrange a third of the noodles over sauce (break the noodles to fit if necessary). Combine cheeses; spoon a third of the mixture over noodles. Repeat layers twice. Top with remaining meat sauce.
3. Cover slow cooker and cook on low 4-5 hours or until noodles are tender.

If you don't have picante sauce on hand for the **Picante Beef Roast**, you can use **salsa** instead. It's more chunky than picante sauce. Try serving the **leftover beef** wrapped in **tortillas** with shredded **cheese** and **refried beans**.

Picante Beef Roast

I created this dish because I love the flavor of taco seasoning and think it shouldn't be reserved just for tacos! My recipe couldn't be easier, and it works great with a pork roast, too.

—**MARGARET THIEL** LEVITTOWN, PA

PREP: 15 MIN. • **COOK:** 8 HOURS
MAKES: 8 SERVINGS

- 1 **beef rump roast or bottom round roast (3 pounds), trimmed**
- 1 **jar (16 ounces) picante sauce**
- 1 **can (15 ounces) tomato sauce**
- 1 **envelope taco seasoning**
- 3 **tablespoons cornstarch**
- ¼ **cup cold water**

1. Cut roast in half; place in a 5-qt. slow cooker. In a large bowl, combine the picante sauce, tomato sauce and taco seasoning; pour over roast. Cover and cook on low for 8-9 hours or until meat is tender.

2. Remove meat to a serving platter; keep warm. Skim fat from cooking juices; transfer 3 cups to a small saucepan. Bring liquid to a boil. Combine cornstarch and water until smooth. Gradually stir into the pan. Bring to a boil; cook and stir for 2 minutes or until thickened. Serve with roast.

Throw-Together Short Ribs

This recipe takes just 15 minutes to prep, and it results in delicious fall-off-the-bone ribs. I like to serve them on a bed of rice.

—**LAMYA ASIFF** DELBURNE, AB

PREP: 15 MIN. • **COOK:** 4¼ HOURS
MAKES: 4 SERVINGS

- ⅓ **cup water**
- ¼ **cup tomato paste**
- 3 **tablespoons brown sugar**
- 1 **tablespoon prepared mustard**
- 2 **teaspoons seasoned salt**
- 2 **teaspoons cider vinegar**
- 1 **teaspoon Worcestershire sauce**
- 1 **teaspoon beef bouillon granules**
- 2 **pounds beef short ribs**
- 1 **small tomato, chopped**
- 1 **small onion, chopped**
- 1 **tablespoon cornstarch**
- 1 **tablespoon cold water**

1. In a 3-qt. slow cooker, combine the first eight ingredients. Add the ribs, tomato and onion. Cover and cook on low for 4-5 hours or until meat is tender.

2. In a small bowl, combine cornstarch and cold water until smooth; gradually stir into cooking juices. Cover and cook on high for 15 minutes or until thickened.

Chipotle Carne Guisada

Chipotle peppers and adobo sauce add smoky heat to tender stewed beef. We serve this hearty dish with tortillas and sometimes rice.

—**ADRIENNE SPENRATH** AUSTIN, TX

PREP: 30 MIN. • **COOK:** 6 HOURS
MAKES: 8 SERVINGS

- 2 **tablespoons canola oil**
- 2½ **pounds beef stew meat**
- 1 **can (8 ounces) tomato sauce**
- ¾ **cup water**
- 2 **chopped chipotle peppers in adobo sauce plus 2 tablespoons sauce**
- 12 **garlic cloves, minced**
- 1 **tablespoon chili powder**
- 1½ **teaspoons ground cumin**
- 1 **teaspoon beef bouillon granules**
- ½ **teaspoon pepper**
- ¼ **teaspoon salt**
  Hot cooked rice or warmed flour tortillas, optional

1. In a large skillet, heat oil over medium-high heat. Brown beef in batches. Transfer meat to a 3-qt. slow cooker. Stir in tomato sauce, water, chipotle peppers, adobo sauce, garlic, chili powder, cumin, bouillon, pepper and salt.

2. Cook, covered, on low 6-8 hours or until meat is tender. If desired, serve with rice.

CHIPOTLE CARNE GUISADA

EAT SMART

Slow Cooker Beef Bourguignonne

I've wanted to make Beef Burgundy ever since I got one of Julia Child's cookbooks, but I wanted to find a way to fix it in a slow cooker. My version of the popular stew is still rich, hearty and delicious, but without all the steps. If you have the time, it's delightful with homemade mashed potatoes.

—CRYSTAL BRUNS ILIFF, CO

PREP: 30 MIN. + MARINATING
COOK: 8 HOURS
MAKES: 12 SERVINGS (⅔ CUP EACH)

- 3 **pounds beef stew meat**
- 1¾ **cups dry red wine**
- 3 **tablespoons olive oil**
- 3 **tablespoons dried minced onion**
- 2 **tablespoons dried parsley flakes**
- 1 **bay leaf**
- 1 **teaspoon dried thyme**
- ¼ **teaspoon pepper**
- 8 **bacon strips, chopped**
- 1 **pound whole fresh mushrooms, quartered**
- 24 **pearl onions, peeled (about 2 cups)**
- 2 **garlic cloves, minced**
- ⅓ **cup all-purpose flour**
- 1 **teaspoon salt**
   Hot cooked whole wheat egg noodles, optional

1. Place beef in a large resealable plastic bag; add the wine, oil and seasonings. Seal bag and turn to coat. Refrigerate overnight.
2. In a large skillet, cook bacon over medium heat until crisp, stirring occasionally. Remove with a slotted spoon; drain on paper towels. Discard drippings, reserving 1 tablespoon in pan. Add mushrooms and onions to drippings; cook and stir over medium-high heat until tender. Add garlic; cook 1 minute longer.
3. Drain beef, reserving marinade; transfer beef to a 4- or 5-qt. slow cooker. Sprinkle beef with flour and salt; toss to coat. Top with the bacon and mushroom mixture. Add the reserved marinade.
4. Cook, covered, on low 8-10 hours or until beef is tender. Discard the bay leaf. If desired, serve the stew with noodles.

PER SERVING ⅔ cup beef mixture (calculated without noodles) equals 289 cal., 15 g fat (5 g sat. fat), 77 mg chol., 350 mg sodium, 8 g carb., 1 g fiber, 25 g pro. **Diabetic Exchanges:** 3 lean meat, 1½ fat, 1 vegetable.

Sweet & Tangy Beef Roast

PREP: 10 MIN. • **COOK:** 7 HOURS + STANDING
MAKES: 8 SERVINGS

- 1 **tablespoon canola oil**
- 1 **boneless beef chuck roast (4 pounds)**
- 2 **medium onions, cut into rings**
- 1 **cup plus 2 tablespoons water, divided**
- ¾ **cup honey barbecue sauce**
- ½ **cup red pepper jelly**
- 3 **tablespoons hoisin sauce**
- 2 **tablespoons cornstarch**

1. In a large skillet, heat oil over medium heat. Brown roast on all sides. Transfer to a 5-qt. slow cooker; add onions and 1 cup water.
2. Combine barbecue sauce, jelly and hoisin sauce; pour over meat. Cook, covered, on low for 7-9 hours or until meat is tender. Remove roast from slow cooker and tent with foil. Let stand 10 minutes before slicing.
3. Meanwhile, skim fat from the cooking juices; transfer juices to a small saucepan. Bring to a boil. Mix cornstarch and remaining water until smooth. Stir into pan. Return to a boil; cook and stir 1-2 minutes or until juices are thickened. Serve with roast and onions.

Hoisin sauce is a thick, sweet and somewhat spicy condiment popular in Chinese cooking. It's often made with fermented **soybeans** (miso), **garlic, spices** and sweet ingredients such as **plums** or **sweet potatoes**.

SLOW COOKER BEEF BOURGUIGNONNE

"While cleaning out the fridge I found barbecue sauce, red pepper jelly and hoisin sauce—the perfect trio for creating this slightly tangy and sweet, utterly delicious roast."
—RACHEL VAN ORDEN ANNVILLE, PA

SWEET & TANGY BEEF ROAST

Slow Cooker Vegetable Beef Stew

Here's a fun variation of beef stew that I came across. With sweet flavor from apricots and butternut squash, it seems to have a South American or Cuban flair. It's wonderful for a chilly fall day.

—**RUTH RODRIGUEZ** FORT MYERS BEACH, FL

PREP: 10 MIN. • **COOK:** 5½ HOURS
MAKES: 4 SERVINGS

- ¾ pound beef stew meat, cut into ½-inch cubes
- 2 teaspoons canola oil
- 1 can (14½ ounces) beef broth
- 1 can (14½ ounces) stewed tomatoes, cut up
- 1½ cups cubed peeled butternut squash
- 1 cup frozen corn, thawed
- 6 dried apricots or peaches, quartered
- ½ cup chopped carrot
- 1 teaspoon dried oregano
- ¼ teaspoon salt
- ¼ teaspoon pepper
- 2 tablespoons cornstarch
- ¼ cup cold water
- 2 tablespoons minced fresh parsley

1. In a large nonstick skillet, brown beef in oil over medium heat.
2. Transfer to a 3-qt. slow cooker. Add the broth, tomatoes, butternut squash, corn, apricots, carrot, oregano, salt and pepper.
3. Cover and cook on high for 5-6 hours or until vegetables and meat are tender.
4. Combine the cornstarch and cold water until smooth; gradually stir into stew. Cover and cook on high for 30 minutes or until thickened. Stir in the parsley.

EASY ROPA VIEJA

FREEZE IT
Easy Ropa Vieja

Use your slow cooker for this meaty Cuban classic, which offers bold flavors without a lot of hands-on time.

—**DENISE NYLAND** PANAMA CITY, FL

PREP: 25 MIN. • **COOK:** 6 HOURS
MAKES: 8 SERVINGS

- 1 boneless beef chuck roast (2 pounds), cut in half
- 2 tablespoons olive oil
- 2 large onions, coarsely chopped
- 2 large green peppers, coarsely chopped
- 4 jalapeno peppers, seeded and minced
- 1 habanero pepper, seeded and minced
- 3 cans (14½ ounces each) diced tomatoes, undrained
- ½ cup water
- 6 garlic cloves, minced
- 2 tablespoons minced fresh cilantro
- 4 teaspoons beef bouillon granules
- 2 teaspoons pepper
- 1½ teaspoons ground cumin
- 1 teaspoon dried oregano
- ½ cup pimiento-stuffed olives, coarsely chopped
  Hot cooked rice, optional

1. In a large skillet, brown beef in oil on all sides. Transfer meat to a 5-qt. slow cooker. Add onions and peppers. Combine tomatoes, water, garlic, cilantro, beef bouillon, pepper, cumin and oregano; pour over vegetables.
2. Cover and cook on low 6-8 hours or until meat is tender. Remove beef; cool slightly. Skim fat from cooking juices; stir in olives. Shred the beef with two forks and return to slow cooker; heat through. Serve with rice if desired.
FREEZE OPTION *Transfer individual portions of stew to freezer containers and freeze. To use, partially thaw in refrigerator overnight. Heat through in a saucepan, stirring occasionally and adding a little water if necessary.*
NOTE *Wear disposable gloves when cutting hot peppers; the oils can burn skin. Avoid touching your face.*

Meat Loaf with Chili Sauce

I used to serve this meat loaf recipe in my cafe. Everyone asked for it. I adapted it for the slow cooker so I could make it at home, where it's quite popular, too.
—**ROBERT COX** LAS CRUCES, NM

PREP: 20 MIN.
COOK: 3 HOURS + STANDING
MAKES: 8 SERVINGS

- 1 large onion, finely chopped
- ½ cup seasoned bread crumbs
- 1 small green pepper, chopped
- 2 eggs, lightly beaten
- ½ cup chili sauce
- 2 tablespoons spicy brown mustard
- 3 to 4 garlic cloves, minced
- ¾ teaspoon salt
- ¼ teaspoon dried oregano
- ¼ teaspoon dried basil
- 2 pounds lean ground beef (90% lean)
  Additional chili sauce, optional

1. Cut four 20x3-in. strips of heavy-duty foil; crisscross so they resemble spokes of a wheel. Place strips on bottom and up sides of a 5-qt. slow cooker. Coat strips with cooking spray.
2. In a large bowl, combine the first 10 ingredients. Add beef; mix lightly but thoroughly. Shape into a 9-in. round loaf. Place loaf in center of strips in slow cooker.
3. Cook, covered, on low 3-4 hours or until a thermometer reads at least 160°. If desired, spoon additional chili sauce over meat loaf; let stand for 10 minutes. Using foil strips as handles, remove meat loaf to a platter.
FREEZE OPTION *Securely wrap and freeze cooled meat loaf in plastic wrap and foil. To use, partially thaw in refrigerator overnight. Unwrap meat loaf; reheat in a greased shallow baking pan in a preheated 350° oven until the meat loaf is heated through and a thermometer inserted in the center reads 165°.*
PER SERVING *1 slice equals 253 cal., 11 g fat (4 g sat. fat), 123 mg chol., 686 mg sodium, 12 g carb., 1 g fiber, 25 g pro.* **Diabetic Exchanges:** *3 lean meat, 1 starch.*

Family-Favorite Beef Roast

You will need only a few ingredients for this tangy roast that feeds a bunch. The rich gravy is delicious on mashed potatoes, too.
—**JEANIE BEASLEY** TUPELO, MS

PREP: 10 MIN. • **COOK:** 6 HOURS
MAKES: 8 SERVINGS

- 1 boneless beef chuck roast (3 to 4 pounds)
- 1 can (14½ ounces) stewed tomatoes, cut up
- 1 can (10¾ ounces) condensed cream of mushroom soup, undiluted
- 1 envelope Lipton beefy onion soup mix
- ¼ cup cornstarch
- ½ cup cold water

1. Place roast in a 5-qt. slow cooker. In a small bowl, combine tomatoes, soup and soup mix; pour over meat. Cover and cook on low for 6-8 hours or until the meat is tender.
2. Remove meat to a serving platter; keep warm. Skim fat from cooking juices; transfer to a large saucepan. Bring liquid to a boil. Combine the cornstarch and water until smooth; stir into pan. Bring to a boil; cook and stir for 2 minutes or until thickened. Serve with roast.

MEAT LOAF WITH CHILI SAUCE

STEAK SAN MARINO

Orange-Spiced Brisket

PREP: 10 MIN. • **COOK:** 7¼ HOURS
MAKES: 6 SERVINGS

- 1 fresh beef brisket (3 pounds)
- 1½ cups orange juice
- 1 small onion, chopped
- ½ cup chopped dates
- 1 cinnamon stick (3 inches)
- 1 garlic clove, minced
- ½ teaspoon ground coriander
- ⅛ teaspoon ground cloves

1. Place brisket in a 6-qt. slow cooker. Mix remaining ingredients; pour over brisket. Cook, covered, on low for 7-9 hours or until tender.

2. Transfer brisket to a platter; keep warm. Discard cinnamon stick. Skim fat from cooking juices. In a blender, cover and process cooking juices until pureed; pour into a small saucepan. Bring to a boil. Cook, uncovered, 13-15 minutes or until thickened, stirring occasionally. Cut beef diagonally across the grain into thin slices; serve with sauce.

FREEZE OPTION *Place brisket in freezer containers; top with sauce. Cool and freeze. To use, partially thaw in refrigerator overnight. Heat through in a covered saucepan, gently stirring occasionally and adding a little water if necessary.*

NOTE *This is a fresh beef brisket, not corned beef.*

If you grow **cilantro**, you can also **harvest its seeds**, known as **coriander.** Let seeds mature on the plant to a light brown color, then **hang herbs** to dry well. Gently **loosen the seeds** and store in a covered jar.

Steak San Marino

As a busy pastor's wife and mother of three, I find that my day runs more smoothly with easy, inexpensive dishes like this. The steak is so tender and flavorful, my kids gobble it up and my husband asks for seconds.

—**LAEL GRIESS** HULL, IA

PREP: 15 MIN. • **COOK:** 7 HOURS
MAKES: 6 SERVINGS

- ¼ cup all-purpose flour
- ½ teaspoon salt
- ½ teaspoon pepper
- 1 beef top round steak (1½ pounds), cut into six pieces
- 2 large carrots, sliced
- 1 celery rib, sliced
- 1 can (8 ounces) tomato sauce
- 2 garlic cloves, minced
- 1 bay leaf
- 1 teaspoon Italian seasoning
- ½ teaspoon Worcestershire sauce
- 3 cups hot cooked brown rice

1. In a large resealable plastic bag, combine the flour, salt and pepper. Add beef, a few pieces at a time, and shake to coat. Transfer to a 4-qt. slow cooker.

2. In a small bowl, combine carrots, celery, tomato sauce, garlic, bay leaf, Italian seasoning and Worcestershire sauce. Pour over beef. Cover and cook on low for 7-9 hours or until beef is tender. Discard the bay leaf. Serve with rice.

FREEZE OPTION *Place the cooked steak and vegetables in freezer containers; top with sauce. Cool and freeze. To use, partially thaw in refrigerator overnight. Heat through in a covered saucepan, gently stirring and adding a little water if necessary.*

ORANGE-SPICED BRISKET

Teriyaki Beef Stew

In the spirit of the old saying "Necessity is the mother of invention," I created this sweet-tangy beef recipe because I had a package of stew meat that needed to be used. After I spotted the ginger beer in the fridge, the rest was history. It's nice to have a new way to serve an affordable cut of meat.

—**LESLIE SIMMS** SHERMAN OAKS, CA

PREP: 20 MIN. • **COOK:** 6½ HOURS
MAKES: 8 SERVINGS

- 2 **pounds beef stew meat**
- 1 **bottle (12 ounces) ginger beer or ginger ale**
- ¼ **cup teriyaki sauce**
- 2 **garlic cloves, minced**
- 2 **tablespoons sesame seeds**
- 2 **tablespoons cornstarch**
- 2 **tablespoons cold water**
- 2 **cups frozen peas, thawed**
  Hot cooked rice, optional

1. In a large nonstick skillet, brown beef in batches. Transfer to a 3-qt. slow cooker.
2. In a small bowl, combine the ginger beer, teriyaki sauce, garlic and sesame seeds; pour over beef. Cover and cook on low for 6-8 hours or until the meat is tender.
3. Combine cornstarch and cold water until smooth; gradually stir into stew. Stir in peas. Cover and cook on high for 30 minutes or until thickened. Serve with rice if desired.
PER SERVING *1 cup stew (calculated without rice) equals 310 cal., 12 g fat (4 g sat. fat), 94 mg chol., 528 mg sodium, 17 g carb., 2 g fiber, 33 g pro. Diabetic Exchanges: 4 lean meat, 1 starch.*

Ginger beer is a gingery **soda pop** that's popular in the **Caribbean**. It doesn't contain any alcohol.

HUNGARIAN GOULASH

Hungarian Goulash

My grandmother used to make this goulash for my mother. Paprika and caraway add wonderful flavor, and the sour cream gives it a traditional creamy richness. It's scrumptious!

—**MARCIA DOYLE** POMPANO, FL

PREP: 20 MIN. • **COOK:** 7 HOURS
MAKES: 12 SERVINGS

- 3 **medium onions, chopped**
- 2 **medium carrots, chopped**
- 2 **medium green peppers, chopped**
- 3 **pounds beef stew meat, cut into 1-inch cubes**
- ¾ **teaspoon salt, divided**
- ¾ **teaspoon pepper, divided**
- 2 **tablespoons olive oil**
- 1½ **cups reduced-sodium beef broth**
- ¼ **cup all-purpose flour**
- 3 **tablespoons paprika**
- 2 **tablespoons tomato paste**
- 1 **teaspoon caraway seeds**
- 1 **garlic clove, minced**
  Dash sugar
- 12 **cups uncooked whole wheat egg noodles**
- 1 **cup (8 ounces) reduced-fat sour cream**

1. Place the onions, carrots and green peppers in a 5-qt. slow cooker. Sprinkle meat with ½ teaspoon salt and ½ teaspoon pepper. In a large skillet, brown meat in oil in batches. Transfer to slow cooker.
2. Add broth to skillet, stirring to loosen browned bits from pan. Combine the flour, paprika, tomato paste, caraway seeds, garlic, sugar and remaining salt and pepper; stir into skillet. Bring to a boil; cook and stir for 2 minutes or until thickened. Pour over meat. Cover and cook on low for 7-9 hours or until meat is tender.
3. Cook noodles according to package directions. Stir sour cream into slow cooker. Drain noodles; serve with goulash.
PER SERVING *⅔ cup goulash with 1 cup noodles equals 388 cal., 13 g fat (4 g sat. fat), 78 mg chol., 285 mg sodium, 41 g carb., 7 g fiber, 31 g pro. Diabetic Exchanges: 3 lean meat, 2 starch, 1 vegetable, 1 fat.*

Chile Colorado Burritos

When I was growing up in Southern California, this was one of my favorite Mexican dishes. It's hard to find now that I live in the Midwest—except in my kitchen!

—**KELLY MCCULLEY** DES MOINES, IA

PREP: 20 MIN. • **COOK:** 6¼ HOURS
MAKES: 8 SERVINGS

- **2 pounds boneless beef chuck roast, cut into 1½-inch pieces**
- **2 cans (10 ounces each) enchilada sauce**
- **1 teaspoon beef bouillon granules**
- **1 can (16 ounces) refried beans, optional**
- **8 flour tortillas (8 inches)**
- **1 cup (4 ounces) shredded Colby-Monterey Jack cheese**
  Chopped green onions, optional

1. In a 4-qt. slow cooker, combine beef, enchilada sauce and bouillon granules. Cook, covered, on low 6-8 hours or until meat is tender.
2. Preheat oven to 425°. Using a slotted spoon, remove meat from sauce. Skim fat from sauce. If desired, spoon about ¼ cup beans across center of each tortilla; top with ⅓ cup meat. Fold bottom and sides of tortilla over filling and roll up.
3. Place in a greased 11x7-in. baking dish. Pour 1 cup of the sauce over top; sprinkle with cheese. Bake burritos, uncovered, 10-15 minutes or until cheese is melted. If desired, sprinkle with green onions.

Sassy Pot Roast

We lost this recipe for several years, so it's even more special to us now that we found it again. I love walking into my home after a long day at the office and smelling this lovely pot roast.

—**SUSAN BURKETT** MONROEVILLE, PA

PREP: 15 MIN. • **COOK:** 8 HOURS
MAKES: 8 SERVINGS

- **1 boneless beef chuck roast (2 pounds)**
- **½ teaspoon salt**
- **½ teaspoon pepper**
- **2 teaspoons olive oil**
- **1 large onion, chopped**
- **1 can (8 ounces) tomato sauce**
- **¼ cup water**
- **¼ cup lemon juice**
- **¼ cup cider vinegar**
- **¼ cup ketchup**
- **2 tablespoons brown sugar**
- **1 tablespoon Worcestershire sauce**
- **½ teaspoon ground mustard**
- **½ teaspoon paprika**

1. Sprinkle beef with salt and pepper. In a large skillet, brown beef in oil on all sides; drain.
2. Transfer to a 4-qt. slow cooker. Sprinkle with onion. Combine the remaining ingredients; pour over meat. Cover and cook on low for 8-10 hours or until meat is tender. Skim fat. If desired, thicken the cooking juices.
PER SERVING *3 ounces cooked beef equals 243 cal., 12 g fat (4 g sat. fat), 74 mg chol., 443 mg sodium, 10 g carb., 1 g fiber, 23 g pro.* **Diabetic Exchange:** *3 lean meat.*

CHILE COLORADO BURRITOS

Poultry

29   32   36

Here are the **heartwarming dishes** your family craves: **creamy** chicken with noodles, **tender** herbed turkey breast and **fresh takes on dinner**, such as tikka masala and a **lightened-up** Cincinnati chili. These easy recipes are so **tempting**, you'll want to try them all!

CHICKEN TIKKA MASALA

Chicken Tikka Masala

This Indian-style dish has flavors that keep me coming back for more —a simple entree spiced with garam masala, cumin and gingerroot that's absolutely amazing.
—**JACLYN BELL** LOGAN, UT

PREP: 25 MIN. • **COOK:** 4¼ HOURS
MAKES: 8 SERVINGS

- 1 can (29 ounces) tomato puree
- 1½ cups (12 ounces) plain yogurt
- ½ large onion, finely chopped
- 2 tablespoons olive oil
- 4½ teaspoons minced fresh gingerroot
- 4 garlic cloves, minced
- 1 tablespoon garam masala
- 2½ teaspoons salt
- 1½ teaspoons ground cumin
- 1 teaspoon paprika
- ¾ teaspoon pepper
- ½ teaspoon cayenne pepper
- ¼ teaspoon ground cinnamon
- 2½ pounds boneless skinless chicken breasts, cut into 1½-inch cubes
- 1 jalapeno pepper, halved and seeded
- 1 bay leaf
- 1 tablespoon cornstarch
- 1 cup heavy whipping cream
  Hot cooked basmati rice
  Chopped fresh cilantro, optional

1. In a 5-qt. slow cooker, combine the first 13 ingredients. Add chicken, jalapeno and bay leaf. Cook, covered, on low 4 hours or until chicken is tender. Remove jalapeno and bay leaf.
2. In a small bowl, mix cornstarch and cream until smooth; gradually stir into sauce. Cook, covered, on high 15-20 minutes or until the sauce is thickened. Serve with rice. If desired, sprinkle with cilantro.
NOTE *Wear disposable gloves when cutting hot peppers; the oils can burn skin. Avoid touching your face.*

Fruity Cranberry Chicken

My husband and son love the flavor of cranberries. This lovely slow-cooked dinner is the one they ask for the most.
—**SANDY BROOKS** TACOMA, WA

PREP: 20 MIN. • **COOK:** 5¼ HOURS
MAKES: 4-6 SERVINGS

- 1 cup fresh or frozen cranberries
- ¾ cup chopped onion
- ½ teaspoon salt
- ¼ teaspoon ground cinnamon
- ¼ teaspoon ground ginger
- 1 broiler/fryer chicken (about 3½ pounds), quartered and skin removed
- 1 cup orange juice
- 1 teaspoon grated orange peel
- 3 tablespoons butter, melted
- 3 tablespoons all-purpose flour
- 2 to 3 tablespoons brown sugar
  Hot cooked noodles

1. In a 3-qt. slow cooker, combine the first five ingredients; top with chicken. Pour orange juice over chicken and sprinkle with orange peel. Cover and cook on low for 5-6 hours or until chicken juices run clear.
2. Remove chicken. When cool enough to handle, remove meat from bones; discard bones. Cut meat into bite-size pieces; set aside.
3. Combine butter and flour until smooth; stir into slow cooker. Cook on high 15 minutes or until thickened. Stir in chicken and brown sugar; heat through. Serve with noodles.

Although **tikka masala** is inspired by **Indian cuisine**, it's far more popular in **Great Britain**, where it is rumored to have originated.

"I love dishes with a few ingredients that you can just throw together, and then let the slow cooker do all the work. This easy chicken dinner is one of my favorites."
—CHRISTINA PETRI ALEXANDRIA, MN

CREAMY CHICKEN
THIGHS & NOODLES

Creamy Chicken Thighs & Noodles

PREP: 10 MIN. • **COOK:** 7 HOURS
MAKES: 8 SERVINGS

- 8 **boneless skinless chicken thighs (about 2 pounds)**
- 2 **cans (10¾ ounces each) condensed cream of mushroom soup, undiluted**
- 1 **can (10¾ ounces) condensed cream of chicken soup, undiluted**
- 1 **cup (8 ounces) sour cream**
- 2 **tablespoons paprika**
- ½ **teaspoon onion powder**
- ¼ **teaspoon salt**
- ¼ **teaspoon cayenne pepper**
  Hot cooked wide egg noodles

Place chicken in a greased 4-qt. slow cooker. In a large bowl, combine soups, sour cream and seasonings; pour over chicken. Cook, covered, on low 7-9 hours or until chicken is tender. Serve with noodles.

The **outermost** part of a **citrus fruit** has the most **desirable** flavor. Be careful **not to grate too far down** into the peel. The lighter-colored **inner part** of the peel, the **pith**, tastes **bitter.**

EAT SMART

Spring-Thyme Chicken Stew

During a long winter (and spring), when my husband and I needed something warm, comforting and bright, this stew was the perfect thing. It reminds me of the days my mom made chicken soup.
—**AMY CHASE** VANDERHOOF, BC

PREP: 15 MIN. • **COOK:** 7 HOURS
MAKES: 4 SERVINGS

- 1 **pound small red potatoes, halved**
- 1 **large onion, finely chopped**
- ¾ **cup shredded carrots**
- 3 **tablespoons all-purpose flour**
- 6 **garlic cloves, minced**
- 2 **teaspoons grated lemon peel**
- 2 **teaspoons dried thyme**
- ½ **teaspoon salt**
- ¼ **teaspoon pepper**
- 1½ **pounds boneless skinless chicken thighs, halved**
- 2 **cups reduced-sodium chicken broth**
- 2 **bay leaves**
- 2 **tablespoons minced fresh parsley**

1. Place potatoes, onion and carrots in a 3-qt. slow cooker. Sprinkle with flour, garlic, lemon peel, thyme, salt and pepper; toss to coat. Place chicken over top. Add broth and bay leaves.
2. Cook, covered, on low 7-9 hours or until chicken and vegetables are tender. Remove bay leaves. Sprinkle servings with parsley.
PER SERVING *1 serving equals 395 cal., 13 g fat (3 g sat. fat), 113 mg chol., 707 mg sodium, 32 g carb., 4 g fiber, 37 g pro.* **Diabetic Exchanges:** *5 lean meat, 2 vegetable, 1½ starch.*

CINCINNATI-STYLE CHILI

Cincinnati-Style Chili

My husband had this type of chili when visiting a friend in Ohio and was super-thrilled when I made it at home. You can have it "two-way," with just chili and spaghetti, but our favorite is "five-way," when you add all three toppings.
—**TARI AMBLER** SHOREWOOD, IL

PREP: 35 MIN. • **COOK:** 6 HOURS
MAKES: 10 SERVINGS

- 2 pounds extra-lean ground turkey
- 2 medium onions, finely chopped
- 4 garlic cloves, minced
- 2 cans (8 ounces each) no-salt-added tomato sauce
- 1 can (14½ ounces) reduced-sodium beef broth
- 2 tablespoons cider vinegar
- ½ ounce unsweetened chocolate, chopped
- 3 tablespoons chili powder
- 1 bay leaf
- 2 teaspoons Worcestershire sauce
- 1 teaspoon ground cumin
- ¾ teaspoon salt
- ¾ teaspoon ground cinnamon
- ¼ teaspoon ground allspice
- ⅛ teaspoon ground cloves
- ⅛ teaspoon cayenne pepper
- 1 package (16 ounces) whole wheat spaghetti

TOPPINGS
- 1 can (16 ounces) kidney beans, rinsed and drained
- 1¼ cups (5 ounces) shredded reduced-fat cheddar cheese
- 1 medium onion, chopped

1. In a nonstick Dutch oven coated with cooking spray, cook turkey, onions and garlic until turkey is no longer pink. Transfer to a 3-qt. slow cooker.
2. In a large bowl, combine tomato sauce, broth, vinegar, chocolate and seasonings; pour over turkey mixture. Cook, covered, on low 6-8 hours.
3. Cook spaghetti according to package directions; drain. Remove bay leaf from chili. For each serving, place ¾ cup spaghetti in a bowl. Top with about ⅔ cup chili, 3 tablespoons kidney beans, 2 tablespoons cheese and 1 tablespoon chopped onion.
PER SERVING *1 serving equals 388 cal., 6 g fat (3 g sat. fat), 47 mg chol., 523 mg sodium, 52 g carb., 10 g fiber, 37 g pro.*

Red, White and Brew Slow-Cooked Chicken

My chicken is a snap to prepare, and the results are always delicious! The beer imparts a tang to the sauce that makes it irresistible. Serve this dish with plenty of crusty bread so you can mop up and enjoy every last drop.
—**GILDA LESTER** MILLSBORO, DE

PREP: 25 MIN. • **COOK:** 6 HOURS
MAKES: 6 SERVINGS

- 1 can (14½ ounces) fire-roasted diced tomatoes, undrained
- 1 medium onion, chopped
- 1 jalapeno pepper, seeded and chopped
- 3 tablespoons brown sugar
- 3 tablespoons balsamic vinegar
- 1 tablespoon ground mustard
- 1 teaspoon dried basil
- ¼ teaspoon crushed red pepper flakes
- 1 cup beer or nonalcoholic beer
- 1 broiler/fryer chicken (3 to 4 pounds), cut up and skin removed
- 1 envelope (1¼ ounces) chili seasoning
  Hot cooked pasta

1. Place the first eight ingredients in a food processor; cover and process until pureed. Stir in beer; set aside.
2. Rub chicken pieces with chili seasoning. Place in a 5-qt. slow cooker. Pour tomato mixture over chicken. Cover and cook on low for 6-7 hours or until chicken is tender.
3. Thicken cooking liquid if desired. Serve chicken with pasta.
NOTE *Wear disposable gloves when cutting hot peppers; the oils can burn skin. Avoid touching your face.*

Tex-Mex Chicken with Black Beans & Rice

I came up with this recipe for my sister, who cooks mostly by throwing canned goods into a pot, when she got her first slow cooker. It's a delicious go-to dish for the busiest day.

—**ELIZABETH DUMONT** BOULDER, CO

PREP: 15 MIN. • **COOK:** 7 HOURS
MAKES: 6 SERVINGS

- 6 **chicken leg quarters, skin removed**
- 1 **envelope taco seasoning, divided**
- 1 **can (14½ ounces) Mexican diced tomatoes, undrained**
- 1 **can (10¾ ounces) condensed cream of chicken soup, undiluted**
- 1 **large onion, chopped**
- 1 **can (4 ounces) chopped green chilies**
- 1 **cup uncooked instant rice**
- 1 **cup canned black beans, rinsed and drained**
- 1 **container (8 ounces) sour cream**
- 1 **cup (4 ounces) shredded cheddar cheese**
- 1½ **cups crushed tortilla chips Minced fresh cilantro**

1. Sprinkle chicken with 1 tablespoon taco seasoning; transfer to a 5- or 6-qt. slow cooker. In a large bowl, combine the tomatoes, soup, onion, chilies and remaining taco seasoning; pour over chicken. Cover and cook on low for 7-9 hours or until chicken is tender.

2. Prepare rice according to package directions. Stir in beans; heat through.

3. Remove chicken from cooking juices; stir sour cream into cooking juices. Serve chicken with the rice mixture and sauce. Sprinkle each serving with cheese, tortilla chips and cilantro.

Sunday Chicken Supper

Here's a hearty, homespun dinner that satisfies the biggest appetites. You're sure to love the convenience of cooking your chicken, veggies and starch all in the same wonderful dish.

—**RUTHANN MARTIN** LOUISVILLE, OH

PREP: 15 MIN. • **COOK:** 6 HOURS
MAKES: 4 SERVINGS

- 4 **medium carrots, cut into 2-inch pieces**
- 1 **medium onion, chopped**
- 1 **celery rib, cut into 2-inch pieces**
- 2 **cups cut fresh green beans (2-inch pieces)**
- 5 **small red potatoes, quartered**
- 1 **broiler/fryer chicken (3 to 3½ pounds), cut up**
- 4 **bacon strips, cooked and crumbled**
- 1½ **cups hot water**
- 2 **teaspoons chicken bouillon granules**
- 1 **teaspoon salt**
- ½ **teaspoon dried thyme**
- ½ **teaspoon dried basil Pinch pepper**

1. In a 5-qt. slow cooker, layer the first seven ingredients in order listed. In a small bowl, combine water, bouillon, salt, thyme, basil and pepper; pour over the top. Do not stir.

2. Cover slow cooker and cook on low for 6-8 hours or until vegetables are tender and chicken juices run clear. Remove chicken and vegetables.

3. Thicken the cooking juices for gravy if desired.

TEX-MEX CHICKEN WITH BLACK BEANS & RICE

TURKEY ROAST WITH WHITE WINE GRAVY

Chicken, Smashed Potatoes & Gravy

PREP: 30 MIN. • **COOK:** 3 HOURS
MAKES: 6 SERVINGS

- 2 **pounds small red potatoes, quartered**
- 3 **tablespoons water**
- 2 **pounds boneless skinless chicken breasts**
- 1 **medium onion, sliced**
- 2 **medium carrots, cut into 2-inch pieces**
- 2 **celery ribs, cut into 2-inch pieces**
- 3 **garlic cloves, minced**
- 2 **bay leaves**
- 1½ **teaspoons pepper, divided**
- 2½ **cups chicken broth**
- ½ **cup white wine or additional chicken broth**
- 4 **ounces cream cheese, softened**
- ¾ **teaspoon salt, divided**
- 3 **tablespoons butter**
- 3 **tablespoons all-purpose flour**
- ½ **cup 2% milk**
  Minced chives, optional

1. In a large microwave-safe bowl, combine potatoes and water. Microwave, covered, on high for 10-12 minutes or just until tender. Cool slightly; drain.
2. Transfer potatoes to a 5-qt. slow cooker. Add chicken, vegetables, garlic, bay leaves and 1 teaspoon pepper. Pour broth and wine over top. Cook, covered, on low for 3-4 hours or until a thermometer reads 165° and potatoes are tender. Remove chicken from slow cooker; tent with foil.
3. Strain cooking juices, reserving potatoes and cooking juices; discard remaining vegetables and bay leaves. In a large bowl, mash potatoes with cream cheese, ¼ teaspoon salt, ¼ teaspoon pepper and enough cooking juices to reach desired consistency; keep warm.
4. In a small saucepan, melt butter over medium heat. Stir in flour until blended; cook and stir 1-2 minutes. Gradually whisk in 1 cup cooking juices, milk and remaining salt and pepper. Bring to a boil, stirring constantly; cook and stir 2-3 minutes or until thickened.
5. Discard remaining cooking juices. Slice chicken; serve with potatoes, gravy and, if desired, chives.

Turkey Roast with White Wine Gravy

The wine you use in this recipe doesn't have to be expensive, but please don't use cooking wine. I've used Sauvignon Blanc with great results. If you have any leftovers, they'll make scrumptious sandwiches the next day.
—TINA MACKISSOCK MANCHESTER, NH

PREP: 20 MIN. • **COOK:** 6 HOURS
MAKES: 8 SERVINGS

- 1 **cup white wine**
- 1 **medium apple, chopped**
- ½ **cup sliced fennel bulb**
- ⅓ **cup chopped celery**
- ⅓ **cup chopped carrot**
- 3 **garlic cloves, minced**
- 1 **teaspoon ground mustard**
- 1 **bay leaf**
- ½ **teaspoon dried rosemary, crushed**
- ½ **teaspoon dried thyme**
- ½ **teaspoon rubbed sage**
- ¼ **teaspoon pepper**
- 1 **package (3 pounds) frozen boneless turkey breast roast, thawed**
- 2 **tablespoons plus 1½ teaspoons cornstarch**
- ½ **cup half-and-half cream**

1. In a 6-qt. slow cooker, combine the wine, apple, fennel, celery, carrot, garlic, mustard and bay leaf. In a small bowl, combine the rosemary, thyme, sage and pepper; rub over turkey. Add turkey to slow cooker. Cover and cook on low for 6-8 hours or until the meat is tender.
2. Remove the turkey to a serving platter and keep warm. Strain the drippings into a measuring cup to measure 1 cup. Skim fat. In a small saucepan, combine cornstarch and cream; stir until smooth. Gradually add the drippings. Bring to a boil; cook and stir for 2 minutes or until thickened. Serve with turkey.
PER SERVING *5 ounces cooked turkey with 3 tablespoons gravy equals 238 cal., 3 g fat (1 g sat. fat), 113 mg chol., 102 mg sodium, 7 g carb., 1 g fiber, 43 g pro. Diabetic Exchanges: 6 lean meat, ½ starch.*

"On chilly days, I crave this yummy chicken with potatoes and gravy. Share it with the family or take it to potlucks and watch it disappear."
—**DEBORAH POSEY** VIRGINIA BEACH, VA

CHICKEN, SMASHED POTATOES & GRAVY

Rosemary Cashew Chicken

Here's a flavorful entree with a hint of citrus and herbs and the delightful crunch of cashews.

—RUTH ANDREWSON LEAVENWORTH, WA

PREP: 15 MIN. • **COOK:** 4 HOURS
MAKES: 4-6 SERVINGS

- 1 broiler/fryer chicken (3 to 4 pounds), cut up, skin removed
- 1 medium onion, thinly sliced
- ⅓ cup thawed orange juice concentrate
- 1 teaspoon dried rosemary, crushed
- 1 teaspoon salt
- ¼ teaspoon cayenne pepper
- 2 tablespoons all-purpose flour
- 3 tablespoons water
- ¼ to ½ cup chopped cashews
    Hot cooked pasta

1. Place chicken in a 3-qt. slow cooker. Combine the onion, orange juice concentrate, rosemary, salt and cayenne; pour over chicken. Cover and cook on low for 4-5 hours or until chicken juices run clear. Remove the chicken and keep warm.

2. In a saucepan, combine flour and water until smooth. Stir in cooking juices. Bring to a boil; cook and stir for 2 minutes or until thickened. Stir in cashews. Pour over chicken. Serve with pasta.

Green peppers are unripened versions of **red, yellow or orange** peppers. They are **less expensive** because they're quicker to get to market. Use **colored peppers** in recipes for more sweetness.

SQUASH 'N' CHICKEN STEW

Squash 'n' Chicken Stew

We created a satisfying stew that's nutritious, loaded with flavor and family friendly. Chicken thighs are slowly simmered with stewed tomatoes, butternut squash, green peppers and onion for meal-in-one convenience.

—*TASTE OF HOME* TEST KITCHEN

PREP: 15 MIN. • **COOK:** 6 HOURS
MAKES: 5 SERVINGS

- 2 pounds boneless skinless chicken thighs, cut into ½-inch pieces
- 1 can (28 ounces) stewed tomatoes, cut up
- 3 cups cubed peeled butternut squash
- 2 medium green peppers, cut into ½-inch pieces
- 1 small onion, sliced and separated into rings
- 1 cup water
- 1 teaspoon salt
- 1 teaspoon ground cumin
- ½ teaspoon ground coriander
- ½ teaspoon pepper
- 2 tablespoons minced fresh parsley
    Hot cooked couscous, optional

In a 5-qt. slow cooker, combine the first 10 ingredients. Cover and cook on low for 6-7 hours or until chicken is no longer pink. Sprinkle with parsley. Serve with couscous if desired.

Soy-Ginger Chicken

This is the first recipe I ever tried making without a cookbook, and it came out so tender and delicious. Garlic, ginger and spices give the rich sauce plenty of authentic Asian flavor.

—**KAEL HARVEY** BROOKLYN, NY

PREP: 25 MIN. • **COOK:** 5 HOURS
MAKES: 4 SERVINGS

- 4 **bone-in chicken thighs (about 1½ pounds), skin removed**
- 4 **chicken drumsticks (about 1 pound), skin removed**
- 2 **medium carrots, sliced**
- 4 **green onions, thinly sliced**
- ⅓ **cup soy sauce**
- 2 **tablespoons brown sugar**
- 1 **piece fresh gingerroot (about 2 inches), peeled and thinly sliced**
- 5 **garlic cloves, minced**
- 1 **tablespoon balsamic vinegar**
- 1 **teaspoon ground coriander**
- ½ **teaspoon pepper**
- 1 **tablespoon cornstarch**
- 1 **tablespoon cold water**
  Hot cooked rice and minced fresh cilantro

1. Place the chicken, carrots and green onions in a 3-qt. slow cooker. Combine the soy sauce, brown sugar, ginger, garlic, vinegar, coriander and pepper in a small bowl. Pour over top. Cover and cook on low 5-6 hours or until chicken is tender.

2. Remove chicken to a serving platter; keep warm. Pour juices into a small saucepan. Bring to a boil. Combine cornstarch and water until smooth; gradually stir into pan. Bring to a boil; cook and stir for 1-2 minutes or until thickened. Serve with chicken and rice; sprinkle servings with cilantro.

Tender Chicken Dinner

Just about anyone would enjoy this family-pleasing dinner of chicken and vegetables. You can put it together fast before you leave for school or work.

—**WANDA SANNER** AMARILLO, TX

PREP: 15 MIN. • **COOK:** 5¼ HOURS
MAKES: 4 SERVINGS

- 4 **boneless skinless chicken breast halves (4 ounces each)**
- 1 **can (14½ ounces) chicken broth**
- 1 **jar (12 ounces) chicken gravy**
- 2 **cups sliced peeled potatoes**
- 1 **package (16 ounces) frozen sliced carrots, thawed**
- 1 **package (16 ounces) frozen cut green beans, thawed**
- 1 **teaspoon pepper**
- 2 **tablespoons cornstarch**
- ⅓ **cup cold water**
- 1 **cup French-fried onions**

1. Place chicken in a 5-qt. slow cooker. Add the broth, gravy, potatoes, carrots, beans and pepper. Cover and cook on low for 5 to 5½ hours or until chicken is tender.

2. Mix cornstarch and water until smooth; stir into cooking juices. Sprinkle with onions. Cover and cook on high for 15 minutes or until thickened.

SOY-GINGER CHICKEN

Chicken & Vegetables with Mustard-Herb Sauce

Here's an almost effortless recipe that makes a delicious chicken dinner. This is classic comfort food.

—MARIE RIZZIO INTERLOCHEN, MI

PREP: 20 MIN. • **COOK:** 6 HOURS
MAKES: 4 SERVINGS

- 4 medium red potatoes, quartered
- 3 medium parsnips, cut into 1-inch pieces
- 2 medium leeks (white portion only), thinly sliced
- ¾ cup fresh baby carrots
- 4 chicken leg quarters, skin removed
- 1 can (10¾ ounces) condensed cream of chicken soup with herbs, undiluted
- 2 tablespoons minced fresh parsley
- 1 tablespoon snipped fresh dill or 1 teaspoon dill weed
- 1 tablespoon Dijon mustard

1. In a 5- or 6-qt. slow cooker, place the potatoes, parsnips, leeks, carrots and chicken; pour soup over top. Cover and cook on low for 6-8 hours or until chicken is tender.

2. Remove chicken and vegetables; cover and keep warm. Stir the parsley, dill and mustard into cooking juices; serve with chicken and vegetables.

Herbed Turkey Breast

Flavorful herbs, spices and citrus enhance tender turkey breast in this special recipe. You can also roast the turkey if you don't want to wait all day. Yum!

—LAURIE MACE LOS OSOS, CA

PREP: 25 MIN. + MARINATING
COOK: 3½ HOURS • **MAKES:** 12 SERVINGS

- 1 can (14½ ounces) chicken broth
- ½ cup lemon juice
- ¼ cup packed brown sugar
- ¼ cup fresh sage
- ¼ cup fresh thyme leaves
- ¼ cup lime juice
- ¼ cup cider vinegar
- ¼ cup olive oil
- 1 envelope onion soup mix
- 2 tablespoons Dijon mustard
- 1 tablespoon minced fresh marjoram
- 1½ teaspoons paprika
- 1 teaspoon garlic powder
- 1 teaspoon pepper
- ½ teaspoon salt
- 2 boneless skinless turkey breast halves (2 pounds each)

1. In a blender, process the first 15 ingredients until blended. Pour into a large resealable plastic bag; add the turkey. Seal bag and turn to coat; refrigerate 8 hours or overnight.

2. Transfer turkey and marinade to a 5-qt. slow cooker. Cover and cook on high for 3½ to 4½ hours or until a thermometer reads 165°.

Save prep work by making **a second batch** of the turkey **marinade** and freezing it for **next time**.

CHICKEN & VEGETABLES WITH MUSTARD-HERB SAUCE

HERBED TURKEY BREAST

Italian Chicken and Peppers

I put this chicken recipe together one day when I had leftover peppers and wanted something easy. To my delight, the taste reminded me of pizza—something I love but can no longer eat! It's great with steamed broccoli.

—BRENDA NOLEN SIMPSONVILLE, SC

PREP: 20 MIN. • **COOK:** 4 HOURS
MAKES: 6 SERVINGS

- 6 **boneless skinless chicken breast halves (4 ounces each)**
- 1 **jar (24 ounces) garden-style spaghetti sauce**
- 1 **medium onion, sliced**
- ½ **each small green, sweet yellow and red peppers, julienned**
- ¼ **cup grated Parmesan cheese**
- 2 **garlic cloves, minced**
- 1 **teaspoon dried oregano**
- 1 **teaspoon dried basil**
- ½ **teaspoon salt**
- ¼ **teaspoon pepper**
- 4½ **cups uncooked spiral pasta**
  Shaved Parmesan cheese, optional

1. Place the chicken in a 3-qt. slow cooker. In a large bowl, combine the spaghetti sauce, onion, peppers, cheese, garlic, oregano, basil, salt and pepper. Pour over chicken. Cover and cook on low for 4-5 hours or until a thermometer reads 170°.

2. Cook pasta according to package directions; drain. Serve with chicken and sauce. Top with shaved Parmesan cheese if desired.

PER SERVING *1 chicken breast half with ¾ cup pasta and ⅔ cup sauce (calculated without shaved Parmesan) equals 396 cal., 7 g fat (2 g sat. fat), 70 mg chol., 770 mg sodium, 50 g carb., 5 g fiber, 32 g pro.*

Chicken in Mushroom Gravy

Cream of mushroom soup makes an easy gravy for tender, juicy chicken breasts. You can also make this with other vegetables, or serve it over thick-sliced potatoes instead of rice.

—VALMA O'NEILL UTICA, MI

PREP: 5 MIN. • **COOK:** 4 HOURS
MAKES: 2 SERVINGS

- 2 **boneless skinless chicken breast halves (6 ounces each)**
- ½ **pound fresh baby carrots, cut in half lengthwise**
- 1 **can (10¾ ounces) condensed cream of mushroom soup, undiluted**
- 1 **can (4 ounces) mushroom stems and pieces, drained**
  Hot cooked rice, optional

Place the chicken in a 1½-qt. slow cooker. Top with carrots, soup and mushrooms. Cover and cook on low for 4-5 hours or until chicken is tender. Serve over rice if desired.

Spicy Shredded Chicken

I love Mexican food, but not the high calorie count that often comes with it. This easy dish is healthy, delicious and a definite crowd-pleaser! I like to serve the chicken with warm tortillas, rice, beans and salsa on the side.

—**HEATHER WALKER** SCOTTSDALE, AZ

PREP: 40 MIN. • **COOK:** 4¼ HOURS
MAKES: 8 SERVINGS

- 2 **tablespoons olive oil**
- 1 **pound boneless skinless chicken thighs**
- 1 **pound boneless skinless chicken breasts**
- 3 **cups reduced-sodium chicken broth, divided**
- 6 **green onions, chopped**
- 1 **medium green pepper, chopped**
- 2 **tablespoons ground cumin**
- 1 **tablespoon garlic powder**
- 1 **tablespoon chili powder**
- 1 **tablespoon paprika**
- 1 **teaspoon cayenne pepper**
- ½ **teaspoon salt**
- ¼ **teaspoon pepper**
- 1 **plum tomato, chopped**

1. In a large skillet, heat the oil over medium-high heat. Brown chicken in batches. Transfer to a 3- or 4-qt. slow cooker. Add 1 cup broth to the pan. Cook, stirring to loosen browned bits from pan.

2. Add onions and green pepper; cook and stir 3-5 minutes or until vegetables are tender. Stir in the seasonings; cook 1-2 minutes. Add tomato and remaining broth; pour over chicken. Cook, covered, on low 4-5 hours or until chicken is tender.

3. Remove chicken from slow cooker. When cool enough to handle, shred meat with two forks; return to slow cooker. Cook, covered, on low for 15-20 minutes longer or until heated through. Serve with a slotted spoon.

FREEZE OPTION *Freeze cooled chicken mixture in freezer containers. To use, partially thaw chicken in the refrigerator overnight. Heat through in a saucepan, stirring occasionally and adding a little reduced-sodium broth or water if necessary.*

PER SERVING *¾ cup equals 202 cal., 10 g fat (2 g sat. fat), 69 mg chol., 436 mg sodium, 5 g carb., 2 g fiber, 24 g pro. **Diabetic Exchanges:** 3 lean meat, 1 fat.*

Chicken in a Pot

At the end of a busy day, your family will appreciate the simple goodness of home-cooked chicken and vegetables. This is one of our favorite meals.

—**ALPHA WILSON** ROSWELL, NM

PREP: 10 MIN. • **COOK:** 7 HOURS
MAKES: 6 SERVINGS

- 3 **medium carrots, chopped**
- 2 **celery ribs with leaves, chopped**
- 2 **medium onions, sliced**
- 1 **broiler/fryer chicken (3 to 4 pounds), cut up**
- ½ **cup chicken broth**
- 1½ **teaspoons salt**
- 1 **teaspoon dried basil**
- ½ **teaspoon pepper**

1. Place the carrots, celery and onions in a 5-qt. slow cooker. Top with the chicken. Combine the remaining ingredients; pour over chicken.

2. Cover slow cooker and cook on low for 7-9 hours or until the chicken and vegetables are tender. Serve with a slotted spoon.

SPICY SHREDDED CHICKEN

WINE-BRAISED CHICKEN WITH PEARL ONIONS

Wine-Braised Chicken with Pearl Onions

PREP: 10 MIN. • **COOK:** 7 HOURS
MAKES: 4 SERVINGS

- 8 **boneless skinless chicken thighs (about 2 pounds)**
- 1 **package (14.4 ounces) pearl onions, thawed**
- 1 **can (10¾ ounces) condensed cream of chicken soup, undiluted**
- ¼ **cup white wine or chicken broth**
- 2 **teaspoons minced fresh parsley**
- 1 **teaspoon dried tarragon**
- ½ **teaspoon salt**
- ¼ **teaspoon dried rosemary, crushed**
  Hot cooked rice or pasta
  Minced fresh parsley, optional

1. Place chicken and onions in a 4-qt. slow cooker. In a small bowl, combine soup, wine and seasonings; pour over chicken and onions. Cook, covered, on low 7-8 hours or until the chicken is tender.

2. Remove chicken; skim fat from cooking juices. Serve cooking juices with chicken and rice. If desired, sprinkle with parsley.

To **keep parsley fresh** for up to a month, trim the stems and place the bunch in a **tumbler** with an inch of **water**. Be sure no loose leaves or greenery are in the water. Tie a **produce bag** around the glass to **trap humidity**; store parsley in the refrigerator.

CHICKEN MOLE

FREEZE IT

Chicken Mole

If you're not familiar with mole, don't be afraid to try this versatile Mexican sauce. I love sharing the recipe because it's a good, simple introduction to mole.
—**DARLENE MORRIS** FRANKLINTON, LA

PREP: 25 MIN. • **COOK:** 6 HOURS
MAKES: 12 SERVINGS

- 12 **bone-in chicken thighs (about 4½ pounds), skin removed**
- 1 **teaspoon salt**

MOLE SAUCE

- 1 **can (28 ounces) whole tomatoes, drained**
- 1 **medium onion, chopped**
- 2 **dried ancho chilies, stems and seeds removed**
- ½ **cup sliced almonds, toasted**
- ¼ **cup raisins**
- 3 **ounces bittersweet chocolate, chopped**
- 3 **tablespoons olive oil**
- 1 **chipotle pepper in adobo sauce**
- 3 **garlic cloves, peeled and halved**
- ¾ **teaspoon ground cumin**
- ½ **teaspoon ground cinnamon**
  Fresh cilantro leaves, optional

1. Sprinkle chicken with salt; place in a 5- or 6-qt. slow cooker. Place the tomatoes, onion, chilies, almonds, raisins, chocolate, oil, chipotle pepper, garlic, cumin and cinnamon in a food processor; cover and process until blended. Pour over chicken.

2. Cover and cook on low 6-8 hours or until chicken is tender; skim fat. Serve chicken with sauce and sprinkle with cilantro if desired.

FREEZE OPTION *Cool chicken in mole sauce. Freeze in freezer containers. To use, partially thaw in the refrigerator overnight. Heat mixture slowly in a covered skillet or Dutch oven until a thermometer inserted in chicken reads 165°, stirring occasionally and adding a little broth or water if necessary.*

Other Entrees

47   52   57

Experience the **joy** of returning home to the **delightful aroma** of one of these **slow-simmered meals**. Savor tender **pork** chops, fruity **ham**, **vegetarian** mains, crowd-pleasing **brunch** dishes and even perfectly poached **salmon**, all cooked up in your favorite appliance.

SUNDAY POT ROAST

Country Cassoulet

This bean stew goes wonderfully with fresh dinner rolls and your favorite green salad. It's a hearty meal that's perfect after a long day in the garden.

—SUZANNE MCKINLEY LYONS, GA

PREP: 20 MIN. + STANDING
COOK: 6 HOURS
MAKES: 8-10 SERVINGS

- 1 **pound dried great northern beans**
- 2 **uncooked garlic-flavored pork sausage links**
- 3 **bacon strips, diced**
- 1½ **pounds boneless pork, cut into 1-inch cubes**
- 1 **pound boneless lamb, cut into 1-inch cubes**
- 1½ **cups chopped onion**
- 3 **garlic cloves, minced**
- 2 **teaspoons salt**
- 1 **teaspoon dried thyme**
- 4 **whole cloves**
- 2 **bay leaves**
- 2½ **cups chicken broth**
- 1 **can (8 ounces) tomato sauce**

1. Rinse and sort beans; soak according to package directions. Drain and rinse beans, discarding the liquid.

2. In a large skillet over medium-high heat, brown sausage links; transfer to a 5-qt. slow cooker. Add bacon to skillet; cook until crisp. Remove with a slotted spoon to slow cooker.

3. In bacon drippings, cook pork and lamb until browned on all sides. Place in slow cooker. Stir in beans and the remaining ingredients.

4. Cover and cook on low for 6-8 hours or until beans are tender. Discard cloves and bay leaves. Remove sausage and cut into ¼-in. slices; gently stir into cassoulet.

Sunday Pot Roast

With the help of a slow cooker, you can prepare a down-home dinner any day of the week, not just on Sundays.

—BRANDY SCHAEFER GLEN CARBON, IL

PREP: 10 MIN. + CHILLING • **COOK:** 8 HOURS
MAKES: 14 SERVINGS

- 1 **teaspoon dried oregano**
- ½ **teaspoon onion salt**
- ½ **teaspoon caraway seeds**
- ½ **teaspoon pepper**
- ¼ **teaspoon garlic salt**
- 1 **boneless pork loin roast (3½ to 4 pounds), trimmed**
- 6 **medium carrots, peeled and cut into 1½-inch pieces**
- 3 **large potatoes, peeled and quartered**
- 3 **small onions, quartered**
- 1½ **cups beef broth**
- ⅓ **cup all-purpose flour**
- ⅓ **cup cold water**
- ¼ **teaspoon browning sauce, optional**

1. In a small bowl, combine the first five ingredients; rub over pork roast. Wrap roast in plastic wrap and refrigerate overnight.

2. Place carrots, potatoes and onions in a 6-qt. slow cooker; add broth. Unwrap roast; place in slow cooker. Cook, covered, on low 8-10 hours or until meat and vegetables are tender.

3. Transfer roast and vegetables to a serving platter; tent with foil. Pour cooking juices into a small saucepan. In a small bowl, mix flour and water until smooth; stir into pan. Bring to a boil; cook and stir 2 minutes or until thickened. If desired, add browning sauce. Serve roast with gravy.

PER SERVING *1 serving equals 233 cal., 5 g fat (2 g sat. fat), 56 mg chol., 249 mg sodium, 21 g carb., 2 g fiber, 24 g pro.* **Diabetic Exchanges:** *3 lean meat, 1½ starch.*

"Ribs slow-cooked with carrots, celery, onions and red potatoes are pure comfort food for us. To add a little zip, we sometimes sprinkle in cayenne."

—ROSE INGALL MANISTEE, MI

COUNTRY RIBS DINNER

Country Ribs Dinner

PREP: 10 MIN. • **COOK:** 6¼ HOURS
MAKES: 4 SERVINGS

- 2 pounds boneless country-style pork ribs
- ½ teaspoon salt
- ¼ teaspoon pepper
- 8 small red potatoes (about 1 pound), halved
- 4 medium carrots, cut into 1-inch pieces
- 3 celery ribs, cut into ½-inch pieces
- 1 medium onion, coarsely chopped
- ¾ cup water
- 1 garlic clove, crushed
- 1 can (10¾ ounces) condensed cream of mushroom soup, undiluted

1. Sprinkle ribs with salt and pepper; transfer to a 4-qt. slow cooker. Add the potatoes, carrots, celery, onion, water and garlic. Cook, covered, on low 6-8 hours or until meat and vegetables are tender.

2. Remove meat and vegetables; skim fat from cooking juices. Whisk soup into cooking juices; return meat and vegetables to slow cooker. Cook, covered, 15-30 minutes longer or until heated through.

Country-style ribs come from the loin end close to the **shoulder**. They are generally considered the **meatiest** type of rib. Country-style ribs are sold in a **bone-in rack** form, as **single ribs** similar to pork chops, and **boneless**.

TANGY PORK CHOPS

Tangy Pork Chops

When my husband and I had our first child, we found this recipe so convenient. I could start it during nap time and we'd enjoy an easy, satisfying dinner that night.
—**KAROL HINES** KITTY HAWK, NC

PREP: 15 MIN. • **COOK:** 5½ HOURS
MAKES: 4 SERVINGS

- 4 bone-in pork loin chops
- ½ teaspoon salt, optional
- ⅛ teaspoon pepper
- 2 medium onions, chopped
- 2 celery ribs, chopped
- 1 large green pepper, sliced
- 1 can (14½ ounces) stewed tomatoes
- ½ cup ketchup
- 2 tablespoons cider vinegar
- 2 tablespoons brown sugar
- 2 tablespoons Worcestershire sauce
- 1 tablespoon lemon juice
- 1 teaspoon beef bouillon granules
- 2 tablespoons cornstarch
- 2 tablespoons cold water
  Hot cooked rice, optional

1. Place chops in a 3-qt. slow cooker; sprinkle with salt if desired and the pepper. Add the onions, celery, green pepper and tomatoes. Combine the ketchup, vinegar, brown sugar, Worcestershire sauce, lemon juice and bouillon; pour over vegetables. Cover and cook on low for 5-6 hours or until meat is tender.

2. Mix cornstarch and water until smooth; stir into liquid in the slow cooker. Cover and cook on high for 30 minutes or until thickened. Serve with rice if desired.

Slow-Cooked Ham with Pineapple Sauce

We serve this dish during the holidays because everyone is crazy about the classic pairing of sweet-tart pineapple and salty ham. It makes appearances at the dinner table all year-round because it's so simple to prepare.

—TERRY ROBERTS YORKTOWN, VA

PREP: 10 MIN. • **COOK:** 6 HOURS
MAKES: 12 SERVINGS

- 1 fully cooked boneless ham (4 to 5 pounds)
- 1 can (20 ounces) unsweetened crushed pineapple, undrained
- 1 cup packed brown sugar
- 1 tablespoon cornstarch
- ¼ teaspoon salt
- 2 tablespoons lemon juice
- 1 tablespoon yellow mustard

1. Place ham in a 5-qt. slow cooker. In a small saucepan, mix the remaining ingredients, stirring to dissolve cornstarch. Bring mixture to a boil, stirring occasionally.
2. Pour over ham, covering completely. Cover and cook on low for 6-8 hours.

EAT SMART

Manchester Stew

While in college, I studied at the University of Manchester in England. At the time, I was a vegetarian and was pleasantly surprised at how delicious and diverse vegetarian food in Britain could be. My favorite meal, served at my favorite restaurant, was Beans Burgundy and, after returning to the States, I created this version. As it simmers in the slow cooker and the enticing aroma fills the kitchen, I'm reminded of my time in England.

—KIMBERLY HAMMOND KINGWOOD, TX

PREP: 25 MIN. • **COOK:** 8 HOURS
MAKES: 6 SERVINGS

- 2 tablespoons olive oil
- 2 medium onions, chopped
- 2 garlic cloves, minced
- 1 teaspoon dried oregano
- 1 cup dry red wine
- 1 pound small red potatoes, quartered
- 1 can (16 ounces) kidney beans, rinsed and drained
- ½ pound sliced fresh mushrooms
- 2 medium leeks (white portion only), sliced
- 1 cup fresh baby carrots
- 2½ cups water
- 1 can (14½ ounces) no-salt-added diced tomatoes
- 1 teaspoon dried thyme
- ½ teaspoon salt
- ¼ teaspoon pepper
  Fresh basil leaves

1. In a large skillet, heat oil over medium-high heat. Add onions; cook and stir 2-3 minutes or until tender. Add garlic and oregano; cook and stir 1 minute longer. Stir in wine. Bring to a boil; cook 3-4 minutes or until liquid is reduced by half.
2. Transfer to a 5-qt. slow cooker. Add potatoes, beans, mushrooms, leeks and carrots. Stir in water, tomatoes, thyme, salt and pepper. Cook, covered, on low 8-10 hours or until potatoes are tender. Garnish with basil.

PER SERVING 1⅔ cups equals 227 cal., 5 g fat (1 g sat. fat), 0 chol., 378 mg sodium, 39 g carb., 8 g fiber, 9 g pro. **Diabetic Exchanges:** 2 starch, 1 vegetable, 1 fat.

SLOW-COOKED HAM WITH PINEAPPLE SAUCE

"My overnight eggs and veggies make a hearty breakfast for those who have to rush out the door. I use sliced potatoes, but frozen potatoes work, too."
—KIMBERLY CLARK-THIRY MOORCROFT, WY

OVERNIGHT VEGETABLE & EGG BREAKFAST

Overnight Vegetable & Egg Breakfast

PREP: 15 MIN. • **COOK:** 7 HOURS
MAKES: 8 SERVINGS

- 4 pounds potatoes, peeled and thinly sliced (about 8 cups)
- 1 medium green pepper, finely chopped
- 1 package (10 ounces) frozen chopped spinach, thawed and squeezed dry
- 1 cup sliced fresh mushrooms
- 1 medium onion, finely chopped
- 8 eggs
- 1 cup water
- 1 cup 2% milk
- 1¼ teaspoons salt
- ¼ teaspoon pepper
- 2 cups (8 ounces) shredded cheddar cheese

1. In a greased 6-qt. slow cooker, layer the first five ingredients. In a large bowl, whisk the eggs, water, milk, salt and pepper; pour over top. Sprinkle with cheese.

2. Cook, covered, on low 7-9 hours or until potatoes are tender and the eggs are set.

FREEZE IT
Smoky Bean Stew

I love to start this satisfying stew in the slow cooker, then spend the afternoon curled up with a good book. It's an effortless meal that always tastes great.
—GLENDA HOLMES RILEY, KS

PREP: 10 MIN. • **COOK:** 4 HOURS
MAKES: 6-8 SERVINGS

- 1 package (16 ounces) miniature smoked sausage links
- 1 can (16 ounces) baked beans
- 2 cups frozen cut green beans
- 2 cups frozen lima beans
- ½ cup packed brown sugar
- ½ cup thinly sliced fresh carrots
- ½ cup chopped onion
- ½ cup ketchup
- 1 tablespoon cider vinegar
- 1 teaspoon prepared mustard

In a 3-qt. slow cooker, combine all ingredients. Cover and cook on high for 4-5 hours or until the vegetables are tender.

FREEZE OPTION *Freeze cooled stew in freezer containers. To use, partially thaw in the refrigerator overnight. Heat through in a saucepan, stirring occasionally and adding a little water if necessary.*

EASY & ELEGANT
POACHED SALMON

Peachy Baby Back Ribs

It's easy to get a smoky outdoor barbecue flavor from your slow cooker. Trust me, I've fooled many people with these ribs.

—MARY LOUISE BURK ROME, GA

PREP: 15 MIN. • **COOK:** 6 HOURS
MAKES: 6 SERVINGS

2 bottles (18 ounces each) hickory smoke-flavored barbecue sauce
1 can (15 ounces) sliced peaches, drained and halved crosswise
1 medium onion, chopped
¾ cup jalapeno pepper jelly
½ cup pickled hot jalapeno slices
6 pounds pork baby back ribs, well-trimmed
1 teaspoon salt
½ teaspoon pepper
Thinly sliced green onions

1. In a large bowl, mix the first five ingredients. Cut the ribs into 3-rib portions; sprinkle with salt and pepper. Place half of the ribs in a 6-qt. slow cooker; top with half of sauce mixture. Repeat layers. Cook, covered, on low 6-8 hours or until tender.
2. Remove ribs from slow cooker; keep warm. Strain cooking juices, reserving peaches and vegetables. Skim fat from cooking juices; thicken if desired. Stir in reserved peaches and vegetables; serve with ribs. Sprinkle with green onions.

EAT SMART
Easy & Elegant Poached Salmon

I adore this recipe because it's healthy and almost effortless. And the salmon always cooks to perfection!

—ERIN CHILCOAT CENTRAL ISLIP, NY

PREP: 10 MIN. • **COOK:** 1½ HOURS
MAKES: 4 SERVINGS

2 cups water
1 cup white wine
1 medium onion, sliced
1 celery rib, sliced
1 medium carrot, sliced
2 tablespoons lemon juice
3 fresh thyme sprigs
1 fresh rosemary sprig
1 bay leaf
½ teaspoon salt
¼ teaspoon pepper
4 salmon fillets (1¼ inches thick and 6 ounces each)
Lemon wedges

1. In a 3-qt. slow cooker, combine the first 11 ingredients. Cook, covered, on low 45 minutes.
2. Carefully place fillets in liquid; add additional warm water (120° to 130°) to cover if needed. Cook, covered, 45-55 minutes or just until fish flakes easily with a fork (a thermometer inserted in fish should read at least 145°). Remove fish from the cooking liquid and serve warm or cold with lemon wedges.
PER SERVING *1 salmon fillet equals 272 cal., 16 g fat (3 g sat. fat), 85 mg chol., 115 mg sodium, 1 g carb., trace fiber, 29 g pro.* **Diabetic Exchange:** *4 lean meat.*

Wild salmon is 20% leaner than farm-raised, and it's higher in **heart-healthy omega-3** fatty acids. It's available fresh from **May to October**, when the fish swim upstream to spawn.

PEACHY BABY BACK RIBS

Gulf Coast Jambalaya Rice

As the stew of the South, jambalaya is a definite staple. For ages, home cooks have been making their own versions of the traditional recipe. This slow-cooked rendition is my favorite.

—JUDY BATSON TAMPA, FL

PREP: 20 MIN. • **COOK:** 3¼ HOURS
MAKES: 8 SERVINGS

- 1 pound boneless skinless chicken breasts, cut into 1-inch cubes
- 1 pound smoked kielbasa, cut into ¼-inch slices
- 2 cups chicken stock
- 1 large green pepper, chopped
- 1 cup chopped sweet onion
- 2 celery ribs, chopped
- 2 garlic cloves, minced
- 2 teaspoons Creole seasoning
- 1 teaspoon seafood seasoning
- 1 teaspoon pepper
- 1 pound uncooked medium shrimp, peeled and deveined
- 2 cups uncooked instant rice

1. Place the first 10 ingredients in a 5-qt. slow cooker. Cook, covered, on low 3-4 hours or until chicken is tender.
2. Stir in shrimp and rice. Cook, covered, 15-20 minutes longer or until shrimp turn pink and rice is tender.
NOTE *The following spices may be substituted for 1 teaspoon Creole seasoning: ¼ teaspoon each salt, garlic powder and paprika; and a pinch each of dried thyme, ground cumin and cayenne pepper.*

GULF COAST JAMBALAYA RICE

EAT SMART

Pork Chop Cacciatore

It's hard to believe that so much flavor can come from such an easy recipe. Serve it with noodles and a simple green salad, and dinner is solved!

—TRACY HIATT GRICE SOMERSET, WI

PREP: 30 MIN. • **COOK:** 8 HOURS
MAKES: 6 SERVINGS

- 6 bone-in pork loin chops (7 ounces each)
- ¾ teaspoon salt, divided
- ¼ teaspoon pepper
- 1 tablespoon olive oil
- 1 cup sliced fresh mushrooms
- 1 small onion, chopped
- 1 celery rib, chopped
- 1 small green pepper, chopped
- 2 garlic cloves, minced
- 1 can (14½ ounces) diced tomatoes
- ½ cup water, divided
- ½ teaspoon dried basil
- 2 tablespoons cornstarch
- 4½ cups cooked egg noodles

1. Sprinkle chops with ½ teaspoon salt and the pepper. In a large skillet, brown the chops in oil in batches. Transfer to a 4-or 5-qt. slow cooker coated with cooking spray. Saute the mushrooms, onion, celery and green pepper in drippings until tender. Add garlic; cook 1 minute longer. Stir in the tomatoes, ¼ cup water, basil and remaining salt; pour over chops.
2. Cover and cook on low for 8-10 hours or until pork is tender. Remove meat to a serving platter; keep warm. Skim fat from cooking juices if necessary; transfer to a small saucepan. Bring liquid to a boil. Combine cornstarch and remaining water until smooth. Gradually stir into the pan. Bring to a boil; cook and stir for 2 minutes or until thickened. Serve with meat and noodles.
PER SERVING *1 pork chop with ¾ cup noodles and ½ cup sauce equals 371 cal., 12 g fat (4 g sat. fat), 110 mg chol., 458 mg sodium, 29 g carb., 3 g fiber, 35 g pro.* **Diabetic Exchanges:** *4 lean meat, 1½ starch, 1 vegetable, ½ fat.*

Slow-Cooked Pork Loin

Sweet apple undertones in the cooking juices lend special flair to tender pork loin. I thicken the juices to make a gravy with true comfort-food appeal.

—**KATHLEEN HENDRICK** ALEXANDRIA, KY

PREP: 20 MIN. • **COOK:** 5 HOURS
MAKES: 12 SERVINGS

- 1 **boneless pork loin roast (3½ to 4 pounds)**
- 1 **tablespoon canola oil**
- 1 **medium onion, chopped**
- 1 **celery rib, cut into 1-inch pieces**
- 1 **envelope brown gravy mix**
- 1 **cup water**
- 1 **cup unsweetened apple juice**
- ½ **cup unsweetened applesauce**
- 2 **teaspoons Worcestershire sauce**
- ½ **teaspoon seasoned salt**
- ½ **teaspoon pepper**

1. Cut roast in half. In a large skillet, brown the roast in oil on all sides. Transfer to a 5-qt. slow cooker. In the same skillet, saute onion and celery until tender; add to slow cooker.
2. In a small bowl, combine gravy mix and water. Stir in the remaining ingredients; pour over pork. Cover and cook on low for 5-6 hours or until meat is tender. Skim fat from cooking juices; thicken if desired. Serve with the roast.
PER SERVING *4 ounces cooked pork with ⅓ cup juices equals 204 cal., 8 g fat (2 g sat. fat), 66 mg chol., 294 mg sodium, 6 g carb., trace fiber, 26 g pro.* **Diabetic Exchanges:** *3 lean meat, ½ starch.*

Sweet and Spicy Jerk Ribs

Here's a no-fuss ribs recipe that the whole family will love. The spicy rub and sweet sauce make it an instant favorite.

—**GERI LESCH** NEW PORT RICHEY, FL

PREP: 10 MIN. • **COOK:** 6 HOURS
MAKES: 5 SERVINGS

- 4½ **pounds pork baby back ribs**
- 3 **tablespoons olive oil**
- ⅓ **cup Caribbean jerk seasoning**
- 3 **cups honey barbecue sauce**
- 3 **tablespoons apricot preserves**
- 2 **tablespoons honey**

1. Cut ribs into serving-size pieces; brush with oil and rub with jerk seasoning. Place in a 5- or 6-qt. slow cooker. Combine the remaining ingredients; pour over ribs.
2. Cover and cook on low 6-8 hours or until meat is tender. Skim fat from sauce before serving.

Creamy Potatoes 'n' Kielbasa

In just five minutes, you can have this hearty meal started in your slow cooker. What's not to love about sausage, hash browns and cheese? Even picky eaters want to dig in!

—**BETH SINE** FAULKNER, MD

PREP: 5 MIN. • **COOK:** 6 HOURS
MAKES: 4-6 SERVINGS

- 1 **package (28 ounces) frozen O'Brien potatoes**
- 1 **pound smoked kielbasa or Polish sausage, sliced**
- 1 **can (10¾ ounces) condensed cream of mushroom soup, undiluted**
- 1 **cup (4 ounces) shredded cheddar cheese**
- ½ **cup water**

In a 3-qt. slow cooker, combine all ingredients. Cover and cook on low for 6-8 hours or until the potatoes are tender.

PORK SATAY WITH RICE NOODLES

Brunch Burritos

I like to use a second slow cooker to keep the tortillas warm and pliable when I serve these hearty burritos. Just place a clean wet cloth in the bottom, then cover it with foil and add your tortillas.
—**BETH OSBURN** LEVELLAND, TX

PREP: 30 MIN. • **COOK:** 4 HOURS
MAKES: 10 SERVINGS

- 1 pound bulk pork sausage, cooked and drained
- ½ pound bacon strips, cooked and crumbled
- 18 eggs, lightly beaten
- 2 cups frozen shredded hash brown potatoes, thawed
- 1 large onion, chopped
- 1 can (10¾ ounces) condensed cheddar cheese soup, undiluted
- 1 can (4 ounces) chopped green chilies
- 1 teaspoon garlic powder
- ½ teaspoon pepper
- 2 cups (8 ounces) shredded cheddar cheese
- 10 flour tortillas (10 inches), warmed
  Optional toppings: jalapeno peppers, salsa or hot pepper sauce

1. In a large bowl, combine the first nine ingredients. Pour half of the egg mixture into a 4- or 5-qt. slow cooker coated with cooking spray. Top with half of the cheese. Repeat layers.
2. Cook, covered, on low 4-5 hours or until center is set and a thermometer reads 160°.
3. Spoon ¾ cup egg mixture across the center of each tortilla. Fold bottom and sides of tortilla over filling and roll up. Add toppings of your choice.

EAT SMART

Pork Satay with Rice Noodles

I love the addition of peanut butter to savory recipes, such as this Thai-inspired dish. Ramp up the flavor by sprinkling minced fresh cilantro and chopped peanuts over the top.
—**STEPHANIE ANDERSON** HORSEHEADS, NY

PREP: 20 MIN. • **COOK:** 4 HOURS
MAKES: 6 SERVINGS

- 1½ pounds boneless pork loin chops, cut into 2-inch pieces
- ¼ teaspoon pepper
- 1 medium onion, halved and sliced
- ⅓ cup creamy peanut butter
- ¼ cup reduced-sodium soy sauce
- ½ teaspoon onion powder
- ½ teaspoon garlic powder
- ½ teaspoon hot pepper sauce
- 1 can (14½ ounces) reduced-sodium chicken broth
- 3 tablespoons cornstarch
- 3 tablespoons cold water
- 9 ounces uncooked thick rice noodles
  Minced fresh cilantro and chopped peanuts, optional

1. Sprinkle pork with pepper. Place in a 3-qt. slow cooker; top with onion. In a small bowl, mix peanut butter, soy sauce, onion powder, garlic powder and pepper sauce; gradually add the broth. Pour over onion. Cook, covered, on low for 4-6 hours or until the pork is tender.
2. Remove pork from slow cooker and keep warm. Skim fat from cooking juices; transfer cooking juices to a large skillet. Bring to a boil. In a small bowl, mix cornstarch and water until smooth and add to pan. Return to a boil; cook and stir 2 minutes or until thickened. Add pork; heat through.
3. Meanwhile, cook rice noodles according to package directions; drain. Serve with the pork mixture. If desired, sprinkle with cilantro and peanuts.
NOTE *Reduced-fat peanut butter is not recommended for this recipe.*
PER SERVING *1 serving equals 411 cal., 14 g fat (4 g sat. fat), 55 mg chol., 700 mg sodium, 41 g carb., 2 g fiber, 30 g pro.* **Diabetic Exchanges:** *3 lean meat, 2½ starch, 1 fat.*

BRUNCH BURRITOS

APRICOT PORK ROAST
WITH VEGETABLES

> "After Sunday evening church service, I like to serve a pork roast that slow-cooks with flavorful jam and veggies. The amazing aroma draws everyone to the table."
> —LISA JAMES VANCOUVER, WA

Apricot Pork Roast with Vegetables

PREP: 20 MIN.
COOK: 3½ HOURS + STANDING
MAKES: 10 SERVINGS

- 1½ pounds potatoes (about 3 medium), peeled and cut into wedges
- 7 medium carrots, sliced
- 1 large onion, quartered
- 1 can (14½ ounces) beef broth
- 1 teaspoon salt
- 1 teaspoon garlic powder
- 1 teaspoon dried thyme
- 1 teaspoon rubbed sage
- ½ teaspoon pepper
- 1 boneless pork loin roast (3 to 4 pounds)
- 1 jar (12 ounces) apricot preserves, divided

1. In a large microwave-safe bowl, combine potatoes and 3 tablespoons water. Microwave, covered, on high for 10-12 minutes or just until tender. Drain and transfer to a 6-qt. slow cooker. Add carrots, onion and beef broth. In a small bowl, mix salt, garlic, thyme, sage and pepper; sprinkle half over vegetables.

2. Rub remaining seasoning mixture over roast; place over vegetables. Spread half of the preserves over roast. Cook, covered, on low 3½ to 4½ hours or until meat is tender (a thermometer inserted in pork should read at least 145°).

3. Remove roast from slow cooker; tent with foil. Let stand for 15 minutes. Serve with vegetables and remaining preserves.

Overnight Cherry-Almond Oatmeal

Would you like breakfast ready for you when the sun comes up? If so, try my hot cereal. It's so simple: Just place the ingredients in the slow cooker and turn it on before you go to bed. In the morning, enjoy a healthy, warm and satisfying dish.
—GERALDINE SAUCIER ALBUQUERQUE, NM

PREP: 10 MIN. • **COOK:** 7 HOURS
MAKES: 6 SERVINGS

- 4 cups vanilla almond milk
- 1 cup steel-cut oats
- 1 cup dried cherries
- ⅓ cup packed brown sugar
- ½ teaspoon salt
- ½ teaspoon ground cinnamon

In a 3-qt. slow cooker coated with cooking spray, combine all the ingredients. Cover and cook on low 7-8 hours or until milk is absorbed.
PER SERVING *¾ cup equals 276 cal., 4 g fat (trace sat. fat), 0 chol., 306 mg sodium, 57 g carb., 4 g fiber, 5 g pro.*

Sweet-Sour Meatballs

For a great meal on busy days, I pop ready-made meatballs in the slow cooker and return later to the heartwarming aroma of this Asian-style specialty! Nothing is more convenient than coming home to dinner that's ready to go.

—LISA STEPANSKI MUNNSVILLE, NY

PREP: 10 MIN. • **COOK:** 5 HOURS
MAKES: 2 SERVINGS

- 16 frozen fully cooked homestyle meatballs (½ ounce each), thawed
- ½ cup sugar
- 2 tablespoons plus 2 teaspoons cornstarch
- ⅓ cup white vinegar
- 1 tablespoon reduced-sodium soy sauce
- ½ medium green pepper, cut into 1-inch pieces
- 1 can (8 ounces) pineapple chunks, undrained
  Hot cooked rice, optional

1. Place meatballs in a 1½-qt. slow cooker. In a small bowl, combine the sugar, cornstarch, vinegar and soy sauce; pour over meatballs. Add green pepper. Cover and cook on low for 4½ hours or until the green pepper is crisp-tender.
2. Stir in the pineapple; cover and cook 30 minutes longer. Serve with rice if desired.

Slow-Cooked Lasagna with Homemade Sauce

I got this recipe from a friend who made it with store-bought marinara. I created a homemade sauce for my rendition, and it's been a hit whenever I serve it— especially at bring-a-dish gatherings.

—SHERI OGANOWSKI DAYTON, OH

PREP: 1½ HOURS • **COOK:** 4 HOURS
MAKES: 10 SERVINGS

- 1 pound ground turkey
- 1 pound bulk Italian sausage
- ¾ cup chopped sweet onion
- 3 garlic cloves, minced
- 3 cans (15 ounces each) tomato sauce
- 1 can (28 ounces) crushed tomatoes, undrained
- ⅓ cup sugar
- 3 tablespoons dried parsley flakes, divided
- 2 teaspoons dried basil
- 3 teaspoons dried oregano, divided
- ½ teaspoon salt, divided
- ¼ cup dry red wine or beef broth
- 3 cups (12 ounces) shredded part-skim mozzarella cheese
- 2½ cups ricotta cheese
- 1 cup grated Parmesan cheese
- 1 package (9 ounces) no-cook lasagna noodles

1. In a Dutch oven, cook the turkey, sausage, onion and garlic over medium heat until the meat is no longer pink; drain. Stir in the tomato sauce, crushed tomatoes, sugar, 2 tablespoons parsley, basil, 2 teaspoons oregano and ¼ teaspoon salt. Bring to a boil. Reduce heat; simmer, uncovered, for 45 minutes. Add wine; cook 15 minutes longer.
2. Meanwhile, in a large bowl, combine cheeses and the remaining parsley, oregano and salt.
3. Spread 2¼ cups meat mixture into a 6-qt. slow cooker. Arrange five noodles over sauce, breaking to fit if necessary. Spread 1⅓ cups cheese mixture over noodles.
4. Repeat the layers twice. Top with remaining meat mixture.
5. Cover and cook on low 4-5 hours or until noodles are tender.

To **quickly peel fresh garlic**, gently **crush** the clove with the flat side of a large **knife blade**. If you don't have a large knife, you can crush the garlic with a **small can**.

SWEET-SOUR MEATBALLS

SOUTHERN LOADED SWEET POTATOES

Southern Loaded Sweet Potatoes

For a taste of a Southern classic, we make sweet potatoes stuffed with pulled pork and coleslaw and manage to sidestep the calorie overload.

—**AMY BURTON** FUQUAY-VARINA, NC

PREP: 15 MIN. • **COOK:** 6 HOURS
MAKES: 8 SERVINGS

- 1 **boneless pork loin roast (2 to 3 pounds)**
- ½ **cup Dijon mustard, divided**
- 1 **tablespoon brown sugar**
- 1 **tablespoon garlic powder**
- 1 **teaspoon cayenne pepper**
- 1 **teaspoon salt, divided**
- 1 **cup reduced-sodium beef broth**
- 8 **medium sweet potatoes (about 5 pounds)**
- 3 **cups coleslaw mix**
- ½ **cup fat-free plain Greek yogurt**
- ½ **cup reduced-fat mayonnaise**
- 2 **tablespoons cider vinegar**
- ½ **teaspoon celery seed**
- ¼ **teaspoon garlic salt**

1. Place roast in a 3-qt. slow cooker. In a small bowl, mix ⅓ cup mustard, brown sugar, garlic powder, cayenne and ½ teaspoon salt; brush over pork. Add broth; cook, covered, on low for 6-8 hours or until meat is tender.
2. Meanwhile, preheat oven to 400°. Scrub potatoes; pierce several times with a fork. Bake 45-50 minutes or until tender.
3. Place coleslaw mix in a large bowl. In a small bowl, whisk the yogurt, mayonnaise, vinegar, celery seed, garlic salt and remaining mustard and salt; pour over coleslaw mix and toss to coat.
4. Remove roast; cool slightly. Shred pork with two forks; return to the slow cooker.
5. With a sharp knife, cut an "X" in each potato. Fluff pulp with a fork. Using a slotted spoon, place pork mixture and coleslaw over each sweet potato.

MEAT LOVER'S PIZZA HOT DISH

Meat Lover's Pizza Hot Dish

I make this hearty casserole for the men who help us out during harvesttime. Every year they say it's the best, hands down. Throw in any pizza toppings your family likes; Canadian bacon, black olives and green peppers are some of our picks.

—**BROOK BOTHUN** CANBY, MN

PREP: 25 MIN. • **COOK:** 3¼ HOURS
MAKES: 10 SERVINGS

- 1 **pound ground beef**
- 1 **pound bulk Italian sausage**
- 1 **medium onion, chopped**
- 1 **cup sliced fresh mushrooms**
- 4 **cans (8 ounces each) no-salt-added tomato sauce**
- 2 **cans (15 ounces each) pizza sauce**
- 1 **package (16 ounces) uncooked penne pasta**
- 1 **cup water**
- 1 **can (6 ounces) tomato paste**
- 1 **package (3½ ounces) sliced pepperoni**
- 1 **teaspoon Italian seasoning**
- 2 **cups (8 ounces) shredded part-skim mozzarella cheese, divided**
- 2 **cups (8 ounces) shredded cheddar cheese, divided**

1. In a large skillet, cook the beef, sausage, onion and mushrooms over medium heat 10-12 minutes or until meat is no longer pink and vegetables are tender, breaking up meat into crumbles; drain.
2. Transfer meat mixture to a greased 6-qt. slow cooker. Stir in tomato sauce, pizza sauce, uncooked pasta, water, tomato paste, pepperoni and Italian seasoning. Cook, covered, on low for 3-4 hours or until pasta is tender.
3. Stir thoroughly; mix in 1 cup mozzarella cheese and 1 cup cheddar cheese. Sprinkle remaining cheese over the top. Cook, covered, for 15-20 minutes longer or until the cheese is melted.

Soups, Sides & Sandwiches

65   68   75

You'll find more than three dozen **special dishes** in this chapter, from **meaty sandwiches** like Philly cheesesteaks and meatballs subs to an **array of steaming soups** such as curried turkey and Maryland crab, to **simple veggie and pasta sides** that **make entertaining a breeze.**

Chunky Chicken Soup

I am a stay-at-home mom and rely on my slow cooker for fast, nutritious meals with minimal prep time and cleanup. I knew this recipe was a hit when I didn't have any leftovers and my husband asked me to make it again.

—NANCY CLOW MALLORYTOWN, ON

PREP: 15 MIN. • **COOK:** 4½ HOURS
MAKES: 7 SERVINGS

- 1½ pounds boneless skinless chicken breasts, cut into 2-inch strips
- 2 teaspoons canola oil
- ⅔ cup finely chopped onion
- 2 medium carrots, chopped
- 2 celery ribs, chopped
- 1 cup frozen corn
- 2 cans (10¾ ounces each) condensed cream of potato soup, undiluted
- 1½ cups chicken broth
- 1 teaspoon dill weed
- 1 cup frozen peas
- ½ cup half-and-half cream

1. In a large skillet over medium-high heat, brown chicken in oil. Transfer to a 5-qt. slow cooker; add the onion, carrots, celery and corn.
2. In a large bowl, whisk the soup, broth and dill until blended; stir into slow cooker. Cover and cook on low for 4 hours or until chicken and vegetables are tender.
3. Stir in peas and cream. Cover and cook 30 minutes longer or until heated through.

If you don't have **dried minced onion** for the minestrone, you can substitute 3 tablespoons of **minced fresh onion** or a scant ½ teaspoon of onion powder.

POTATO MINESTRONE

Potato Minestrone

When I prepare this savory soup, I only have to slice some bread and toss a salad to have dinner ready. For a thicker soup, mash half of the garbanzo beans before adding them to the slow cooker.

—PAULA ZSIRAY LOGAN, UT

PREP: 10 MIN. • **COOK:** 8½ HOURS
MAKES: 12 SERVINGS (ABOUT 3 QUARTS)

- 2 cans (14½ ounces each) chicken or vegetable broth
- 1 can (28 ounces) crushed tomatoes
- 1 can (16 ounces) kidney beans, rinsed and drained
- 1 can (15 ounces) garbanzo beans or chickpeas, rinsed and drained
- 1 can (14½ ounces) beef broth
- 2 cups frozen cubed hash brown potatoes, thawed
- 1 tablespoon dried minced onion
- 1 tablespoon dried parsley flakes
- 1 teaspoon salt
- 1 teaspoon dried oregano
- ½ teaspoon garlic powder
- ½ teaspoon dried basil
- ½ teaspoon dried marjoram
- 1 package (10 ounces) frozen chopped spinach, thawed and drained
- 2 cups frozen peas and carrots, thawed

In a 5-qt. slow cooker, combine the first 13 ingredients. Cover and cook on low for 8 hours. Stir in the spinach, peas and carrots; cook 30 minutes or until heated thorough.

SPICY
LENTIL SOUP

Slow Cooker Meatball Sandwiches

Our approach to meatball sandwiches is a simple one—cook the meatballs low and slow, load into hoagie buns and top with provolone and pepperoncini.

—STACIE NICHOLLS SPRING CREEK, NV

PREP: 5 MIN. • **COOK:** 3 HOURS
MAKES: 8 SERVINGS

- 2 packages (12 ounces each) frozen fully cooked Italian meatballs, thawed
- 2 jars (24 ounces each) marinara sauce
- 8 hoagie buns, split
- 8 slices provolone cheese
  Sliced pepperoncini, optional

1. Place meatballs and sauce in a 3- or 4-qt. slow cooker. Cook, covered, on low 3-4 hours until meatballs are heated through.
2. On each bun bottom, layer meatballs, cheese and, if desired, pepperoncini; replace tops.

Applesauce Sweet Potatoes

Use your slow cooker during the holidays to not only free up oven space, but to save time, too! Everyone will think you worked hard on this dish, but it is really very simple. Sweet potatoes are a must on our family's menu.

—PAMELA ALLEN MARYSVILLE, OH

PREP: 15 MIN. • **COOK:** 4 HOURS
MAKES: 8 SERVINGS

- 2 pounds sweet potatoes, peeled and sliced
- 1½ cups unsweetened applesauce
- ⅔ cup packed brown sugar
- 3 tablespoons butter, melted
- 1 teaspoon ground cinnamon
- ½ cup chopped glazed pecans, optional

Place sweet potatoes in a 4-qt. slow cooker. Combine the applesauce, brown sugar, butter and cinnamon; pour over sweet potatoes. Cover and cook on low for 4-5 hours or until sweet potatoes are tender. Sprinkle with pecans if desired. Serve with a slotted spoon.

Spicy Lentil Soup

I've finally found a lentil soup my husband goes for. Adjust the spice level to your taste, and present this yummy soup with warm pita bread.

—EVA BARKER LEBANON, NH

PREP: 25 MIN. • **COOK:** 9 HOURS
MAKES: 14 SERVINGS (3½ QUARTS)

- 1½ pounds potatoes, peeled and cubed (about 5 cups)
- 1 large onion, chopped
- 2 large carrots, chopped
- 2 celery ribs, chopped
- ¼ cup olive oil
- 4 teaspoons ground cumin
- 2 teaspoons chili powder
- 1 teaspoon salt
- 1 teaspoon ground coriander
- 1 teaspoon coarsely ground pepper
- ½ teaspoon ground turmeric
- ½ teaspoon cayenne pepper
- 5 garlic cloves, minced
- 2 cartons (32 ounces each) reduced-sodium chicken broth
- 2 cans (15 ounces each) tomato sauce
- 1 package (16 ounces) dried lentils, rinsed
- ¼ cup lemon juice

1. Place potatoes, onion, carrots and celery in a 6-qt. slow cooker. In a small skillet, heat oil over medium heat. Add seasonings; cook and stir 2 minutes. Add garlic; cook 1-2 minutes longer. Transfer to slow cooker.
2. Stir in broth, tomato sauce and lentils. Cook, covered, on low for 9-11 hours or until lentils are tender. Stir in lemon juice.

**SLOW-COOKED
REUBEN BRATS**

"Sauerkraut gives these beer-simmered brats a big flavor boost, but the special chili sauce and melted cheese put them way over the top. Top your favorite burger with some of the chili sauce; you won't be sorry!"

—ALANA SIMMONS JOHNSTOWN, PA

Slow-Cooked Reuben Brats

PREP: 30 MIN. • **COOK:** 7¼ HOURS
MAKES: 10 SERVINGS

- 10 uncooked bratwurst links
- 3 cans (12 ounces each) light beer or nonalcoholic beer
- 1 large sweet onion, sliced
- 1 can (14 ounces) sauerkraut, rinsed and well drained
- ¾ cup mayonnaise
- ¼ cup chili sauce
- 2 tablespoons ketchup
- 1 tablespoon finely chopped onion
- 2 teaspoons sweet pickle relish
- 1 garlic clove, minced
- ⅛ teaspoon pepper
- 10 hoagie buns, split
- 10 slices Swiss cheese

1. In a large skillet, brown bratwurst in batches; drain. In a 5-qt. slow cooker, combine beer, sliced onion and sauerkraut; add bratwurst. Cook, covered, on low 7-9 hours or until sausages are cooked through.

2. Preheat oven to 350°. In a small bowl, mix mayonnaise, chili sauce, ketchup, chopped onion, relish, garlic and pepper until blended. Spread over the cut sides of buns; top with cheese, bratwurst and sauerkraut mixture. Place on an ungreased baking sheet. Bake 8-10 minutes or until the cheese is melted.

Veggie-Sausage Cheese Soup

I took this soup to a potluck at work, where it was well received—and was the only dish prepared by a guy! The great combination of textures and flavors had everyone asking for the recipe.

—RICHARD GRANT HUDSON, NH

PREP: 55 MIN. • **COOK:** 6½ HOURS
MAKES: 16 SERVINGS (4 QUARTS)

- 2 medium onions, finely chopped
- 1 each medium green and sweet red peppers, chopped
- 2 celery ribs, chopped
- 1 tablespoon olive oil
- 4 garlic cloves, minced
- 1 pound smoked kielbasa or Polish sausage, cut into ¼-inch slices
- 2 medium potatoes, diced
- 1 can (14¾ ounces) cream-style corn
- 1 can (14½ ounces) chicken broth
- 1 can (10¾ ounces) condensed cream of mushroom soup, undiluted
- 2 medium carrots, sliced
- 1 cup whole kernel corn
- 1 cup sliced fresh mushrooms
- 1 tablespoon Worcestershire sauce
- 1 tablespoon Dijon mustard
- 1 tablespoon dried basil
- 1 tablespoon dried parsley flakes
- ½ teaspoon pepper
- 2 cups (8 ounces) shredded sharp cheddar cheese
- 1 can (12 ounces) evaporated milk

1. In a large skillet, saute the onions, peppers and celery in oil until tender. Add garlic; cook 1 minute longer.

2. Transfer to a 5-qt. slow cooker. Stir in the sausage, potatoes, cream-style corn, broth, soup, carrots, corn, mushrooms, Worcestershire sauce, Dijon mustard and seasonings. Cover and cook on low for 6-8 hours or until vegetables are tender.

3. Stir in cheese and milk. Cook on low 30 minutes longer or until cheese is melted. Stir until blended.

Slow-Cooked Boston Beans

These slow-cooked beans have a little more zip than usual Boston baked beans, and rum is my secret ingredient. My grandfather would add extra black pepper to his serving, so I now add extra pepper to the entire recipe.

—**ANN SHEEHY** LAWRENCE, MA

PREP: 10 MIN. + SOAKING • **COOK:** 9 HOURS
MAKES: 8 SERVINGS

- 1 **pound dried navy beans**
- ¼ **pound sliced salt pork belly or bacon strips, chopped**
- 1½ **cups water**
- 1 **medium onion, chopped**
- ½ **cup molasses**
- ⅓ **cup packed brown sugar**
- ⅓ **cup rum or unsweetened apple juice**
- 2 **teaspoons ground mustard**
- ½ **teaspoon salt**
- ½ **teaspoon pepper**

1. Sort beans and rinse in cold water. Place beans in a large bowl; add water to cover by 2 in. Let stand, covered, overnight.

2. Drain and rinse beans, discarding liquid. Transfer beans to a greased 3-qt. slow cooker; add salt pork. In a small bowl, combine the remaining ingredients. Stir into slow cooker.

3. Cook, covered, on low 9-11 hours or until beans are tender.

FREEZE OPTION *Freeze cooled beans in freezer containers. To use, partially thaw in refrigerator overnight. Heat beans through in a saucepan, stirring occasionally and adding a little water or broth if necessary.*

SLOW-COOKED BOSTON BEANS

Shredded Barbecue Beef

I work for the Delaware Department of Transportation, and I often prepare this simple dish to bring to the office for lunchtime get-togethers and even during storm emergencies.

—**JAN WALLS** DOVER, DE

PREP: 20 MIN. • **COOK:** 6 HOURS
MAKES: 12 SERVINGS

- 1 **teaspoon celery salt**
- 1 **teaspoon garlic powder**
- 1 **teaspoon onion powder**
- 1 **fresh beef brisket (3 to 4 pounds)**
- 3 **tablespoons liquid smoke, optional**
- 1 **tablespoon hot pepper sauce**
- 1 **bottle (18 ounces) barbecue sauce**
- 12 **sandwich rolls, split**

1. Combine the celery salt, garlic powder and onion powder; rub over brisket. Place in a 5-qt. slow cooker.

2. Combine liquid smoke if desired and hot pepper sauce; pour over brisket. Cover and cook on low for 6-8 hours or until the brisket is tender.

3. Remove beef and cool slightly. Discard all but ½ cup cooking juices; whisk barbecue sauce into cooking juices. Shred meat with two forks; return to slow cooker and mix well. Heat through. Serve about ⅓ cup meat mixture on each roll.

NOTE *This is a fresh beef brisket, not corned beef.*

"I love spicy food, so I think this chili really hits the spot. A lot of my friends say it's a little too spicy for them. So if you're sensitive to chili peppers, start out with one or two chipotles and go up from there."
—**STEVEN SCHEND** GRAND RAPIDS, MI

CHIPOTLE BEEF CHILI

Chipotle Beef Chili

PREP: 15 MIN. • **COOK:** 6 HOURS
MAKES: 8 SERVINGS (ABOUT 2½ QUARTS)

- 2 **pounds beef flank steak, cut into 1-inch pieces**
- 2 **to 4 chipotle peppers in adobo sauce, chopped**
- ¼ **cup chopped onion**
- 1 **tablespoon chili powder**
- 2 **garlic cloves, minced**
- 1 **teaspoon salt**
- ½ **teaspoon ground cumin**
- 3 **cans (15 ounces each) tomato puree**
- 1 **can (14½ ounces) beef broth**
- ¼ **cup minced fresh cilantro**

In a 4- or 5-qt. slow cooker, combine the first nine ingredients. Cook, covered, on low 6-8 hours or until meat is tender. Stir in cilantro.

FREEZE OPTION *Freeze cooled chili in freezer containers. To use, partially thaw in refrigerator overnight. Heat chili through in a saucepan, stirring occasionally and adding a little broth or water if necessary.*

PER SERVING *1¼ cups equals 230 cal., 9 g fat (4 g sat. fat), 54 mg chol., 668 mg sodium, 12 g carb., 2 g fiber, 25 g pro.* **Diabetic Exchanges: 3 lean meat, 2 vegetable.**

To **freeze soup** or chili in handy **single-serving packets**, line a measuring cup with a small **freezer bag** to hold the bag upright, then fill with soup. Freeze the bags flat, then **stack them** for efficient storage.

SLOW-COOKED RANCH POTATOES

Slow-Cooked Ranch Potatoes

Even after seven years, my family still asks for this tasty potato and bacon side dish. Try it once and I'll bet your family will be hooked, too.

—LYNN IRELAND LEBANON, WI

PREP: 15 MIN. • **COOK:** 7 HOURS
MAKES: 10 SERVINGS

- 6 **bacon strips, chopped**
- 2½ **pounds small red potatoes, cubed**
- 1 **package (8 ounces) cream cheese, softened**
- 1 **can (10¾ ounces) condensed cream of potato soup, undiluted**
- ¼ **cup 2% milk**
- 1 **envelope buttermilk ranch salad dressing mix**
- 3 **tablespoons thinly sliced green onions**

1. In a large skillet, cook bacon over medium heat until crisp, stirring occasionally. Remove with a slotted spoon; drain on paper towels. Drain drippings, reserving 1 tablespoon.

2. Place potatoes in a 3-qt. slow cooker. In a bowl, beat cream cheese, soup, milk, dressing mix and reserved drippings until blended; stir into potatoes. Sprinkle with bacon.

3. Cook, covered, on low 7-8 hours or until potatoes are tender. Top with green onions.

Turkey Sausage Soup with Fresh Vegetables

Our family is big on soup. This favorite is quick to make, very tasty and gives me plenty of time to have fun with my kids and grandkids while it slow-cooks.

—NANCY HEISHMAN LAS VEGAS, NV

PREP: 30 MIN. • **COOK:** 6 HOURS
MAKES: 10 SERVINGS (3½ QUARTS)

- 1 package (19½ ounces) Italian turkey sausage links, casings removed
- 3 large tomatoes, chopped
- 1 can (15 ounces) garbanzo beans or chickpeas, rinsed and drained
- 3 medium carrots, thinly sliced
- 1½ cups cut fresh green beans (1-inch pieces)
- 1 medium zucchini, quartered lengthwise and sliced
- 1 large sweet red or green pepper, chopped
- 8 green onions, chopped
- 4 cups chicken stock
- 1 can (12 ounces) tomato paste
- ½ teaspoon seasoned salt
- ⅓ cup minced fresh basil

1. In a large skillet, cook the sausage over medium heat 8-10 minutes or until no longer pink, breaking into crumbles; drain and transfer to a 6-qt. slow cooker.

2. Add tomatoes, beans, carrots, green beans, zucchini, pepper and green onions. In a large bowl, whisk stock, tomato paste and seasoned salt; pour over vegetables.

3. Cook, covered, on low 6-8 hours or until vegetables are tender. Just before serving, stir in basil.

FREEZE OPTION *Freeze cooled soup in freezer containers. To use, partially thaw in refrigerator overnight. Heat soup through in a saucepan, stirring occasionally and adding a little stock if necessary.*

PER SERVING *1⅓ cups equals 167 cal., 5 g fat (1 g sat. fat), 20 mg chol., 604 mg sodium, 21 g carb., 5 g fiber, 13 g pro.* **Diabetic Exchanges:** *2 lean meat, 2 vegetable, 1/2 starch.*

Nebraska Creamed Corn

I brought this super-easy recipe to a school potluck once, and it was gone in no time. I've been asked to bring it to every function since.

—JESSICA MAXWELL ENGLEWOOD, NJ

PREP: 10 MIN. • **COOK:** 3 HOURS
MAKES: 9 SERVINGS

- 2 packages (one 16 ounces, one 12 ounces) frozen corn, thawed
- 1 package (8 ounces) cream cheese, cubed
- ¾ cup shredded cheddar cheese
- ¼ cup butter, melted
- ¼ cup heavy whipping cream
- ½ teaspoon salt
- ¼ teaspoon pepper

In a 3- or 4-qt. slow cooker, combine all the ingredients. Cook, covered, on low 3 to 3½ hours or until cheese is melted and corn is tender. Stir just before serving.

Add a small can of **chopped green chilies** to the creamed **corn** if you like **a little heat.**

NEBRASKA CREAMED CORN

Italian Sloppy Joes

I wanted to make sloppy joes for a work potluck without using canned sloppy joe sauce. I had a few ingredients on hand, and this recipe was born. It's also good over pasta.
—**HOPE WASYLENKI** GAHANNA, OH

PREP: 30 MIN. • **COOK:** 4 HOURS
MAKES: 36 SERVINGS

- 2 **pounds lean ground beef (90% lean)**
- 2 **pounds bulk Italian sausage**
- 2 **medium green peppers, chopped**
- 1 **large onion, chopped**
- 4 **cups spaghetti sauce**
- 1 **can (28 ounces) diced tomatoes, undrained**
- ½ **pound sliced fresh mushrooms**
- 1 **can (6 ounces) tomato paste**
- 2 **garlic cloves, minced**
- 2 **bay leaves**
- 36 **hamburger buns, split**

1. Cook the beef, sausage, peppers and onion in a Dutch oven over medium heat until meat is no longer pink; drain. Transfer to a 6-qt. slow cooker. Stir in the spaghetti sauce, tomatoes, mushrooms, tomato paste, garlic and bay leaves.
2. Cover slow cooker and cook on high for 4-5 hours or until flavors are blended. Discard the bay leaves. Serve meat mixture on buns, ½ cup on each.
FREEZE OPTION *Freeze cooled meat mixture in freezer containers. To use, partially thaw in refrigerator overnight. Heat mixture through in a saucepan, stirring occasionally and adding a little broth or water if necessary.*

EASY PHILLY CHEESESTEAKS

Easy Philly Cheesesteaks

Since we live in a rural area where there aren't any restaurants, I thought it would be fun to make this classic sandwich at home. For an extra flavor boost, add a splash of steak sauce.
—**LENETTE A. BENNETT** COMO, CO

PREP: 20 MIN. • **COOK:** 6 HOURS
MAKES: 6 SERVINGS

- 2 **medium onions, halved and sliced**
- 2 **medium sweet red or green peppers, halved and sliced**
- 1½ **pounds beef top sirloin steak, cut into thin strips**
- 1 **envelope onion soup mix**
- 1 **can (14½ ounces) reduced-sodium beef broth**
- 6 **hoagie buns, split**
- 12 **slices provolone cheese, halved Pickled hot cherry peppers, optional**

1. Place onions and red peppers in a 4- or 5-qt. slow cooker. Add beef, soup mix and broth. Cook, covered, on low 6-8 hours or until meat is tender.
2. Arrange buns on a baking sheet, cut side up. Using tongs, place the meat mixture on bun bottoms; top with cheese.
3. Broil 2-3 in. from the heat for 30-60 seconds or until cheese is melted and bun tops are toasted. If desired, serve with cherry peppers.

SOUTHWEST PULLED PORK

1. In a 3-qt. slow cooker, combine the first eight ingredients. Cover and cook on low for 8-10 hours.

2. Stir in macaroni. Cover and cook 30 minutes longer or until macaroni is tender. Garnish with cheese if desired.

Beef Vegetable Soup

This nicely seasoned soup tastes so good, especially on a chilly day. I like being able to do the prep work in the morning and then let the soup simmer all day.

—**JEAN HUTZELL** DUBUQUE, IA

PREP: 20 MIN. • **COOK:** 9 HOURS
MAKES: 7 SERVINGS

- 1 **pound lean ground beef (90% lean)**
- 1 **medium onion, chopped**
- ½ **teaspoon salt**
- ¼ **teaspoon pepper**
- 3 **cups water**
- 3 **medium potatoes, peeled and cut into ¾-inch cubes**
- 1 **can (14½ ounces) Italian diced tomatoes, undrained**
- 1 **can (11½ ounces) V8 juice**
- 1 **cup chopped celery**
- 1 **cup sliced carrots**
- 2 **tablespoons sugar**
- 1 **tablespoon dried parsley flakes**
- 2 **teaspoons dried basil**
- 1 **bay leaf**

1. In a nonstick skillet, cook beef and onion over medium heat until meat is no longer pink; drain. Stir in salt and pepper.

2. Transfer to a 5-qt. slow cooker. Add the remaining ingredients. Cover and cook on low for 9-11 hours or until the vegetables are tender. Discard bay leaf before serving.

PER SERVING 1⅓ cups equals 210 cal., 5 g fat (2 g sat. fat), 32 mg chol., 537 mg sodium, 26 g carb., 3 g fiber, 15 g pro. **Diabetic Exchanges:** 2 lean meat, 2 vegetable, 1 starch.

Southwest Pulled Pork

I made this recipe on a whim one Sunday when friends called me in the morning and said they wanted to drop by in the afternoon. I was able to feed them and my neighbors a casual supper. If you have time, you can coat the roast with the rub and refrigerate it several hours before cooking for even more flavor.

—**DEB LEBLANC** PHILLIPSBURG, KS

PREP: 20 MIN. • **COOK:** 8 HOURS
MAKES: 14 SERVINGS

- 1 **boneless pork shoulder butt roast (4 pounds)**
- 2 **tablespoons chili powder**
- 1 **tablespoon brown sugar**
- 1½ **teaspoons ground cumin**
- 1 **teaspoon salt**
- ½ **teaspoon pepper**
- ½ **teaspoon cayenne pepper**
- 1 **large sweet onion, coarsely chopped**
- 2 **cans (4 ounces each) chopped green chilies**
- 1 **cup chicken broth**
- 14 **kaiser rolls, split**

1. Cut roast in half. In a small bowl, combine the chili powder, brown sugar, cumin, salt, pepper and cayenne; rub over meat. Transfer to a 5-qt. slow cooker. Top with onion and chilies. Pour broth around meat.

2. Cover slow cooker and cook on low for 8-10 hours or until tender. Remove roast; cool slightly. Skim fat from the cooking juices.

3. Shred pork with two forks and return to slow cooker; heat through. Serve on rolls, ½ cup on each.

Meaty Tomato Soup

As an elementary school librarian and church choir director, I've come to rely on—and thoroughly enjoy—the homemade convenience of slow-cooked meals. A sorority sister shared this recipe with me.

—**ANN BOST** ELKHART, TX

PREP: 20 MIN. • **COOK:** 8½ HOURS
MAKES: 10 SERVINGS (2½ QUARTS)

- 1 **can (28 ounces) diced tomatoes, undrained**
- 2 **cans (8 ounces each) tomato sauce**
- 2 **cups water**
- ½ **pound ground beef, cooked and drained**
- ½ **pound bulk pork sausage, cooked and drained**
- 2 **tablespoons dried minced onion**
- 2 **teaspoons chicken bouillon granules**
- ¾ **teaspoon garlic salt**
- ¾ **cup uncooked elbow macaroni Shredded cheddar cheese, optional**

Spicy Kielbasa Soup

Should you have any left over, this soup is great reheated because the flavors have had more time to blend. I like to serve steaming bowls of it with fresh rye bread.

—CAROL CUSTER CLIFTON PARK, NY

PREP: 15 MIN. • **COOK:** 8 HOURS
MAKES: 5 SERVINGS

- ½ pound reduced-fat smoked turkey kielbasa, sliced
- 1 medium onion, chopped
- 1 medium green pepper, chopped
- 1 celery rib with leaves, thinly sliced
- 4 garlic cloves, minced
- 2 cans (14½ ounces each) reduced-sodium chicken broth
- 1 can (15½ ounces) great northern beans, rinsed and drained
- 1 can (14½ ounces) stewed tomatoes, cut up
- 1 small zucchini, sliced
- 1 medium carrot, shredded
- 1 tablespoon dried parsley flakes
- ¼ teaspoon crushed red pepper flakes
- ¼ teaspoon pepper

1. In a nonstick skillet, cook kielbasa over medium heat until lightly browned. Add the onion, green pepper and celery; cook and stir for 3 minutes. Add garlic; cook 1 minute longer.

2. Transfer to a 5-qt. slow cooker. Stir in the remaining ingredients. Cover and cook on low for 8-9 hours or until vegetables are tender.

Spoon Bread

Enjoy an easy take on this Southern specialty by using your slow cooker. It's an excellent side dish for Thanksgiving, Easter or any special feast.

—TASTE OF HOME TEST KITCHEN

PREP: 20 MIN. • **COOK:** 4 HOURS
MAKES: 8 SERVINGS

- 1 package (8 ounces) cream cheese, softened
- 2 tablespoons sugar
- 2 eggs, beaten
- 1 cup 2% milk
- 2 tablespoons butter, melted
- ½ teaspoon salt
- ¼ teaspoon cayenne pepper
- ⅛ teaspoon pepper
- 2 cups frozen corn
- 1 can (14¾ ounces) cream-style corn
- 1 cup yellow cornmeal
- 1 cup (4 ounces) shredded Monterey Jack cheese
- 3 green onions, thinly sliced

1. In a large bowl, beat cream cheese and sugar until smooth. Gradually beat in eggs. Beat in milk, butter, salt, cayenne and pepper until blended. Stir in the remaining ingredients.

2. Pour into a greased 3-qt. slow cooker. Cover and cook on low for 4-5 hours or until a toothpick inserted in center comes out clean.

SPICY KIELBASA SOUP

COCONUT-LIME CHICKEN CURRY SOUP

Polynesian Pulled Chicken

PREP: 15 MIN. • **COOK:** 3¼ HOURS
MAKES: 6 SERVINGS

- 2 **pounds boneless skinless chicken breasts**
- 1 **cup barbecue sauce**
- 1 **cup crushed pineapple, undrained**
- 1 **medium onion, chopped**
- ¾ **cup frozen pepper strips, thawed**
- ¼ **cup flaked coconut**
- 1 **tablespoon minced garlic**
- 1 **tablespoon reduced-sodium soy sauce**
- 1 **teaspoon salt**
- 1 **tablespoon cornstarch**
- ¼ **cup water**
- 6 **hoagie buns, split**
  Minced fresh cilantro, optional

1. In a 3- or 4-qt. slow cooker, combine the first nine ingredients. Cook, covered, on low 3-4 hours or until a thermometer reads 165°. Remove chicken; cool slightly.
2. Meanwhile, in a small bowl, mix cornstarch and water until smooth; gradually stir into cooking juices. Cook, covered, on high 15-20 minutes or until sauce is thickened. Shred the chicken with two forks. Return to slow cooker; heat through.
3. Serve with buns and, if desired, sprinkle with cilantro.
FREEZE OPTION *Freeze cooled meat mixture in freezer containers. To use, partially thaw in refrigerator overnight. Heat chicken through in a saucepan, stirring occasionally and adding a little broth or water if necessary. Serve on buns. If desired, sprinkle with cilantro.*

Coconut-Lime Chicken Curry Soup

I created this chicken recipe to replicate the flavors of my favorite curry dish—slightly sweet with just the right amount of spicy heat. When served with a garnish of green onions and toasted coconut, the soup makes the perfect cold-weather meal.

—LISA RENSHAW KANSAS CITY, MO

PREP: 15 MIN. • **COOK:** 4¼ HOURS
MAKES: 8 SERVINGS (2½ QUARTS)

- 2 **cans (13.66 ounces each) light coconut milk**
- 2 **cans (4 ounces each) chopped green chilies**
- 8 **green onions, sliced**
- 2 **teaspoons grated lime peel**
- ½ **cup lime juice**
- ¼ **cup sweet chili sauce**
- 6 **garlic cloves, minced**
- 4 **teaspoons curry powder**
- ½ **teaspoon salt**
- 2 **pounds boneless skinless chicken thighs, cut into ½-inch pieces**
- 3 **cups cooked basmati rice**
  Minced fresh cilantro

1. Place the first nine ingredients in a 4- or 5-qt. slow cooker; stir in chicken. Cook, covered, on low 4-5 hours or until chicken is tender.
2. Skim fat; stir in cooked rice. Cook, covered, on low 15-30 minutes or until heated through. Sprinkle servings with cilantro.

> "I love the aroma of pork as it cooks but don't eat pork, so I make pulled chicken with coconut and pineapple for a Polynesian twist."
>
> —**BECKY WALCH** MANTECA, CA

**POLYNESIAN
PULLED CHICKEN**

**ZESTY ITALIAN
BEEF SANDWICHES**

Zesty Italian Beef Sandwiches

It's so easy to build a zesty sandwich when you pile on the shredded beef, pickles and smoked provolone. Can't find smoked provolone? I use regular, too.

—**CRYSTAL SCHLUETER** NORTHGLENN, CO

PREP: 15 MIN. • **COOK:** 8 HOURS
MAKES: 6 SERVINGS

- 1 **boneless beef chuck roast (3 to 4 pounds)**
- 1 **can (10½ ounces) condensed French onion soup, undiluted**
- ½ **cup cider vinegar**
- 2 **tablespoons reduced-sodium soy sauce**
- 1 **tablespoon brown sugar**
- ½ **cup mayonnaise**
- 1 **tablespoon horseradish mustard or spicy brown mustard**
- 1 **tablespoon chili garlic sauce**
- 6 **Italian rolls, split**
- 6 **thin slices red onion**
- 18 **sweet pickle slices**
- 6 **slices smoked provolone cheese**

1. Place roast in a 5- or 6-qt. slow cooker. In a small bowl, mix soup, vinegar, soy sauce and brown sugar; pour over roast. Cook, covered, on low 8-10 hours or until meat is tender.
2. Remove roast; cool slightly. Shred meat with two forks. Return meat to slow cooker; heat through. In a small bowl, mix mayonnaise, mustard and chili sauce; spread on roll bottoms. Layer with onion, pickles, shredded beef and cheese. Replace tops.

Curried Turkey Soup

This colorful soup is a delight to serve the day after Thanksgiving. Best of all, it cooks up in the slow cooker, which allows you to get a jump on holiday shopping.

—**HOLLY BAUER** WEST BEND, WI

PREP: 40 MIN. • **COOK:** 8 HOURS
MAKES: 6 SERVINGS (2½ QUARTS)

- 4½ **cups chicken broth**
- 1 **can (14½ ounces) diced tomatoes, undrained**
- 2 **medium carrots, chopped**
- 2 **celery ribs, chopped**
- 1 **medium onion, chopped**
- 1 **medium green pepper, chopped**
- 1 **medium tart apple, peeled and chopped**
- 1 **tablespoon curry powder**
- ½ **teaspoon salt**
- ½ **teaspoon pepper**
- ¼ **cup all-purpose flour**
- ½ **cup unsweetened apple juice or additional chicken broth**
- 3 **cups cubed cooked turkey**
- 3 **cups hot cooked rice**

1. Combine the first ten ingredients in a 4- or 5-qt. slow cooker. Cover and cook on low for 7-8 hours or until vegetables are tender. Mix flour and apple juice until smooth; stir into soup. Cover and cook on high for 30 minutes or until soup is thickened.
2. Stir in turkey and heat through. Serve with rice.

Sweet 'n' Sour Beans

These flavorful beans are popular on both sides of the border. The recipe came from a friend in Alaska, then traveled with me to Mexico, where I lived for five years. Now it's a potluck favorite here in my Arkansas community.

—BARBARA SHORT MENA, AR

PREP: 20 MIN. • **COOK:** 3 HOURS
MAKES: 20 SERVINGS (½ CUP EACH)

- 8 bacon strips, diced
- 2 medium onions, halved and thinly sliced
- 1 cup packed brown sugar
- ½ cup cider vinegar
- 1 teaspoon salt
- 1 teaspoon ground mustard
- ½ teaspoon garlic powder
- 1 can (28 ounces) baked beans, undrained
- 1 can (16 ounces) kidney beans, rinsed and drained
- 1 can (15 ounces) pinto beans, rinsed and drained
- 1 can (15 ounces) lima beans, rinsed and drained
- 1 can (15½ ounces) black-eyed peas, rinsed and drained

1. In a large skillet, cook the bacon over medium heat until crisp. Remove with slotted spoon to paper towels. Drain, reserving 2 tablespoons drippings. Saute onions in the drippings until tender. Add brown sugar, vinegar, salt, mustard and garlic powder. Bring to a boil.
2. In a 5-qt. slow cooker, combine beans and peas. Add the onion mixture and bacon; mix well. Cover and cook on high 3-4 hours or until heated through.

> "This simple chowder is a regular part of our Christmas Eve dinner. We enjoy it along with a pot of chili, breadsticks, raw veggies and an array of baked goodies. It's an easy-to-serve, easy-to-clean-up meal between our church service and gift exchange."
> —MARLENE MUCKENHIRN DELANO, MN

Seafood Chowder

PREP: 15 MIN. • **COOK:** 4¼ HOURS
MAKES: 8 SERVINGS (2 QUARTS)

- 1 can (10¾ ounces) condensed cream of potato soup, undiluted
- 1 can (10¾ ounces) condensed cream of mushroom soup, undiluted
- 2½ cups milk
- 4 medium carrots, finely chopped
- 2 medium potatoes, peeled and cut into ¼-inch cubes
- 1 large onion, finely chopped
- 2 celery ribs, finely chopped
- 1 can (6½ ounces) chopped clams, drained
- 1 can (6 ounces) medium shrimp, drained
- 4 ounces imitation crabmeat, flaked
- 5 bacon strips, cooked and crumbled

1. In a 3-qt. slow cooker, combine soups and milk. Stir in the vegetables. Cover and cook on low for 4-5 hours.
2. Stir in clams, shrimp and crab; cover and cook 15-20 minutes or until heated through. Garnish each serving with bacon.

SWEET 'N' SOUR BEANS

EASY SLOW COOKER
MAC & CHEESE

Easy Slow Cooker Mac & Cheese

My sons always cheer, "You're the best mom in the world!" whenever I make this creamy mac-and-cheese perfection. Does it get any better than that?

—**HEIDI FLEEK** HAMBURG, PA

PREP: 25 MIN. • **COOK:** 1 HOUR
MAKES: 8 SERVINGS

- 2 **cups uncooked elbow macaroni**
- 1 **can (10¾ ounces) condensed cheddar cheese soup, undiluted**
- 1 **cup 2% milk**
- ½ **cup sour cream**
- ¼ **cup butter, cubed**
- ½ **teaspoon onion powder**
- ¼ **teaspoon white pepper**
- ⅛ **teaspoon salt**
- 1 **cup (4 ounces) shredded cheddar cheese**
- 1 **cup (4 ounces) shredded fontina cheese**
- 1 **cup (4 ounces) shredded provolone cheese**

1. Cook macaroni according to package directions for al dente. Meanwhile, in a large saucepan, combine soup, milk, sour cream, butter and seasonings; cook and stir over medium-low heat until blended. Stir in cheeses until melted.

2. Drain macaroni; transfer to a greased 3-qt. slow cooker. Stir in cheese mixture. Cook, covered, on low 1-2 hours or until heated through.

Serve the **saucy macaroni** as a side dish to **rotisserie chicken** or quick-to-heat **ham steaks**. It would be popular at **reunions** and **potlucks**, or even **Thanksgiving**.

Pulled BBQ Pork

After years of vacationing on the North Carolina coast, I became hooked on the region's pork barbecue. The version I developed is a favorite at potluck dinners.

—**JOSEPH SARNOSKI** WEST CHESTER, PA

PREP: 15 MIN. • **COOK:** 10 HOURS
MAKES: 8 SERVINGS

- 2 **medium onions, finely chopped**
- 1 **tablespoon canola oil**
- 6 **garlic cloves, minced**
- 1 **teaspoon crushed red pepper flakes**
- 1 **teaspoon pepper**
- 1 **can (14½ ounces) diced tomatoes, undrained**
- ¼ **cup packed brown sugar**
- ¼ **cup cider vinegar**
- 2 **tablespoons hot pepper sauce**
- 1 **tablespoon Worcestershire sauce**
- 1 **teaspoon ground cumin**
- 1 **boneless pork shoulder butt roast (3 to 4 pounds)**
- 8 **kaiser rolls, split**

1. In a large skillet, saute onions in oil until tender. Add the garlic, pepper flakes and pepper; cook 1 minute longer. Stir in the tomatoes, brown sugar, vinegar, hot pepper sauce, Worcestershire and cumin. Cook over medium heat until heated through and sugar is dissolved.

2. Cut roast in half. Place in a 5-qt. slow cooker; pour sauce over the top. Cover and cook on low for 10-12 hours or until meat is tender. Remove roast; cool slightly. Skim fat from cooking juices. Shred meat with two forks and return to the slow cooker. Heat through. With a slotted spoon, place ¾ cup meat mixture on each roll.

PULLED BBQ PORK

COMFORTING CHEESY POTATOES

Maryland-Style Crab Soup

PREP: 20 MIN. • **COOK:** 6¼ HOURS
MAKES: 8 SERVINGS (3 QUARTS)

- 2 cans (14½ ounces each) diced tomatoes with green peppers and onions, undrained
- 2 cups water
- 1½ pounds potatoes, cut into ½-inch cubes (about 5 cups)
- 2 cups cubed peeled rutabaga
- 2 cups chopped cabbage
- 1 medium onion, finely chopped
- 1 medium carrot, sliced
- ½ cup frozen corn, thawed
- ½ cup frozen lima beans, thawed
- ½ cup frozen peas, thawed
- ½ cup cut fresh green beans (1-inch pieces)
- 4 teaspoons seafood seasoning
- 1 teaspoon celery seed
- 1 vegetable bouillon cube
- ¼ teaspoon salt
- ¼ teaspoon pepper
- 1 pound fresh or lump crabmeat, drained

1. In a 6-qt. slow cooker, combine the first 16 ingredients. Cook, covered, on low 6-8 hours or until vegetables are tender.

2. Stir in crab. Cook, covered, on low for 15 minutes longer or until soup is heated through.

NOTE *This recipe was prepared with Knorr vegetable bouillon.*

Comforting Cheesy Potatoes

As a four-generation Idaho family, we love our potatoes and cook with them in every way possible. I have served this dish for weddings, family dinners and more. It has become a favorite of many.

—**KARLA KIMBALL** EMMETT, ID

PREP: 10 MIN. • **COOK:** 4 HOURS
MAKES: 8 SERVINGS

- 1 can (10¾ ounces) condensed cream of chicken soup, undiluted
- 1 cup (8 ounces) sour cream
- 1 small onion, finely chopped
- ¼ cup butter, melted
- ¾ teaspoon salt
- ¼ teaspoon pepper
- 1 package (32 ounces) frozen cubed hash brown potatoes, thawed
- 2 cups (8 ounces) shredded cheddar cheese, divided

In a 4-qt. slow cooker, combine the first six ingredients. Stir in hash browns and 1½ cups cheese. Cook, covered, on low 4-5 hours or until potatoes are tender, sprinkling with remaining cheese during the last 5 minutes.

Celery seed is a classic addition to **seafood** dishes, **slaws** and **pickles**. The seeds are **herbaceous, crunchy** and slightly **bitter**. They come from a type of flavorful **Asian celery.**

"Try this hearty soup that incorporates the best of vegetable soup and flavorful crab. Whole crabs and claws can be broken into pieces and dropped into the soup, which is my personal preference. I serve the soup with saltine crackers and a cold beer."
—**FREELOVE KNOTT** PALM BAY, FL

MARYLAND-STYLE CRAB SOUP

Mexican Chicken Chili

Corn and black beans give this satisfying chili Mexican flair the whole family will love. Adjust the cayenne if you have small children or are looking for a little less zip.

—STEPHANIE RABBITT-SCHAPP
CINCINNATI, OH

PREP: 30 MIN. • **COOK:** 5 HOURS
MAKES: 6 SERVINGS

- 1 **pound boneless skinless chicken breasts, cubed**
- 1 **tablespoon canola oil**
- 2 **cans (14½ ounces each) diced tomatoes, undrained**
- 2 **cups frozen corn**
- 1 **can (15 ounces) black beans, rinsed and drained**
- 1 **can (14½ ounces) reduced-sodium chicken broth**
- 1 **can (4 ounces) chopped green chilies**
- 2 **tablespoons chili powder**
- 1 **tablespoon ground cumin**
- ½ **teaspoon salt**
- ¼ **teaspoon cayenne pepper**

In a large skillet, brown chicken in oil. Transfer to a 5-qt. slow cooker. Stir in the remaining ingredients. Cover and cook on low for 5-6 hours or until chicken is no longer pink.

French Dip

For a sandwich with more pizzazz than the traditional French dip, give this recipe a try. Soy sauce and herbs give the meaty broth a wonderful flavor with just a few ingredients.

—MARGARET MCNEIL GERMANTOWN, TN

PREP: 15 MIN. • **COOK:** 5 HOURS
MAKES: 8 SERVINGS

- 1 **beef chuck roast (3 pounds), trimmed**
- 2 **cups water**
- ½ **cup reduced-sodium soy sauce**
- 1 **teaspoon dried rosemary, crushed**
- 1 **teaspoon dried thyme**
- 1 **teaspoon garlic powder**
- 1 **bay leaf**
- 3 **to 4 whole peppercorns**
- 8 **French rolls, split**

1. Place the roast in a 5-qt. slow cooker. Add the water, soy sauce and seasonings. Cover and cook on high for 5-6 hours or until beef is tender.
2. Remove meat from broth; shred with two forks and keep warm. Strain broth; skim fat. Pour broth into small cups for dipping. Serve beef on rolls.

FRENCH DIP

CHUTNEY-GLAZED CARROTS

Chutney-Glazed Carrots

Carrots slow-cooked with chutney, Dijon and ginger make a zippy side dish for a barbecue or potluck. We love to serve these carrots with grilled chicken or roast beef.

—NANCY HEISHMAN LAS VEGAS, NV

PREP: 15 MIN. • **COOK:** 4 HOURS
MAKES: 4 SERVINGS

- ⅓ **cup mango chutney**
- 2 **tablespoons sugar**
- 2 **tablespoons minced fresh parsley**
- 2 **tablespoons white wine or unsweetened apple juice**
- 1 **tablespoon Dijon mustard**
- 1 **tablespoon butter, melted**
- 1 **garlic clove, minced**
- ½ **teaspoon salt**
- ¼ **teaspoon ground ginger**
- ¼ **teaspoon pepper**
- 1 **pound fresh carrots, cut into ¼-inch slices (about 4 cups)**

1. Place the first 10 ingredients in a 3-qt. slow cooker. Add the carrots; toss to combine.

2. Cook, covered, on low for 4-5 hours or until the carrots are tender. Stir before serving.

Cabbage-Pork Chowder

The traditional flavors of German food blend beautifully in a hearty, simple soup. I sometimes use garlic ring bologna in place of the stew meat.

—RUTH ANN STELFOX RAYMOND, AB

PREP: 20 MIN. • **COOK:** 6 HOURS
MAKES: 6 SERVINGS

- 1 **pound pork stew meat**
- 1 **tablespoon canola oil**
- 3 **cups coarsely chopped cabbage**
- 2 **cans (10¾ ounces each) condensed cream of celery soup, undiluted**
- 1½ **cups apple juice**
- 2 **medium red potatoes, cut into 1-inch pieces**
- 3 **medium carrots, sliced**
- ¼ **teaspoon caraway seeds**
- ¼ **teaspoon pepper**
- ½ **cup 2% milk**

1. In a large skillet over medium-high heat, brown pork in oil on all sides; drain. Place in a 3-qt. slow cooker; stir in the cabbage, soup, apple juice, potatoes, carrots, caraway and pepper.

2. Cover and cook on low 6-8 hours or until pork and vegetables are tender. Stir in milk; heat through.

EAT SMART
Bean Soup with Cornmeal Dumplings

This soup's great Southwestern flavor makes it a real winner with my family. I love it because I can have the soup already cooking when I get home from work. Then I simply make the dumplings and dinner's almost ready.

—JOAN HALLFORD FORT WORTH, TX

PREP: 15 MIN. • **COOK:** 6½ HOURS
MAKES: 6 SERVINGS

- 2 **cans (14½ ounces each) chicken broth**
- 1 **package (16 ounces) frozen mixed vegetables**
- 1 **can (15 ounces) black beans, rinsed and drained**
- 1 **can (15 ounces) pinto beans, rinsed and drained**
- 1 **can (14½ ounces) diced tomatoes, undrained**
- 1 **medium onion, chopped**
- 1 **tablespoon chili powder**
- 1 **tablespoon minced fresh cilantro**
- 4 **garlic cloves, minced**
- ¼ **teaspoon pepper**

CORNMEAL DUMPLINGS
- ½ **cup all-purpose flour**
- ½ **cup shredded cheddar cheese**
- ⅓ **cup cornmeal**
- 1 **tablespoon sugar**
- 1 **teaspoon baking powder**
- 1 **egg**
- 2 **tablespoons milk**
- 2 **teaspoons canola oil**

1. In a 5-qt. slow cooker, combine the first 10 ingredients. Cover and cook on low for 6-8 hours or until vegetables are tender.

2. For dumplings, combine the flour, cheese, cornmeal, sugar and baking powder in a large bowl. In another bowl, combine the egg, milk and oil; add to dry ingredients just until moistened (batter will be stiff).

3. Drop by heaping tablespoons onto the soup. Cover and cook on high for 30 minutes (without lifting the cover) or until a toothpick inserted into a dumpling comes out clean.

PER SERVING *1 serving equals 334 cal., 6 g fat (3 g sat. fat), 46 mg chol., 774 mg sodium, 55 g carb., 12 g fiber, 16 g pro.*

Snacks & Sweets

82 86 91

What could make a **special occasion** even better than the crowd-pleasing **snacks**, hot **drinks**, warm, cheesy **dips** and pretty **desserts** you'll find here? The fact that they're all made in the slow cooker! These **clever recipes** get you **out of the kitchen** fast and **into the party**.

PORK PICADILLO LETTUCE WRAPS

EAT SMART

Sweet & Sour Turkey Meatballs

Here's a welcome potluck or buffet recipe for Christmas parties that's easy, seasonal and delicious.

—**CHRISTINE WENDLAND** BROWNS MILLS, NJ

PREP: 30 MIN. • **COOK:** 2 HOURS
MAKES: ABOUT 5 DOZEN

- 4 **thick-sliced peppered bacon strips**
- 1 **egg, beaten**
- ½ **cup seasoned bread crumbs**
- 3 **tablespoons minced fresh cilantro**
- 1 **teaspoon salt**
- 1 **teaspoon white pepper**
- 2 **pounds ground turkey**
- 1 **jar (18 ounces) apricot preserves**
- 1 **can (14½ ounces) diced tomatoes, undrained**
- 1 **bottle (8 ounces) taco sauce**
- ½ **cup pomegranate juice**

1. Place bacon in a food processor; cover and process until finely chopped. In a large bowl, combine the egg, bread crumbs, cilantro, salt and pepper. Crumble turkey and bacon over mixture and mix well. Shape into 1-in. balls.
2. Place meatballs in two ungreased 15x10x1-in. baking pans. Bake at 400° for 8-10 minutes or until no longer pink.
3. In a 4-qt. slow cooker, combine the preserves, tomatoes, taco sauce and juice. Stir in meatballs. Cover and cook on high for 2-3 hours or until heated through.
PER SERVING *1 meatball equals 68 cal., 4 g fat (1 g sat. fat), 14 mg chol., 114 mg sodium, 7 g carb., trace fiber, 3 g pro.*

Pork Picadillo Lettuce Wraps

Warm pork and cool, crisp lettuce are a combination born in culinary heaven. My spin on a lettuce wrap is chock-full of scrumptious flavor.

—**JANICE ELDER** CHARLOTTE, NC

PREP: 30 MIN. • **COOK:** 2½ HOURS
MAKES: 2 DOZEN

- 3 **garlic cloves, minced**
- 1 **tablespoon chili powder**
- 1 **teaspoon salt**
- ½ **teaspoon pumpkin pie spice**
- ½ **teaspoon ground cumin**
- ½ **teaspoon pepper**
- 2 **pork tenderloins (1 pound each)**
- 1 **large onion, chopped**
- 1 **small Granny Smith apple, peeled and chopped**
- 1 **small sweet red pepper, chopped**
- 1 **can (10 ounces) diced tomatoes and green chilies, undrained**
- ½ **cup golden raisins**
- ½ **cup chopped pimiento-stuffed olives**
- 24 **Bibb or Boston lettuce leaves**
- ¼ **cup slivered almonds, toasted**

1. Mix garlic and seasonings; rub over pork. Transfer to a 5-qt. slow cooker. Add onion, apple, sweet pepper and tomatoes. Cook, covered, on low for 2½ to 3 hours or until meat is tender.
2. Remove pork; cool slightly. Shred meat into bite-size pieces; return to slow cooker. Stir in raisins and olives; heat through. Serve in lettuce leaves; sprinkle with almonds.

With small, round, **buttery** leaves, Bibb lettuce is ideal for **lettuce wraps**. Tuna, chicken salad and taco meat all make **tasty fillings**.

Slow Cooker Candied Nuts

I like giving spiced nuts as holiday gifts. This slow cooker recipe with ginger and cinnamon is so good, you just might use it all year long.

—YVONNE STARLIN HERMITAGE, TN

PREP: 10 MIN. • **COOK:** 2 HOURS
MAKES: 4 CUPS

- ½ cup butter, melted
- ½ cup confectioners' sugar
- 1½ teaspoons ground cinnamon
- ¼ teaspoon ground ginger
- ¼ teaspoon ground allspice
- 1½ cups pecan halves
- 1½ cups walnut halves
- 1 cup unblanched almonds

1. In a greased 3-qt. slow cooker, mix butter, confectioners' sugar and spices. Add nuts; toss to coat. Cook, covered, on low 2-3 hours or until nuts are crisp, stirring once.

2. Transfer nuts to waxed paper to cool completely. Store in an airtight container.

Dress up a holiday **gift** tin by including a recipe card for the **sweet treats** the recipient will find inside. Secure the **recipe** with a **festive magnet**.

EAT SMART
Slow Cooker Honey Granola

PREP: 10 MIN.
COOK: 2 HOURS + COOLING
MAKES: ABOUT 8 CUPS

- 4 **cups old-fashioned oats**
- 1 **cup sunflower kernels**
- 1 **cup flaked coconut**
- ½ **teaspoon salt**
- ½ **cup canola oil**
- ½ **cup honey**
- 1 **cup chopped dried pineapple**
- 1 **cup chopped dried mangoes**

1. In a 3-qt. slow cooker, combine oats, sunflower kernels, coconut and salt. In a small bowl, whisk oil and honey until blended. Stir into oats mixture. Cook, covered, on high for 2 hours, stirring well every 20 minutes.

2. Remove granola to baking sheets, spreading evenly; cool completely. Stir in pineapple and mangoes. Store in airtight containers.

PER SERVING ½ cup equals 295 cal., 15 g fat (3 g sat. fat), 0 chol., 167 mg sodium, 38 g carb., 4 g fiber, 5 g pro.

"It's so simple to put this granola together, and it really helps with breakfast on busy mornings. The recipe is flexible, so change up the fruits to your own preference."
—**ARISA CUPP** WARREN, OR

EAT SMART
Sweet Onion & Red Bell Pepper Topping

As soon as the spring Vidalia onions hit the market, this is one of the first recipes I make. I use it on hot dogs, bruschetta, cream cheese and crackers—it is indeed that versatile.
—**PAT HOCKETT** OCALA, FL

PREP: 15 MIN. • **COOK:** 4 HOURS
MAKES: 16 SERVINGS (¼ CUP EACH)

- 4 **large sweet onions, thinly sliced (about 8 cups)**
- 4 **large sweet red peppers, thinly sliced (about 6 cups)**
- ½ **cup cider vinegar**
- ¼ **cup packed brown sugar**
- 2 **tablespoons canola oil**
- 2 **tablespoons honey**
- 2 **teaspoons celery seed**
- ¾ **teaspoon crushed red pepper flakes**
- ½ **teaspoon salt**

In a 5- or 6-qt. slow cooker, combine all ingredients. Cook, covered, on low 4-5 hours or until vegetables are tender. Serve with a slotted spoon.
PER SERVING ¼ cup equals 76 cal., 2 g fat (trace sat. fat), 0 chol., 84 mg sodium, 14 g carb., 2 g fiber, 1 g pro.
Diabetic Exchange: 1 starch.

SLOW COOKER HONEY GRANOLA

HOT SPICED
LEMON DRINK

Caribbean Chipotle Pork Sliders

One of our favorite pulled pork recipes combines the heat of chipotle peppers with cool tropical coleslaw. The robust flavors make these sliders a big hit with guests.

—**KADIJA BRIDGEWATER** DEERFIELD BEACH, FL

PREP: 35 MIN. • **COOK:** 8 HOURS
MAKES: 20 SERVINGS

- 1 **large onion, quartered**
- 1 **boneless pork shoulder butt roast (3 to 4 pounds)**
- 2 **finely chopped chipotle peppers in adobo sauce plus 3 tablespoons sauce**
- ¾ **cup honey barbecue sauce**
- ¼ **cup water**
- 4 **garlic cloves, minced**
- 1 **tablespoon ground cumin**
- 1 **teaspoon salt**
- ¼ **teaspoon pepper**

COLESLAW
- 2 **cups finely chopped red cabbage**
- 1 **medium mango, peeled and chopped**
- 1 **cup pineapple tidbits, drained**
- ¾ **cup chopped fresh cilantro**
- 1 **tablespoon lime juice**
- ¼ **teaspoon salt**
- ⅛ **teaspoon pepper**
- 20 **Hawaiian sweet rolls, split and toasted**

1. Place onion in a 5-qt. slow cooker. Cut roast in half; place over onion. In a small bowl, combine chipotle peppers, adobo sauce, barbecue sauce, water, garlic, cumin, salt and pepper; pour over meat. Cook, covered, on low for 8-10 hours or until meat is tender.
2. Remove roast; cool slightly. Skim fat from cooking juices. Shred pork with two forks. Return pork to slow cooker; heat through.
3. For coleslaw, in a large bowl, combine cabbage, mango, pineapple, cilantro, lime juice, salt and pepper. Place ¼ cup pork mixture on each roll bottom; top with 2 tablespoons coleslaw. Replace tops.

Hot Spiced Lemon Drink

I received this recipe from a woman in our church. She's an excellent cook who has shared several slow cooker recipes with us. We really enjoy the sweet-tangy flavor of this warm citrus punch.

—**MANDY WRIGHT** SPRINGVILLE, UT

PREP: 10 MIN. • **COOK:** 2 HOURS
MAKES: ABOUT 3 QUARTS

- 2½ **quarts water**
- 2 **cups sugar**
- 1½ **cups orange juice**
- ½ **cup plus 2 tablespoons lemon juice**
- ¼ **cup pineapple juice**
- 1 **cinnamon stick (3 inches)**
- ½ **teaspoon whole cloves**

In a 5-qt. slow cooker, combine the water, sugar and juices. Place the cinnamon stick and cloves on a double thickness of cheesecloth; bring up corners of cloth and tie with kitchen string to form a bag. Place in slow cooker. Cover and cook on low for 2-3 hours or until heated through. Discard spice bag.

Paddy's Reuben Dip

This slow-cooked spread tastes just like the popular Reuben sandwich. Even when I double the recipe, I end up with an empty dish.

—**MARY JANE KIMMES** HASTINGS, MN

PREP: 5 MIN. • **COOK:** 2 HOURS
MAKES: ABOUT 4 CUPS

- 4 **packages (2 ounces each) thinly sliced deli corned beef, finely chopped**
- 1 **package (8 ounces) cream cheese, cubed**
- 1 **can (8 ounces) sauerkraut, rinsed and drained**
- 1 **cup (8 ounces) sour cream**
- 1 **cup (4 ounces) shredded Swiss cheese**
  Rye bread or crackers

In a 1½-qt. slow cooker, combine the first five ingredients. Cover and cook on low for 2 hours or until cheese is melted; stir until blended. Serve warm with bread or crackers.

CARIBBEAN CHIPOTLE
PORK SLIDERS

PINK GRAPEFRUIT CHEESECAKE

let cheesecake stand, covered, in slow cooker 1 hour. Center of cheesecake will be just set and top will appear dull.
5. Remove springform pan from slow cooker; remove foil from pan. Cool cheesecake on a wire rack 1 hour. Loosen sides from pan with a knife. Refrigerate overnight, covering when completely cooled. Remove rim from the pan.
NOTE *Six-inch springform pans are available at* **wilton.com.** *If desired, top cheesecake with orange and grapefruit sections and sliced kumquats.*

Cranberry Hot Wings

Chicken wings get a special treatment of cranberry sauce, citrus and a hint of hot sauce in this no-fuss recipe. The wings are a tangy way to heat up a winter night.
—**ROBIN HAAS** CRANSTON, RI

PREP: 50 MIN. • **COOK:** 2 HOURS
MAKES: ABOUT 2½ DOZEN

- 1 **can (14 ounces) jellied cranberry sauce, cubed**
- 2 **tablespoons ground mustard**
- 2 **tablespoons hot pepper sauce**
- 2 **tablespoons reduced-sodium soy sauce**
- 2 **tablespoons honey**
- 1 **tablespoon cider vinegar**
- 2 **teaspoons garlic powder**
- 1 **teaspoon grated orange peel**
- 3 **pounds chicken wings**
  Blue cheese salad dressing and celery sticks

1. In a 5-qt. slow cooker, combine the first eight ingredients. Cover and cook on low for 45 minutes or until cranberry sauce is melted.
2. Meanwhile, cut wings into three sections; discard wing tip sections. Place wings on a greased broiler pan. Broil 4-6 in. from the heat for 15-20 minutes or until lightly browned, turning occasionally.
3. Transfer wings to slow cooker; toss to coat. Cover and cook on high for 2-3 hours or until tender. Serve with dressing and celery.
NOTE *Uncooked chicken wing sections (wingettes) may be substituted for whole chicken wings.*

Pink Grapefruit Cheesecake

Cheesecake from a slow cooker? It's true! I experimented a few times to turn this classic dessert into a slow-cooker hit. Give it a try—you'll be amazed at the results!
—**KRISTA LANPHIER** MILWAUKEE, WI

PREP: 20 MIN. • **COOK:** 2 HOURS + CHILLING
MAKES: 6 SERVINGS

- ¾ **cup graham cracker crumbs**
- 1 **tablespoon plus ⅔ cup sugar, divided**
- 1 **teaspoon grated grapefruit peel**
- ¼ **teaspoon ground ginger**
- 2½ **tablespoons butter, melted**
- 2 **packages (8 ounces each) cream cheese, softened**
- ½ **cup sour cream**
- 2 **tablespoons pink grapefruit juice**
- 2 **eggs, lightly beaten**

1. Place a greased 6-in. springform pan on a double thickness of heavy-duty foil (about 12 in. square). Wrap foil securely around pan. Pour 1 in. water into a 6-qt. slow cooker. Layer two 24-in. pieces of aluminum foil. Starting with a long side, fold up foil to create a 1-in.-wide strip; roll into a coil. Place in slow cooker to form a rack for the cheesecake.
2. In a small bowl, mix cracker crumbs, 1 tablespoon sugar, peel and ginger; stir in butter. Press onto bottom and about 1 in. up sides of prepared pan.
3. In a large bowl, beat cream cheese and remaining sugar until smooth. Beat in sour cream and grapefruit juice. Add eggs and beat on low speed just until combined.
4. Pour into crust. Place springform pan on top of coil. Cover slow cooker with a double layer of paper towels; place lid securely over towels. Cook, covered, on high 2 hours. Do not remove lid; turn off slow cooker and

Minty Hot Fudge Sundae Cake

The best part about dessert from the slow cooker is that when dining is done, a hot treat is ready to serve. In this case, a chocolaty, gooey, minty treat!
—**TERRI MCKITRICK** DELAFIELD, WI

PREP: 15 MIN. • **COOK:** 4 HOURS
MAKES: 12 SERVINGS

- 1¾ cups packed brown sugar, divided
- 1 cup all-purpose flour
- 5 tablespoons baking cocoa, divided
- 2 teaspoons baking powder
- ½ teaspoon salt
- ½ cup evaporated milk
- 2 tablespoons butter, melted
- ½ teaspoon vanilla extract
- ⅛ teaspoon almond extract
- 1 package (4.67 ounces) mint Andes candies
- 1¾ cups boiling water
- 4 teaspoons instant coffee granules
  Vanilla ice cream, whipped cream and maraschino cherries

1. In a large bowl, combine 1 cup brown sugar, flour, 3 tablespoons cocoa, baking powder and salt. In another bowl, combine the milk, butter and extracts. Stir into dry ingredients just until moistened. Transfer to a 3-qt. slow cooker coated with cooking spray. Sprinkle with the candies.

2. Combine the water, coffee granules and remaining brown sugar and cocoa; pour over batter (do not stir). Cover and cook on high for 4 to 4½ hours or until a toothpick inserted near center of cake comes out clean. Serve with ice cream, whipped cream and cherries.

Hot Crab Dip

I have a large family, work full time and coach soccer and football, so I appreciate recipes that are easy to assemble, like this one. The rich and creamy dip is a fun appetizer for holiday gatherings.
—**TERI RASEY** CADILLAC, MI

PREP: 5 MIN. • **COOK:** 3 HOURS
MAKES: ABOUT 5 CUPS

- ½ cup milk
- ⅓ cup salsa
- 3 packages (8 ounces each) cream cheese, cubed
- 2 packages (8 ounces each) imitation crabmeat, flaked
- 1 cup thinly sliced green onions
- 1 can (4 ounces) chopped green chilies
  Assorted crackers

In a small bowl, combine milk and salsa. Transfer to a greased 3-qt. slow cooker. Stir in cream cheese, crab, onions and chilies. Cover and cook on low for 3-4 hours, stirring every 30 minutes. Serve with crackers.

Dark brown sugar contains more **molasses** than **light** or **golden brown** sugar. The types are generally **interchangeable** in recipes. But if you prefer **a bolder flavor**, choose dark brown sugar.

CINNAMON-RAISIN
BANANA BREAD PUDDING

Cinnamon-Raisin Banana Bread Pudding

My family likes to top this luscious dessert with berries, chopped nuts, ice cream, whipped cream or caramel. If I'm making it for adults only, I add a little rum to the milk mixture for extra flavor.

—AYSHA SCHURMAN AMMON, ID

PREP: 10 MIN. • **COOK:** 2½ HOURS
MAKES: 8 SERVINGS

- 4 eggs
- 2¼ cups 2% milk
- ¾ cup mashed ripe banana (about 1 large)
- ¼ cup packed brown sugar
- ⅓ cup butter, melted
- 1 teaspoon vanilla extract
- 1 loaf (1 pound) cinnamon-raisin bread, cut into 1-inch cubes
- ½ cup chopped pecans, toasted
  Vanilla ice cream, optional

1. In a large bowl, whisk the first six ingredients. Stir in bread and pecans. Transfer mixture to a greased 4-qt. slow cooker.
2. Cook, covered, on low 2½ to 3 hours or until a knife inserted near the center comes out clean. Serve warm, with ice cream if desired.

Most **vanilla** comes from Madagascar and Reunion Island—formerly known as the **Bourbon Islands**—off the southeast coast of Africa. Bourbon vanilla is celebrated for its **strong, clear** vanilla flavor and **creamy** finish.

Cheesy Pizza Fondue

I keep the ingredients for this fun dip on hand, so I'm always ready for a gathering. No one can resist it.

—NEL CARVER MOSCOW, ID

PREP: 10 MIN. • **COOK:** 4 HOURS
MAKES: 4 CUPS

- 1 jar (29 ounces) meatless spaghetti sauce
- 2 cups (8 ounces) shredded part-skim mozzarella cheese
- ¼ cup shredded Parmesan cheese
- 2 teaspoons dried oregano
- 1 teaspoon dried minced onion
- ¼ teaspoon garlic powder
  Cubed Italian bread

1. In a 1½-qt. slow cooker, combine the spaghetti sauce, cheeses, oregano, onion and garlic powder.
2. Cover and cook on low 4-6 hours or until heated through and cheese is melted. Serve with bread.

CHEESY PIZZA FONDUE

Slow Cooker Cider

There's no last-minute rush when you slowly simmer this fragrant fall classic.

—ALPHA WILSON ROSWELL, NM

PREP: 5 MIN. • **COOK:** 2 HOURS
MAKES: 2 QUARTS

- 2 cinnamon sticks (3 inches)
- 1 teaspoon whole cloves
- 1 teaspoon whole allspice
- 2 quarts apple cider
- ½ cup packed brown sugar
- 1 orange, sliced

1. Place cinnamon, cloves and allspice on a double thickness of cheesecloth; bring up corners of cloth and tie with a string to form a bag.
2. Place cider and brown sugar in a 3-qt. slow cooker; stir until sugar dissolves. Add spice bag. Place orange slices on top. Cover and cook on low for 2-3 hours or until heated through. Discard spice bag.

Chicken Sliders with Sesame Slaw

These tangy chicken sliders have an Asian style that tingles the taste buds. At our potlucks, they quickly vanish.

—**PRISCILLA YEE** CONCORD, CA

PREP: 25 MIN. • **COOK:** 6 HOURS
MAKES: 20 SERVINGS

- 1 medium onion, coarsely chopped
- 3 pounds boneless skinless chicken thighs
- ½ cup ketchup
- ¼ cup reduced-sodium teriyaki sauce
- 2 tablespoons dry sherry or reduced-sodium chicken broth
- 2 tablespoons minced fresh gingerroot
- ½ teaspoon salt

SESAME SLAW

- ¼ cup mayonnaise
- 1 tablespoon rice wine vinegar
- 1 tablespoon sesame oil
- 1 teaspoon Sriracha Asian hot chili sauce
- 3 cups coleslaw mix
- ⅓ cup dried cherries or cranberries
- 2 tablespoons minced fresh cilantro
- 20 slider buns or dinner rolls, split

1. Place onion and chicken in a 4-qt. slow cooker. In a small bowl, mix ketchup, teriyaki sauce, sherry, ginger and salt. Pour over chicken. Cook, covered, on low 6-7 hours or until a thermometer reads 170°.
2. Remove chicken; cool slightly. Skim fat from cooking juices. Shred chicken with two forks. Return chicken to slow cooker. Meanwhile, in a small bowl, whisk mayonnaise, vinegar, sesame oil and chili sauce until blended. Stir in coleslaw mix, cherries and cilantro. Using a slotted spoon, place ¼ cup chicken mixture on each bun bottom; top with about 2 tablespoons slaw. Replace tops.

FREEZE IT

Old-Fashioned Peach Butter

Cinnamon and cloves add down-home flavor to this spread for toast or biscuits. Using the slow cooker eliminates much of the stirring required when simmering fruit butter on the stovetop.

—**MARILOU ROBINSON** PORTLAND, OR

PREP: 25 MIN. • **COOK:** 9 HOURS + COOLING
MAKES: 9 CUPS

- 14 cups coarsely chopped peeled fresh or frozen peaches (about 5½ pounds)
- 2½ cups sugar
- 4½ teaspoons lemon juice
- 1½ teaspoons ground cinnamon
- ¾ teaspoon ground cloves
- ½ cup quick-cooking tapioca

1. In a large bowl, combine the peaches, sugar, lemon juice, cinnamon and cloves. Transfer to a 5-qt. slow cooker. Cover and cook on low for 8-10 hours or until peaches are very soft, stirring occasionally.
2. Stir in tapioca. Cook, uncovered, on high for 1 hour or until thickened. Pour into jars or freezer containers; cool to room temperature, about 1 hour. Cover and refrigerate up to 3 weeks or freeze up to 1 year.

FREEZE OPTION *Thaw peach butter in the refrigerator for 1-2 days; use within 3 weeks.*

CHICKEN SLIDERS WITH SESAME SLAW

> "For my niece's annual Halloween party, I make glazed meatballs and deliver them in the slow cooker so they're spicy, sweet and ready to eat."
> —**GAIL BORCZYK** BOCA RATON, FL

SWEET AND SPICY ASIAN MEATBALLS

FREEZE IT

Sweet and Spicy Asian Meatballs

PREP: 1 HOUR • **COOK:** 3 HOURS
MAKES: ABOUT 5 DOZEN

- 1 egg, lightly beaten
- ½ medium onion, finely chopped
- ⅓ cup sliced water chestnuts, minced
- 3 tablespoons minced fresh cilantro
- 1 jalapeno pepper, seeded and finely chopped
- 3 tablespoons reduced-sodium soy sauce
- 4 garlic cloves, minced
- 1 tablespoon minced fresh gingerroot
- ⅔ cup panko (Japanese) bread crumbs
- 2 pounds ground pork

SAUCE

- 2 cups sweet-and-sour sauce
- ¼ cup barbecue sauce
- ¼ cup duck sauce
- 2 tablespoons chicken broth
- 1 tablespoon minced fresh cilantro
- 1 tablespoon reduced-sodium soy sauce
- 2 garlic cloves, minced
- 1½ teaspoons minced fresh gingerroot
  Thinly sliced green onions, optional

1. Preheat oven to 375°. In a large bowl, combine the first eight ingredients; stir in bread crumbs. Add pork; mix lightly but thoroughly. Shape into 1¼-in. balls. Place on a greased rack in a 15x10x1-in. baking pan. Bake for 18-22 minutes or until lightly browned.

2. Transfer meatballs to a 4-qt. slow cooker. In small bowl, mix the first eight sauce ingredients. Pour over meatballs. Cook, covered, on low for 3-4 hours or until meatballs are cooked through. If desired, sprinkle with green onions.

FREEZE OPTION *Freeze the cooled meatball mixture in freezer containers. To use, partially thaw in refrigerator overnight. Heat through in a covered saucepan, gently stirring and adding a little broth or water if necessary. Sprinkle with green onions.*

NOTE *Wear disposable gloves when cutting hot peppers; the oils can burn skin. Avoid touching your face.*

CREAMY BEEF & POTATOES, PAGE 113

"One of my husband's favorite childhood memories was eating his Grandma Barney's Tater Tot casserole. One day I started preparing it, sure that I had some Tots on hand. Instead, I found O'Brien potatoes. Dinner turned out great! Now I always make it this way."

—HEATHER MATTHEWS KELLER, TX
about her recipe, Creamy Beef & Potatoes, on page 113

Stovetop Suppers

Beef & Ground Beef

97   105   108

It's easy to toss together **a pleasing meal** with the delectable beef recipes that follow. From veggie-packed **stir-fries** to convenient one-pot **pasta dinners** and **stick-to-your-ribs stews** and **chili**, you're sure to discover **delicious new dishes** your family will cherish.

SOUTHWESTERN GOULASH

Meatball Chili with Dumplings

My family enjoys this delicious recipe—it's like a spicy meatball stew with fluffy cornmeal dumplings!

—SARAH YODER MIDDLEBURY, IN

PREP: 20 MIN. • **COOK:** 1½ HOURS
MAKES: 6 SERVINGS

- 1 egg, beaten
- ¾ cup finely chopped onion, divided
- ¼ cup dry bread crumbs or rolled oats
- 5 teaspoons beef bouillon granules, divided
- 3 teaspoons chili powder, divided
- 1 pound ground beef
- 3 tablespoons all-purpose flour
- 1 tablespoon canola oil
- 1 can (28 ounces) diced tomatoes, undrained
- 1 garlic clove, minced
- ½ teaspoon ground cumin
- 1 can (16 ounces) kidney beans, rinsed and drained

CORNMEAL DUMPLINGS
- 1½ cups biscuit/baking mix
- ½ cup yellow cornmeal
- ⅔ cup milk

1. In a large bowl, combine egg, ¼ cup chopped onion, bread crumbs, 3 teaspoons bouillon and 1 teaspoon chili powder; crumble beef over mixture and mix well. Shape into twelve 1½-in. meatballs. Roll in flour.
2. Heat oil in a skillet; brown meatballs. Drain on paper towels. Meanwhile, in a large saucepan, combine the tomatoes, garlic and cumin with the remaining onion, bouillon and chili powder. Add meatballs. Cover and cook over low heat for 1 hour. Stir in beans.
3. Combine dumpling ingredients. Drop by spoonfuls onto chili; cook on low, uncovered, for 10 minutes. Cover and cook 10-12 minutes longer or until a toothpick inserted in dumpling comes out clean.

EAT SMART **FREEZE IT**
Southwestern Goulash

I had some extra cilantro in the fridge and didn't want to throw it away. Instead, I came up with a Southwest-inspired dish using the ingredients I had on hand. The whole family loved it.

—VIKKI REBHOLZ WEST CHESTER, OH

START TO FINISH: 30 MIN.
MAKES: 6 SERVINGS

- 1 cup uncooked elbow macaroni
- 1 pound lean ground beef (90% lean)
- 1 medium onion, chopped
- 1 can (28 ounces) diced tomatoes, undrained
- ⅔ cup frozen corn
- 1 can (8 ounces) tomato sauce
- 1 can (4 ounces) chopped green chilies
- ½ teaspoon ground cumin
- ½ teaspoon pepper
- ¼ teaspoon salt
- ¼ cup minced fresh cilantro

1. Cook the macaroni according to package directions. Meanwhile, in a Dutch oven over medium heat, cook beef and onion until meat is no longer pink; drain. Stir in the tomatoes, corn, tomato sauce, chilies, cumin, pepper and salt. Bring to a boil. Reduce heat; simmer, uncovered, for 3-5 minutes to allow flavors to blend.
2. Drain macaroni; add to the meat mixture and heat through. Stir in the cilantro.

FREEZE OPTION *Freeze individual portions of cooled goulash in freezer containers. To use, partially thaw in refrigerator overnight. Heat through in a saucepan, stirring occasionally and adding a little water if necessary.*
PER SERVING *1⅓ cups equals 224 cal., 6 g fat (2 g sat. fat), 37 mg chol., 567 mg sodium, 24 g carb., 4 g fiber, 19 g pro.* **Diabetic Exchanges:** *2 lean meat, 2 vegetable, 1 starch.*

**BEEF & SPINACH
LO MEIN**

"If you like a good stir-fry, this dish will definitely satisfy. I discovered the recipe at an international luncheon and it's now a favorite go-to meal."
—**DENISE PATTERSON** BAINBRIDGE, OH

Beef & Spinach Lo Mein

START TO FINISH: 30 MIN.
MAKES: 5 SERVINGS

- ¼ cup hoisin sauce
- 2 tablespoons soy sauce
- 1 tablespoon water
- 2 teaspoons sesame oil
- 2 garlic cloves, minced
- ¼ teaspoon crushed red pepper flakes
- 1 pound beef top round steak, thinly sliced
- 6 ounces uncooked spaghetti
- 4 teaspoons canola oil, divided
- 1 can (8 ounces) sliced water chestnuts, drained
- 2 green onions, sliced
- 1 package (10 ounces) fresh spinach, coarsely chopped
- 1 red chili pepper, seeded and thinly sliced

1. In a small bowl, mix the first six ingredients. Remove ¼ cup mixture to a large bowl; add beef and toss to coat. Marinate at room temperature 10 minutes.

2. Cook spaghetti according to package directions. Meanwhile, in a large skillet, heat 1½ teaspoons canola oil. Add half of the beef mixture; stir-fry for 1-2 minutes or until no longer pink. Remove from the pan. Repeat with an additional 1½ teaspoons oil and the remaining beef mixture.

3. Stir-fry water chestnuts and green onions in remaining canola oil for 30 seconds. Stir in the spinach and remaining hoisin mixture; cook until spinach is wilted. Return beef to pan; heat through.

4. Drain spaghetti; add to the beef mixture and toss to combine. Sprinkle with chili pepper.

NOTE *Wear disposable gloves when cutting hot peppers; the oils can burn skin. Avoid touching your face.*

PER SERVING *1⅓ cups equals 363 cal., 10 g fat (2 g sat. fat), 51 mg chol., 652 mg sodium, 40 g carb., 4 g fiber, 28 g pro.* **Diabetic Exchanges:** *3 lean meat, 2 vegetable, 1½ starch, 1 fat.*

Gyro Salad with Tzatziki Dressing

If you're fond of gyros, you'll enjoy this garden-fresh salad showcasing feta cheese, olives, tomatoes and a creamy cucumber dressing. Try it with lamb instead of beef for an authentic taste.
—*TASTE OF HOME* TEST KITCHEN

START TO FINISH: 30 MIN.
MAKES: 4-6 SERVINGS

DRESSING
- 1 cucumber, peeled and coarsely shredded
- ½ teaspoon salt
- ½ cup sour cream
- ¾ cup (6 ounces) plain yogurt
- 2 tablespoons white vinegar
- 1 garlic clove, minced
- ½ teaspoon dill weed
- ¼ teaspoon cracked black pepper

SALAD
- ½ pound ground beef or lamb
- 1 small onion, chopped
- 1 teaspoon Greek seasoning or oregano leaves
- 1 package (10 ounces) hearts of romaine salad mix
- 2 tomatoes, chopped
- 1 package (4 ounces) crumbled feta cheese
- ½ cup pitted Greek olives, drained
  Toasted pita bread wedges

1. In a large bowl, sprinkle cucumber with salt; mix well. Let stand for 5 minutes. Drain. Stir in remaining dressing ingredients. Cover and refrigerate.

2. In a large skillet over medium-high heat, cook beef, onion and Greek seasoning until meat is no longer pink; drain.

3. Arrange salad mix on a large serving platter; top with tomatoes, cheese, olives and beef. Spoon the dressing over the salad. Serve immediately with pita wedges.

GYRO SALAD WITH TZATZIKI DRESSING

BEEFY SHELLS AND CHEESE

Spicy Beef with Peppers

I've enjoyed cooking and baking since I was a girl— and my husband and I now have eight grandchildren. But this recipe is actually one of his signature dishes. We've served it at family dinners, picnics and potlucks.

—**PATRICIA ANN FREDELL** ORION, IL

START TO FINISH: 25 MIN.
MAKES: 4-6 SERVINGS

- 2 **tablespoons cornstarch, divided**
- 4 **tablespoons dry sherry or beef broth, divided**
- 4 **tablespoons soy sauce, divided**
- 1 **garlic clove, minced**
- ½ **to 1 teaspoon crushed red pepper flakes**
- 1 **pound beef top sirloin steak, thinly sliced**
- ½ **cup cold water**
- 3 **tablespoons canola oil, divided**
- 1 **green pepper, sliced**
- 1 **sweet red pepper, sliced**
  Cooked rice or chow mein noodles

1. In a small bowl, combine 1 tablespoon cornstarch with 2 tablespoons sherry, 2 tablespoons soy sauce, garlic and pepper flakes. Add beef and toss to coat. Set aside.
2. In another bowl, combine water with remaining cornstarch, sherry and soy sauce. Set aside.
3. In wok or skillet, heat 1 tablespoon oil on medium-high. Add peppers; stir-fry 3 minutes. Remove peppers to a platter.
4. Add remaining oil and half of the beef; stir-fry until no longer pink. Remove and stir-fry remaining beef.
5. Return peppers and beef to the pan. Stir the cornstarch mixture and add to pan; bring to a boil, stirring constantly. Cook 1 minute or until thickened. Serve stir-fry with rice.

Beefy Shells and Cheese

My simple, family-pleasing dinner starts with boxed macaroni and cheese. I like to top it with shredded Monterey Jack or cheddar for even more cheesy goodness.
—**LOUISE GRAYBIEL** TORONTO, ON

START TO FINISH: 30 MIN.
MAKES: 6 SERVINGS

- 1 **pound ground beef**
- 1 **package (12 ounces) shells and cheese dinner mix**
- 2 **cups water**
- 1¼ **cups salsa**
- 1 **can (15 ounces) black beans, rinsed and drained**
- 1 **to 2 teaspoons chili powder**
- ⅛ **teaspoon salt**

1. In a large skillet, cook beef over medium heat until no longer pink; drain. Set aside cheese sauce packet from dinner mix. Add shells and water to skillet. Bring to a boil; cover and simmer for 10-12 minutes or until pasta is tender.
2. Stir in the salsa, beans, chili powder, salt and contents of cheese sauce packet. Remove from the heat; cover and let stand for 5 minutes.

Greek-Style Ravioli

Here's a flavorful Greek twist on an Italian classic. It's an easy weekday meal that's become one of our favorites. My husband and I enjoy it with garlic cheese toast.
—**HETTI WILLIAMS** RAPID CITY, SD

START TO FINISH: 25 MIN.
MAKES: 2 SERVINGS

- 12 **frozen cheese ravioli**
- ⅓ **pound lean ground beef (90% lean)**
- 1 **cup canned diced tomatoes with basil, oregano and garlic**
- 1 **cup fresh baby spinach**
- ¼ **cup sliced ripe olives, drained**
- ¼ **cup crumbled feta cheese**

1. Cook ravioli according to package directions. Meanwhile, in a small skillet, cook beef over medium heat until no longer pink; drain. Stir in tomatoes. Bring to a boil. Reduce heat; simmer, uncovered, for 10 minutes.
2. Drain ravioli. Add the ravioli, spinach and olives to beef mixture; heat through. Sprinkle with the feta cheese.

Pizzeria Burgers

When my children were teens, they asked for these delicious burgers every week! I like to fix them because they don't take much work and kids of all ages adore them.

—AMY LAPOINTE NORTH FOND DU LAC, WI

START TO FINISH: 30 MIN.
MAKES: 6 SERVINGS

- ¾ cup pizza sauce, divided
- ¼ cup dry bread crumbs
- ¼ teaspoon dried oregano
- 1 teaspoon salt
  Dash pepper
- 1½ pounds ground beef
- ¼ pound bulk pork sausage
- 6 slices part-skim mozzarella cheese
- 6 sandwich rolls, split

1. Combine ½ cup pizza sauce, bread crumbs, oregano, salt and pepper in a large bowl. Crumble beef and sausage over mixture and mix well. Shape into six patties.

2. Cook patties in a large skillet over medium heat for 5-7 minutes on each side or until a thermometer reads 160° and juices run clear. Top with remaining pizza sauce and cheese. Cover and cook 2 minutes longer or until cheese is melted. Serve on rolls.

Lentil Stew

Since lentils don't require the long soaking time that dried beans do, you can begin making this hearty stew just an hour before supper—not the night before! Our family likes it served with a basket of homemade breadsticks.

—CAROL WOLFER LEBANON, OR

PREP: 5 MIN. • **COOK:** 50 MIN.
MAKES: 6 SERVINGS

- 1 cup dried lentils, rinsed
- 2½ cups water
- 2 teaspoons beef bouillon granules
- ½ pound ground beef, cooked and drained
- 2 medium carrots, sliced
- 2 cups tomato juice
- ½ teaspoon dried oregano
- ½ cup chopped onion
- 2 celery ribs, chopped
- 1 garlic clove, minced

1. In a large saucepan, bring the lentils, water and bouillon to a boil. Reduce heat; simmer, uncovered, for 20 minutes.

2. Stir in the remaining ingredients. Return to a boil; reduce the heat and simmer 20-30 minutes longer or until lentils and vegetables are tender.

Crumb-Coated Cubed Steaks

I always buy steaks like this that are already tenderized at the meat counter. Fresh tomato slices, mashed potatoes and black-eyed peas complete this meal.

—AGNES WARD STRATFORD, ON

START TO FINISH: 30 MIN.
MAKES: 4 SERVINGS

- 1 egg
- ½ cup milk
- ¾ cup crushed saltines (about 25 crackers)
- ⅔ cup all-purpose flour
- ¾ teaspoon salt
- ¼ teaspoon baking powder
- ¼ teaspoon cayenne pepper
- ¼ teaspoon pepper
- 4 beef cubed steaks (4 ounces each)
- 3 tablespoons canola oil

GRAVY

- 2 tablespoons all-purpose flour
- 1⅓ cups milk
- ¼ teaspoon salt
- ¼ teaspoon pepper

1. In a shallow bowl, whisk egg and milk. In another shallow bowl, combine the cracker crumbs, flour, salt, baking powder, cayenne and pepper. Dip steaks in egg mixture, then in crumb mixture.

2. In a large skillet, cook steaks in oil over medium heat for 3-4 minutes on each side or until no longer pink. Remove and keep warm.

3. For gravy, stir flour into the pan until blended. Gradually add milk, stirring to loosen browned bits from pan. Bring to a boil; cook and stir for 2 minutes or until thickened. Season the gravy with salt and pepper. Serve with steaks.

PIZZERIA BURGERS

WIENER SCHNITZEL

Cashew Curried Beef

This recipe is a favorite with my whole family. The ingredients are a wonderful mix of sweet, salty and spicy.

—JENNIFER FRIDGEN EAST GRAND FORKS, MN

PREP: 20 MIN. • **COOK:** 20 MIN.
MAKES: 5 SERVINGS

- 1 **pound beef top sirloin steak, thinly sliced**
- 2 **tablespoons canola oil, divided**
- 1 **can (13.66 ounces) coconut milk, divided**
- 1 **tablespoon red curry paste**
- 2 **tablespoons packed brown sugar**
- 2 **tablespoons fish sauce or soy sauce**
- 8 **cups chopped bok choy**
- 1 **small sweet red pepper, sliced**
- ½ **cup salted cashews**
- ½ **cup minced fresh cilantro**
      Hot cooked brown rice

1. In a large skillet, saute beef in 1 tablespoon oil until no longer pink. Remove from skillet and set aside.
2. Spoon ½ cup cream from top of coconut milk and place in the pan. Add the remaining oil; bring to a boil. Add the curry paste; cook and stir for 5 minutes or until oil separates from coconut milk mixture.
3. Stir in the brown sugar, fish sauce and remaining coconut milk. Bring to a boil. Reduce the heat; simmer, uncovered, for 5 minutes or until slightly thickened. Add bok choy and red pepper; return to a boil. Cook and stir 2-3 minutes longer or until the vegetables are tender.
4. Stir in the cashews, cilantro and beef; heat through. Serve with rice.
NOTE *This recipe was tested with regular (full-fat) coconut milk. Light coconut milk contains less cream.*

Wiener Schnitzel

I like to chill the veal for 30 minutes after coating it. This makes the recipe more convenient as I prepare the side dishes.

—EMMA WEST LEOMA, TN

START TO FINISH: 25 MIN.
MAKES: 4 SERVINGS

- 4 **veal cutlets (4 ounces each)**
- ¾ **teaspoon salt**
- ¾ **teaspoon pepper**
- ½ **cup all-purpose flour**
- 2 **eggs, lightly beaten**
- ¾ **cup dry bread crumbs**
- ¼ **cup butter**
- 4 **lemon slices**

1. Sprinkle veal with salt and pepper. Place the flour, eggs and bread crumbs in separate shallow bowls. Coat veal with flour, then dip in eggs and coat with crumbs.
2. In a large skillet over medium heat, cook the veal in butter for 2-3 minutes on each side or until no longer pink. Serve with lemon.

Southwestern Roast Beef Sandwiches

When we have leftover roast beef, I like to make these tasty grilled sandwiches. They get their zip from green chilies and pepper jack.

—STEPHANIE STOKLEY SPRINGFIELD, MO

START TO FINISH: 15 MIN.
MAKES: 2 SERVINGS

- 2 **teaspoons butter, softened**
- 4 **slices white bread**
- 2 **slices cooked roast beef (2¼ ounces each)**
- 2 **slices pepper jack cheese**
- 2 **canned whole green chilies, halved**

1. Butter one side of each bread slice. On the unbuttered side of two slices, layer beef, cheese and chilies; top with remaining bread, buttered side up.
2. In a large nonstick skillet or griddle coated with cooking spray, toast the sandwiches for 4 minutes on each side or until golden brown.

SKILLET BEEF STROGANOFF

Skillet Beef Stroganoff

I don't recall where I got this recipe, but I've been making it for 40 years. The recipe card is stained and tattered from so much use. I really like the addition of horseradish, which gives the dish that extra zing.
—ALJENE WENDLING SEATTLE, WA

PREP: 25 MIN. • **COOK:** 1¼ HOURS
MAKES: 6 SERVINGS

- 5 cups sliced fresh mushrooms
- 1 large onion, sliced
- 1 tablespoon reduced-fat butter
- ⅓ to ½ cup hot water
- 1 tablespoon prepared horseradish
- ½ teaspoon salt
- ⅛ teaspoon pepper
- ¼ cup all-purpose flour
- 1 beef flank steak (1¼ pounds), cut into 2-inch strips
- 1 cup (8 ounces) reduced-fat sour cream
  Hot cooked noodles

1. In a large skillet, saute mushrooms and onion in butter until tender. With a slotted spoon, transfer to a large bowl; stir in the water, horseradish, salt and pepper. Set aside.

2. Place flour in a large resealable plastic bag. Add beef, a few pieces at a time. Seal bag; shake to coat.

3. In the same skillet, brown beef in batches. Return all of the beef to the pan; top with mushroom mixture.

4. Bring to a boil. Reduce the heat; cover and simmer for 1¼ to 1½ hours or until the beef is tender, stirring occasionally. Remove from the heat; stir in sour cream. Serve with noodles.

NOTE *This recipe was tested with Land O'Lakes light stick butter.*

FREEZE OPTION *Before adding sour cream, freeze cooled beef in a freezer container. To use, partially thaw in refrigerator overnight. Heat through in a saucepan, stirring occasionally. Reduce heat to low. Stir in sour cream; heat through.*

PER SERVING *⅔ cup (calculated without noodles) equals 246 cal., 11 g fat (6 g sat. fat), 62 mg chol., 302 mg sodium, 11 g carb., 1 g fiber, 24 g pro.* **Diabetic Exchanges:** *3 lean meat, 1 starch, 1 fat.*

Change-of-Pace Burgers

Please the whole family with an all-American meal at home. These burgers are filled with a tantalizing blend of vegetables and offer a great new way to serve up a classic.
—NITA SMITH BELLEFONTE, PA

START TO FINISH: 20 MIN.
MAKES: 4 SERVINGS

- ¼ cup finely chopped onion
- ¼ cup finely chopped green pepper
- 3 tablespoons chopped fresh mushrooms
- 3 tablespoons chili sauce
- 1 pound ground beef
- 4 hamburger buns, split
  Ketchup and mustard, optional

1. In a large bowl, combine the onion, green pepper, mushrooms and chili sauce. Crumble beef over mixture and mix well. Shape into four patties.

2. In a large skillet, cook patties over medium heat for 5-6 minutes on each side or until a thermometer reads 160° and juices run clear. Serve burgers on buns with ketchup and mustard if desired.

Fast Italian Stew

Here's a heartwarming dinner that features nutritious escarole. Let it cook just a few minutes at the end to preserve the vitamins. You can substitute kale if desired.

—TASTE OF HOME TEST KITCHEN

PREP: 20 MIN. • **COOK:** 30 MIN.
MAKES: 6 SERVINGS

- 1 **pound ground beef**
- ½ **pound bulk mild Italian sausage**
- 1 **cup chopped onion**
- 1 **can (15 ounces) cannellini or white kidney beans, rinsed and drained**
- 2 **cups cut fresh green beans**
- 1 **can (14½ ounces) Italian stewed tomatoes, undrained**
- 1 **cup vegetable broth**
- 1 **can (6 ounces) tomato paste**
- 2 **teaspoons dried oregano**
- 1 **teaspoon salt**
- ½ **teaspoon pepper**
- 1 **bunch escarole, trimmed and torn**
- ½ **cup shredded Parmesan cheese**

1. In a Dutch oven, cook the beef, sausage and onion over medium heat until meat is no longer pink; drain. Add the cannellini beans, green beans, tomatoes, broth, tomato paste, oregano, salt and pepper.

2. Bring to a boil. Reduce heat; cover and simmer for 15 minutes. Add the escarole; cover and simmer 5 minutes longer or until wilted. Sprinkle each serving with Parmesan cheese.

Hearty Salisbury Steaks

I love serving Salisbury steak with mashed potatoes and vegetables. With so much irresistible down-home taste, this meal disappears fast!

—DOROTHY BAYES SARDIS, OH

START TO FINISH: 30 MIN.
MAKES: 5 SERVINGS

- 1 **medium onion, finely chopped**
- ½ **cup crushed saltines (about 15 crackers)**
- ¼ **cup egg substitute**
- ½ **teaspoon pepper**
- 1 **pound lean ground beef (90% lean)**
- 1 **tablespoon canola oil**
- 2 **cups water**
- 1 **envelope reduced-sodium onion soup mix**
- 2 **tablespoons all-purpose flour**

1. In a large bowl, combine onion, saltines, egg substitute and pepper. Add beef; mix lightly but thoroughly. Shape into five patties.

2. In a large skillet, heat oil over medium heat. Add the patties; cook 3-4 minutes on each side or until lightly browned. Remove patties and keep warm; discard drippings.

3. Combine water, soup mix and flour; stir into skillet. Bring to a boil. Return patties to skillet. Reduce heat; simmer, covered, 5-7 minutes or until meat is no longer pink.

FREEZE OPTION *Freeze individual cooled steak with some gravy in resealable freezer bags. To use, partially thaw in refrigerator overnight. Microwave, covered, on high in a microwave-safe dish until heated through, gently stirring and adding a little water if necessary.*

PER SERVING *1 patty with ¼ cup gravy equals 233 cal., 10 g fat (3 g sat. fat), 45 mg chol., 418 mg sodium, 14 g carb., 1 g fiber, 20 g pro.* **Diabetic Exchanges:** *2 lean meat, 1 starch, 1 fat.*

HEARTY SALISBURY STEAKS

"This iconic sandwich is the ultimate in Philly and a best-seller at Pat's King of Steaks Restaurant. Patrons praise its thinly cut beef and the crusty Italian rolls."
—FRANK OLIVIERI PHILADELPHIA, PA

PAT'S KING OF STEAKS
PHILLY CHEESE STEAK

Pat's King of Steaks Philly Cheese Steak

START TO FINISH: 20 MIN.
MAKES: 4 SERVINGS

- 1 large onion, sliced
- ½ pound sliced fresh mushrooms, optional
- 1 small green pepper, sliced, optional
- 1 small sweet red pepper, sliced, optional
- 6 tablespoons canola oil, divided
- 1½ pounds beef ribeye steaks, thinly sliced
- 4 crusty Italian rolls, split
  Process cheese sauce
  Ketchup, optional

1. In a large skillet, saute the onion and, if desired, mushrooms and peppers in 3 tablespoons oil until tender. Remove and keep warm. In the same pan, saute beef in remaining oil in batches for 45-60 seconds or until meat reaches desired doneness.
2. On each roll bottom, layer the beef, onion mixture, cheese and, if desired, ketchup. Replace tops.

Cornstarch needs just a few minutes of **boiling** to **thicken** a sauce, gravy or dessert filling. **If it cooks too long**, the cornstarch will begin to **lose its thickening** power. Carefully **follow the recipe** for the best results.

Hamburger Stir-Fry

Here's a quick, easy teriyaki stir-fry that uses hamburger instead of the traditional beef strips. It has a nice sauce and is different enough to be a treat for the taste buds.

—KATHIE AND JOHN HORST WESTFIELD, NY

START TO FINISH: 25 MIN.
MAKES: 4 SERVINGS

- 1 tablespoon sugar
- 1 tablespoon cornstarch
- 1 tablespoon ground mustard
- ⅓ cup cold water
- ⅓ cup reduced-sodium teriyaki sauce
- 1 pound lean ground beef (90% lean)
- 1 package (16 ounces) frozen asparagus stir-fry vegetable blend
- 1 medium onion, halved and thinly sliced
- 2 teaspoons canola oil
- 2 cups hot cooked rice
- 2 teaspoons sesame seeds

1. In a small bowl, combine the sugar, cornstarch and mustard. Stir in water and teriyaki sauce until smooth; set aside.
2. In a large nonstick skillet or wok, cook beef until no longer pink; drain and set aside. In the same pan, stir-fry the vegetable blend and onion in oil until crisp-tender.
3. Stir cornstarch mixture and add to the pan. Bring to a boil; cook and stir for 1-2 minutes or until thickened. Add beef; heat through. Serve with rice. Sprinkle with sesame seeds.
PER SERVING *1 cup stir-fry with ½ cup rice equals 399 cal., 12 g fat (4 g sat. fat), 56 mg chol., 516 mg sodium, 42 g carb., 3 g fiber, 28 g pro.* **Diabetic Exchanges:** *3 lean meat, 2 starch, 2 vegetable, ½ fat.*

HAMBURGER STIR-FRY

Peppered Beef Tenderloin Steaks

I found this recipe when I first started experimenting with herbs and rubs to flavor meats. It quickly became a family favorite. The fancy, flavorful onions make tenderloin steaks even more special.

—KARIN WOODBURY OCALA, FL

PREP: 10 MIN. • **COOK:** 35 MIN.
MAKES: 4 SERVINGS

- 2 teaspoons olive oil, divided
- 2 large red onions, cut into ½-inch slices
- 1 teaspoon salt, divided
- 2 tablespoons balsamic vinegar
- ½ teaspoon sugar
- 2 teaspoons coarsely ground pepper
- 1½ teaspoons dried thyme
- 4 beef tenderloin steaks (4 ounces each)

1. Heat 1 teaspoon oil in a large nonstick skillet coated with cooking spray; add onions. Cook and stir over medium heat for 25-30 minutes or until tender and browned. Stir in ½ teaspoon salt, vinegar and sugar. Remove and keep warm.

2. Combine the pepper, thyme and remaining salt; rub over steaks. In the same skillet, cook steaks 4-7 minutes on each side or until meat reaches desired doneness (for medium-rare, a thermometer should read 145°; medium, 160°; well-done, 170°). Serve with onions.

Indian Fry Bread Tacos

Our son-in-law is half Comanche and half Kiowa, and this recipe is similar to one he uses. I downsized it for two.

—LADONNA REED PONCA CITY, OK

PREP: 20 MIN. + STANDING • **COOK:** 15 MIN.
MAKES: 2 SERVINGS

- ¾ cup all-purpose flour
- ½ teaspoon baking powder
- ¼ teaspoon salt
- ⅓ cup hot water
- ½ pound lean ground beef (90% lean)
- 2 tablespoons taco seasoning
- ⅓ cup water
  Oil for frying
- 2 tablespoons chopped lettuce
- 2 tablespoons chopped tomato
- 2 tablespoons salsa
- 2 tablespoons sour cream

1. In a small bowl, combine the flour, baking powder and salt; stir in hot water to form a soft dough. Cover and let stand for 1 hour.

2. In a small skillet, cook beef over medium heat until no longer pink; drain. Stir in taco seasoning and water; simmer, uncovered, for 10 minutes. Keep warm.

3. Divide dough in half. On a lightly floured surface, roll each portion into a 4-in. circle.

4. In an electric skillet, heat 1 in. of oil to 350°. Fry bread circles in hot oil for 3-4 minutes on each side or until golden; drain on paper towels. Top each with meat mixture, lettuce and tomato. Serve tacos with salsa and sour cream.

INDIAN FRY BREAD TACOS

"The beauty of this dish is that it comes together all in one pot, with a simple homemade sauce. Allspice and mace add a little interest to the recipe, but you could use Italian seasoning instead."
—CAROL BENZEL-SCHMIDT STANWOOD, WA

ONE-POT SPAGHETTI DINNER

One-Pot Spaghetti Dinner

PREP: 10 MIN. • **COOK:** 25 MIN.
MAKES: 4 SERVINGS

- **1 pound lean ground beef (90% lean)**
- **1¾ cups sliced fresh mushrooms**
- **3 cups tomato juice**
- **1 can (14½ ounces) no-salt-added diced tomatoes, drained**
- **1 can (8 ounces) no-salt-added tomato sauce**
- **1 tablespoon dried minced onion**
- **½ teaspoon salt**
- **½ teaspoon garlic powder**
- **½ teaspoon ground mustard**
- **¼ teaspoon pepper**
- **⅛ teaspoon ground allspice**
- **⅛ teaspoon ground mace, optional**
- **6 ounces uncooked multigrain spaghetti, broken into pieces**
- **Fresh mozzarella cheese pearls or shaved Parmesan cheese, optional**

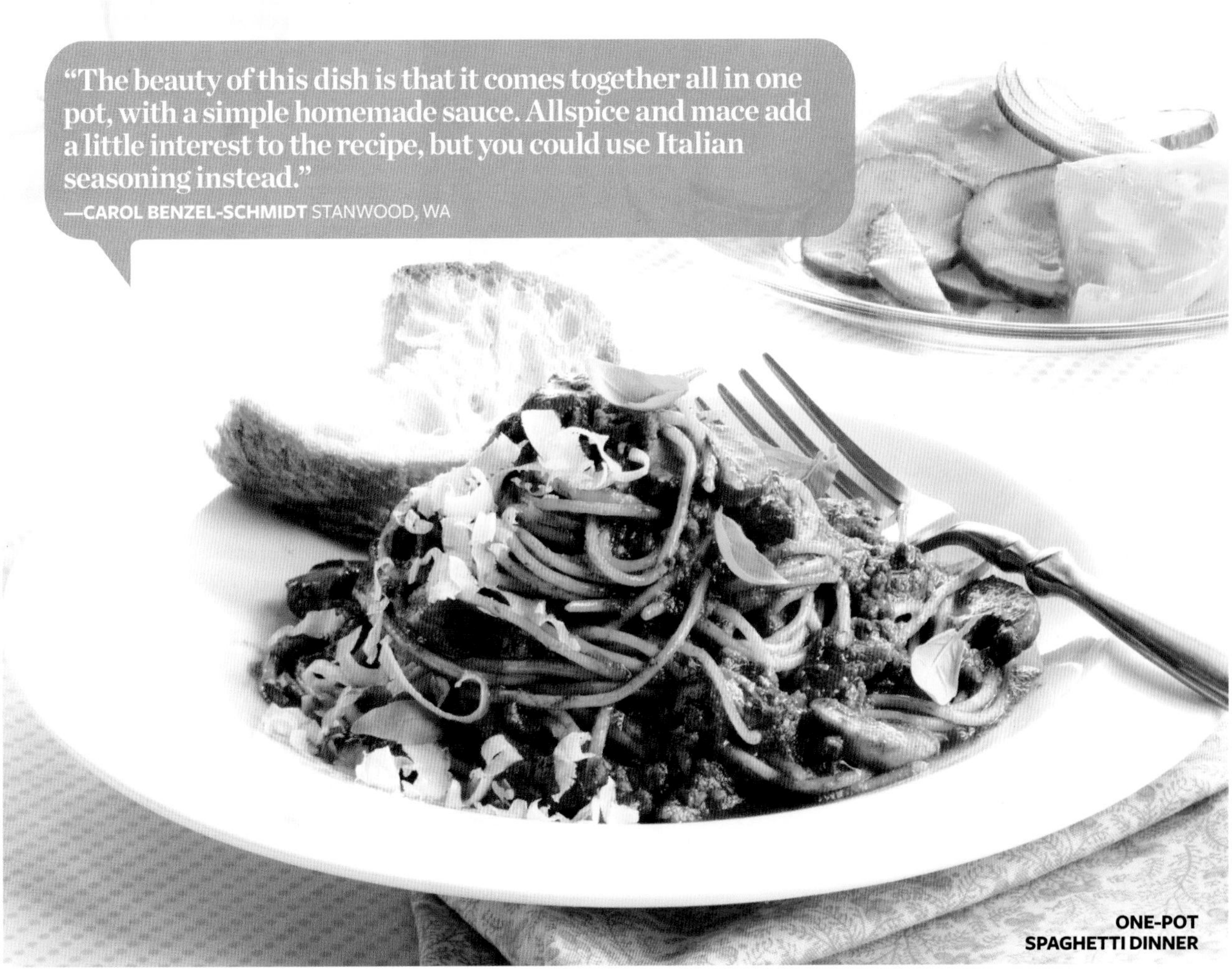

1. In a Dutch oven, cook beef and mushrooms over medium heat until meat is no longer pink; drain. Add tomato juice, tomatoes, tomato sauce, onion and seasonings.

2. Bring to a boil. Stir in spaghetti. Simmer, covered, 12-15 minutes or until spaghetti is tender. If desired, serve with cheese.

EAT SMART

Stovetop Meat Loaves

Who says meat loaf has to bake in the oven for hours? For this convenient recipe, all you need is your stovetop and 30 minutes. It's a quick, simple dish to make for one or two people.
—**EMILY SUND** GENESEO, IL

START TO FINISH: 30 MIN.
MAKES: 2 SERVINGS

- **3 tablespoons 2% milk**
- **2 tablespoons quick-cooking oats**
- **1 tablespoon chopped onion**
- **¼ teaspoon salt**
- **½ pound lean ground beef**
- **½ teaspoon cornstarch**
- **½ cup Italian tomato sauce**
- **¼ cup cold water**

1. In a small bowl, combine the milk, oats, onion and salt. Crumble beef over mixture and mix well. Shape into two loaves.

2. In a small nonstick skillet, brown loaves on all sides; drain. Combine the cornstarch, tomato sauce and water until smooth. Pour over meat loaves. Bring to a boil. Reduce heat to medium-low; cover and cook for 15-20 minutes or until meat is no longer pink.

PER SERVING *1 meat loaf equals 259 cal., 10 g fat (4 g sat. fat), 71 mg chol., 922 mg sodium, 16 g carb., 2 g fiber, 25 g pro.* ***Diabetic Exchanges:*** *3 lean meat, 1 starch.*

ITALIAN MACARONI

Layered Taco Salad

I came up with this taco salad to make my kids happy. Make it with ground beef, turkey or chicken—it's equally good.

—**BETTY NICKELS** TAMPA, FL

START TO FINISH: 25 MIN.
MAKES: 6 SERVINGS

- 1 **pound lean ground beef (90% lean)**
- 2 **tablespoons reduced-sodium taco seasoning**
- 1 **cup salsa**
- 1 **tablespoon lime juice**
- 6 **ounces baked tortilla chips (about 70 chips)**
- 12 **cups chopped iceberg lettuce**
- 6 **plum tomatoes, seeded and chopped**
- 1 **can (15 ounces) black beans, rinsed and drained**
- 1½ **cups (6 ounces) shredded reduced-fat Mexican cheese blend**
- 1 **large sweet yellow or red pepper, thinly sliced**
- 1 **medium red onion, thinly sliced**
- ⅓ **cup fat-free sour cream**

1. In a large nonstick skillet, cook beef over medium heat 6-8 minutes or until no longer pink, breaking into crumbles; drain. Sprinkle taco seasoning over beef; stir to combine. In a small bowl, mix the salsa and lime juice.

2. Arrange tortilla chips on a serving platter; layer with lettuce, tomatoes, beans, cheese, yellow pepper, beef mixture, onion, salsa mixture and sour cream. Serve immediately.

Italian Macaroni

I love how tasty this is and quick it is to prepare. I've shared it with many friends over the years. It makes a good vegetarian dish with meat substitute.

—**LAILA ZVEJNIEKS** STONEY CREEK, ON

START TO FINISH: 25 MIN.
MAKES: 5 SERVINGS

- 1 **pound ground beef**
- 1 **can (28 ounces) diced tomatoes, undrained**
- 2 **cups water**
- 1 **envelope onion soup mix**
- 1 **teaspoon Italian seasoning**
- ¼ **teaspoon crushed red pepper flakes, optional**
- 2 **cups uncooked elbow macaroni**
- ½ **cup grated Parmesan cheese**
- 1 **cup (4 ounces) shredded part-skim mozzarella cheese**

1. In a Dutch oven, cook beef over medium heat until no longer pink; drain. Add the tomatoes, water, soup mix, Italian seasoning and, if desired, pepper flakes. Bring to a boil. Stir in macaroni. Reduce heat; cover and simmer for 8-9 minutes or until macaroni is tender.

2. Remove from the heat; stir in Parmesan cheese. Sprinkle with mozzarella cheese. Cover and let stand for 2 minutes or until cheese is melted.

To quickly **seed a tomato**, cut it into **wedges**. Then swipe your finger over each wedge to remove the **gel pocket** and its **seeds**.

LAYERED TACO SALAD

Italian-Style Beef Liver

My family loves liver, but I get tired of serving the standard liver and onions. Here, a rich tomato sauce gives the dish an exciting makeover.

—**MINA DYCK** BOISSEVAIN, MB

PREP: 10 MIN. • **COOK:** 35 MIN.
MAKES: 4 SERVINGS

- ⅓ **cup all-purpose flour**
- ¼ **teaspoon salt**
- 1 **pound beef liver, cut into bite-size pieces**
- 4 **teaspoons canola oil, divided**
- 1 **cup thinly sliced onion**
- ½ **cup chopped celery**
- 2 **cans (14½ ounces each) diced tomatoes, undrained**
- 1 **bay leaf**
- 2 **tablespoons chopped fresh parsley**
- 1 **tablespoon minced fresh basil or 1 teaspoon dried basil**
- 1 **teaspoon salt**
- ¼ **teaspoon pepper**
  Hot cooked spaghetti
  Grated Parmesan cheese

1. Combine flour and salt; toss with liver. Heat 2 teaspoons oil in a large skillet; cook liver until no longer pink. Remove and set aside.
2. In the same skillet, saute onion and celery in remaining oil until tender. Stir in tomatoes, bay leaf, parsley, basil, salt and pepper. Cover and simmer for 20 minutes, stirring occasionally. Add liver and heat through. Discard bay leaf.
3. Serve mixture over spaghetti; sprinkle with cheese.

> You can make the **gnocchi** recipe even quicker by substituting **two packages** of ready-to-use gnocchi from the **pasta aisle**.

GNOCCHI WITH MEAT SAUCE

Gnocchi with Meat Sauce

This dish from my mother-in-law is the Italian version of a meat-and-potatoes meal. I recently served it to friends, and they immediately wanted the recipe.

—**KARIN NOLTON** ORTONVILLE, MI

PREP: 30 MIN. • **COOK:** 15 MIN.
MAKES: 6 SERVINGS

- ½ **pound lean ground beef (90% lean)**
- 1 **large onion, finely chopped**
- 4 **garlic cloves, minced**
- 2 **cans (15 ounces each) tomato sauce**
- 1 **can (14½ ounces) diced tomatoes**
- 1 **teaspoon dried oregano**
- 1 **teaspoon dried basil**
- ½ **teaspoon dried rosemary, crushed**
- 1 **to 2 teaspoons sugar**
- ½ **teaspoon salt**
- ⅛ **teaspoon pepper**

GNOCCHI

- 2 **cups mashed potato flakes**
- 1½ **cups boiling water**
- 2 **eggs, beaten**
- 1½ **cups all-purpose flour**
- ¼ **teaspoon salt**
  Grated Parmesan cheese, optional

1. In a large saucepan, cook the beef, onion and garlic over medium heat until meat is no longer pink; drain. Stir in the tomato sauce, diced tomatoes and seasonings. Bring to a boil. Reduce heat; cover and simmer for 15-20 minutes to allow flavors to blend.
2. Place potato flakes in a large bowl; stir in boiling water until blended. Stir in eggs. Add flour and salt all at once; stir just until combined. Divide into fourths; turn each onto a floured surface. Roll into ¾-in.-thick ropes; cut ropes into ¾-in. pieces.
3. Bring a large saucepan of water to a boil. Cook gnocchi in batches for 30-60 seconds or until gnocchi float. Remove with a slotted spoon. Place in a large bowl; top with sauce. Gently stir to coat. Sprinkle with cheese if desired.

Saucy Beef with Broccoli

Whenever I'm looking for a fast entree, I turn to this beef and broccoli stir-fry. It features the traditional Chinese flavors of garlic, ginger, green onions and soy sauce.
—**ROSA EVANS** ODESSA, MO

START TO FINISH: 30 MIN.
MAKES: 2 SERVINGS

- 1 tablespoon cornstarch
- ½ cup reduced-sodium beef broth
- ¼ cup sherry or additional beef broth
- 2 tablespoons reduced-sodium soy sauce
- 1 tablespoon brown sugar
- 1 garlic clove, minced
- 1 teaspoon minced fresh gingerroot
- ½ pound beef top sirloin steak, cut into ¼-inch strips
- 2 teaspoons canola oil, divided
- 2 cups fresh broccoli florets
- 8 green onions, cut into 1-inch pieces

1. In a large bowl, combine the first seven ingredients; set aside. In a large nonstick skillet or wok, stir-fry beef in 1 teaspoon oil for 1-2 minutes or until no longer pink. Remove the beef and keep warm.

2. In the same pan, stir-fry broccoli in the remaining oil for 4-5 minutes or until crisp-tender. Add green onions; cook 2 minutes longer. Return beef to the pan.

3. Stir cornstarch mixture and gradually add to the pan. Bring to a boil; cook and stir for 1-2 minutes or until thickened. Reduce heat to low; cover and cook for 3 minutes or until meat and vegetables are tender.

SAUCY BEEF WITH BROCCOLI

EAT SMART
Weeknight Beef Skillet

This hearty family fare is brimming with veggies and good nutrition. It just might become one of your family's favorites!
—**CLARA COULSON MINNEY** WASHINGTON COURT HOUSE, OH

START TO FINISH: 30 MIN.
MAKES: 4 SERVINGS

- 3 cups uncooked yolk-free whole wheat noodles
- 1 pound lean ground beef (90% lean)
- 1 medium green pepper, finely chopped
- 1 package (16 ounces) frozen mixed vegetables, thawed and drained
- 1 can (15 ounces) tomato sauce
- 1 tablespoon Worcestershire sauce
- 1½ teaspoons Italian seasoning
- 2 teaspoons sugar
- ¼ teaspoon salt
- ¼ cup minced fresh parsley

1. Cook noodles according to package directions. Meanwhile, in a large nonstick skillet over medium heat, cook beef and pepper until meat is no longer pink; drain.

2. Stir in the mixed vegetables, tomato sauce, Worcestershire sauce, Italian seasoning, sugar and salt; heat through. Drain noodles; serve with meat mixture. Sprinkle with parsley.

PER SERVING *1¼ cups beef mixture with ¾ cup noodles equals 389 cal., 9 g fat (3 g sat. fat), 56 mg chol., 800 mg sodium, 49 g carb., 10 g fiber, 31 g pro.* **Diabetic Exchanges:** *3 starch, 3 lean meat, 1 vegetable.*

Creamy Beef & Potatoes

One of my husband's favorite childhood memories was eating his Grandma Barney's Tater Tot casserole. One day I started preparing it, sure that I had some Tots on hand. Instead, I found O'Brien potatoes. Dinner turned out great! Now I always make it this way.

—HEATHER MATTHEWS KELLER, TX

START TO FINISH: 20 MIN.
MAKES: 4 SERVINGS

- 4 cups frozen O'Brien potatoes
- 1 tablespoon water
- 1 pound ground beef
- ½ teaspoon salt
- ¼ teaspoon pepper
- 2 cans (10¾ ounces each) condensed cream of mushroom soup, undiluted
- ⅔ cup 2% milk
- 2 cups (8 ounces) shredded Colby-Monterey Jack cheese

1. Place potatoes and water in a microwave-safe bowl. Microwave, covered, on high for 8-10 minutes or until tender, stirring twice.
2. Meanwhile, in a Dutch oven, cook beef over medium heat 6-8 minutes or until no longer pink, breaking into crumbles; drain. Stir in the salt and pepper. In a small bowl, whisk soup and milk until blended; add to beef. Stir in potatoes. Sprinkle with cheese. Reduce heat to low; cook, covered, until cheese is melted.
NOTE *This recipe was tested in a 1,100-watt microwave.*

Mediterranean Steak & Egg Pitas

Traditional steak and eggs get a fun Mediterranean makeover in this easy entree. These pitas are loaded with satisfying flavor!

—TASTE OF HOME TEST KITCHEN

START TO FINISH: 25 MIN.
MAKES: 4 SERVINGS

- 1 pound beef top sirloin steak, cut into ½-inch cubes
- ½ teaspoon Greek seasoning
- ¼ teaspoon salt
- ¼ teaspoon pepper
- 2 teaspoons olive oil
- 4 large eggs
- 4 whole pita breads, warmed
- 2 medium tomatoes, chopped
- 1 can (2¼ ounces) sliced ripe olives, drained
- ⅔ cup crumbled garlic and herb feta cheese

1. Sprinkle beef with the Greek seasoning, salt and pepper. In a large skillet, saute beef in oil for 4-6 minutes or until no longer pink. Remove from the heat; keep warm.
2. In a large nonstick skillet coated with cooking spray, fry eggs as desired. Spoon steak over pita breads; top with tomatoes, olives, cheese and eggs.

For a simple **Southwest** take on the **steak and eggs,** substitute Mexican **seasoning,** corn **tortillas** and **queso fresco** for the Greek seasoning, pitas and feta.

Poultry

118   123   126

Solve any **dinnertime** dilemma with these **fabulous chicken** and **turkey** dishes. Whether you're in the mood for **crunchy** turkey tostadas, **down-home** chicken and dumplings, or a **cool, crisp** main-dish salad that won't overheat the kitchen, you'll find the tasty choice right here.

SMOTHERED TERIYAKI CHICKEN BREASTS

Creamed Turkey over Rice

When I buy a turkey for our family of five, I choose the largest one I can find so we're sure to have plenty of leftovers. This recipe, one of our favorite ways to enjoy leftover turkey, is simple to prepare and absolutely delicious.

—**KATHI PARKER** CRAIG, CO

START TO FINISH: 30 MIN.
MAKES: 4 SERVINGS

- 1 **medium onion, chopped**
- ½ **cup chopped celery**
- ¼ **cup butter**
- ¼ **cup all-purpose flour**
- 1½ **cups chicken broth**
- 2 **cups cubed cooked turkey**
- 1 **cup milk**
- ½ **cup cubed Swiss cheese**
- 1 **tablespoon diced pimientos, drained**
- ½ **teaspoon salt**
- ¼ **teaspoon pepper**
- ¼ **teaspoon ground nutmeg**
  Hot cooked long grain and wild rice mix

1. In a large skillet, saute onion and celery in butter until tender. Stir in flour until blended. Gradually stir in broth. Bring to a boil; cook and stir for 2 minutes.
2. Reduce heat; stir in the turkey, milk, cheese, pimientos, salt, pepper and nutmeg. Cook until cheese is melted and mixture is heated through. Serve over rice.

For a **classic comfort-food variation** on the turkey, omit the pimientos, stir in 1 cup of **frozen peas**, and serve the mixture over **biscuits** instead of rice.

FREEZE IT
Smothered Teriyaki Chicken Breasts

I top teriyaki chicken breasts with tender mushrooms and onions, then smother them with melted Muenster cheese.

—**SALLY NIELSEN** QUINCY, IL

START TO FINISH: 30 MIN.
MAKES: 4 SERVINGS

- 2 **cups sliced fresh mushrooms**
- 1 **medium onion, thinly sliced**
- 2 **tablespoons canola oil, divided**
- ¼ **cup reduced-sodium teriyaki sauce**
- 1 **tablespoon brown sugar**
- ½ **teaspoon garlic powder**
- ½ **teaspoon ground ginger**
- 4 **boneless skinless chicken breast halves (6 ounces each)**
- 4 **slices Muenster or Swiss cheese**

1. Saute mushrooms and onion in 1 tablespoon oil in a large skillet until tender. Stir in the teriyaki sauce, brown sugar, garlic and ginger; heat through. Remove and keep warm.
2. Flatten chicken to ¼-in. thickness. Cook chicken in remaining oil in the same skillet over medium heat for 2-3 minutes on each side or until no longer pink.
3. Top with mushroom mixture and cheese. Cover and let stand until cheese is melted.
FREEZE OPTION *Before adding cheese, cool chicken and mushroom sauce. Place in freezer containers and top with mushroom sauce. To use, partially thaw in refrigerator overnight. Slowly heat chicken through in a covered skillet until a thermometer inserted in chicken reads 165°, stirring occasionally and adding a little broth or water if necessary. Top with cheese and proceed as directed.*

FREEZE IT

Tangy Turkey Tostadas

My husband and I have busy schedules, so I often turn to this nutritious variation on fast-food tacos. They're so tasty and easy to make. I serve them with a tossed green salad and Spanish rice.

—JULIE HUNTINGTON MEMPHIS, TN

START TO FINISH: 25 MIN.
MAKES: 8 SERVINGS

- 1¼ pounds lean ground turkey
- ¾ cup sliced fresh mushrooms
- 1 medium green pepper, chopped
- 1 small onion, chopped
- 2 garlic cloves, minced
- 1 can (16 ounces) kidney beans, rinsed and drained
- 1 cup salsa
- 1 can (4 ounces) chopped green chilies
- 1 tablespoon chili powder
- 1 teaspoon ground cumin
- ½ teaspoon salt
- 4 drops hot pepper sauce
- 1½ cups (6 ounces) reduced-fat Mexican cheese blend
- ½ cup frozen corn, thawed
- 16 tostada shells
- 2 cups shredded lettuce
- 1 cup chopped tomatoes
- ¼ cup minced fresh cilantro

1. In a large skillet, cook turkey, mushrooms, pepper and onion over medium heat 6-8 minutes or until turkey is no longer pink and vegetables are tender, breaking turkey into crumbles; drain. Stir in garlic; cook 1 minute longer.

2. Stir in beans, salsa, green chilies, chili powder, cumin, salt and pepper sauce. Cook, uncovered, 4-5 minutes or until heated through. Add cheese and corn; heat through. Spread about ⅓ cup filling over each tostada shell. Sprinkle with lettuce, tomatoes and cilantro.

FREEZE OPTION *Freeze cooled meat mixture in freezer containers. To use, partially thaw in refrigerator overnight. Heat through in a saucepan, stirring occasionally and adding a little water if necessary. Serve on tostada shells with toppings.*

Chicken Pecan Wraps

Pecans add a nice crunch to these simple chicken wraps. Spice them up a bit with medium or hot salsa if that's your preference.

—JUDY FRAKES BLAIR, NE

START TO FINISH: 10 MIN.
MAKES: 4 SERVINGS

- 1 pound boneless skinless chicken breasts, cut into 1-inch cubes
- ¼ cup chopped onion
- ¼ teaspoon ground cumin
- 1 tablespoon butter
- ¼ cup chopped pecans
- 3 tablespoons sour cream
- 4 flour tortillas (10 inches), warmed
- 1 cup (4 ounces) shredded cheddar cheese
- 1 cup salsa
  Shredded lettuce, optional

1. In a large skillet over medium heat, cook chicken, onion and cumin in butter until chicken is no longer pink.

2. Reduce heat to low. Add pecans and sour cream; heat through. Spoon about ½ cupful down the center of each tortilla; layer with cheese, salsa and, if desired, lettuce. Roll up.

Couscous Chicken Salad

Here's a perfect speedy lunch. It's easy to make, and you can keep most of the ingredients on hand for a fresh, healthy meal. For a vegetarian dish, substitute marinated tofu for the chicken and vegetable broth for the chicken broth.
—**LINDA BAGGETT** ARCATA, CA

START TO FINISH: 25 MIN.
MAKES: 9 SERVINGS

- 1 **can (14½ ounces) reduced-sodium chicken broth**
- ⅓ **cup water**
- 1¾ **cups uncooked couscous**
- 3 **cups cubed cooked chicken breasts**
- 1 **can (14 ounces) water-packed artichoke hearts, rinsed, drained and chopped**
- 2 **medium tomatoes, chopped**
- 1 **medium sweet red pepper, chopped**
- 1 **small cucumber, sliced**
- ½ **cup minced fresh parsley**
- ½ **cup crumbled feta cheese**
- 3 **green onions, sliced**
- ¼ **teaspoon pepper**
- ¾ **cup fat-free Italian salad dressing**

1. In a large saucepan, bring broth and water to a boil. Stir in couscous. Cover and remove from the heat; let stand for 5 minutes. Fluff with a fork.
2. Stir in the chicken, artichokes, tomatoes, red pepper, cucumber, parsley, cheese, onions and pepper. Drizzle with dressing and toss to coat. Refrigerate until serving.

Blueberry-Dijon Chicken

Blueberries and chicken may seem like a strange combination, but prepare to be dazzled. I add a sprinkling of minced fresh basil as the finishing touch.
—**SUSAN MARSHALL** COLORADO SPRINGS, CO

START TO FINISH: 30 MIN.
MAKES: 4 SERVINGS

- 4 **boneless skinless chicken breast halves (6 ounces each)**
- ¼ **teaspoon salt**
- ¼ **teaspoon pepper**
- 1 **tablespoon butter**
- ½ **cup blueberry preserves**
- ⅓ **cup raspberry vinegar**
- ¼ **cup fresh or frozen blueberries**
- 3 **tablespoons Dijon mustard**
  Minced fresh basil or tarragon, optional

1. Sprinkle chicken with salt and pepper. In a large skillet, cook chicken in butter over medium heat for 6-8 minutes on each side or until a thermometer reads 170°. Remove and keep warm.

2. In the same skillet, combine the preserves, vinegar, blueberries and mustard, stirring to loosen browned bits from pan. Bring to a boil; cook and stir until thickened. Serve with chicken. Sprinkle with basil if desired.
PER SERVING *1 chicken breast half with 2 tablespoons sauce equals 331 cal., 7 g fat (3 g sat. fat), 102 mg chol., 520 mg sodium, 31 g carb., trace fiber, 34 g pro.* **Diabetic Exchanges:** *5 lean meat, 1½ starch, ½ fat.*

Sweet **blueberries,** tangy **vinegar** and zesty **Dijon** create a delightful flavor combination. The sauce would also be tasty with **smoked turkey or ham.**

BLUEBERRY-DIJON CHICKEN

TROPICAL CHICKEN

Tropical Chicken

This attractive dish makes a convenient all-in-one meal. I serve it often, and my family never seems to tire of it. They like the way the sweetness of the pineapple balances the garlic and hot red pepper.

—**LEAH JOHNSON** PEARL CITY, HI

PREP: 20 MIN. • **COOK:** 1¼ HOURS
MAKES: 6 SERVINGS

- 1 **broiler/fryer chicken (3½ to 4 pounds), cut up**
- 3 **tablespoons canola oil, divided**
- ¾ **cup chopped onion**
- 2 **garlic cloves, minced**
- 3 **medium tomatoes, peeled and chopped**
- 3 **cups fresh or canned pineapple chunks**
- 1 **can (8 ounces) sliced water chestnuts, drained**
- ¼ **cup pineapple juice**
- 1 **hot red pepper (4½ to 5 inches), seeded and chopped**
- ¾ **teaspoon salt**
- ¼ **teaspoon pepper**
- ½ **pound fresh snow peas**
- 1 **tablespoon minced chives**
  Hot cooked rice

1. In a large skillet over medium heat, brown chicken in 2 tablespoons oil; remove and set aside.

2. In the same skillet, saute onion in remaining oil until tender. Add garlic; cook 1 minute longer. Add the tomatoes, pineapple, water chestnuts, pineapple juice, hot pepper, salt and pepper.

3. Return chicken to the pan; bring to a boil. Reduce heat; cover and simmer for 45 minutes. Add peas and chives; cover and simmer for 10-15 minutes or until peas are tender and chicken juices run clear. Thicken pan juices if desired. Serve with rice.

FREEZE OPTION *Freeze cooled chicken mixture in freezer containers. To use, partially thaw in refrigerator overnight. Heat through in a covered saucepan, gently stirring and adding a little broth or water if necessary.*

NOTE *Wear disposable gloves when cutting hot peppers; the oils can burn skin. Avoid touching your face.*

Turkey & Vegetable Pasta

PREP: 25 MIN. • **COOK:** 35 MIN.
MAKES: 6 SERVINGS

- 1¾ **cups uncooked penne or gemelli pasta (about 6 ounces)**
- 1 **tablespoon olive oil**
- 3 **celery ribs, chopped**
- 1 **cup chopped sweet onion**
- 1 **cup chopped red onion**
- 1 **cup chopped fresh broccoli**
- 1 **cup chopped carrots**
- 3 **garlic cloves, minced**
- 1 **tablespoon minced fresh parsley**
- 1 **tablespoon minced fresh tarragon or 1 teaspoon dried tarragon**
- 1 **teaspoon poultry seasoning**
- 1 **teaspoon lemon-pepper seasoning**
- ¼ **teaspoon white pepper**
- 1½ **cups sliced baby portobello mushrooms**
- 1 **cup frozen peas**
- 2 **cups cubed cooked turkey**
- 1½ **cups vegetable broth**
- 1 **can (10¾ ounces) condensed cream of mushroom soup, undiluted**
- ⅔ **cup plain Greek yogurt**
- 2 **tablespoons reduced-fat cream cheese**
- 1 **tablespoon Worcestershire sauce**

1. Cook pasta according to package directions; drain. Meanwhile, in a Dutch oven, heat oil over medium-high heat. Add celery, onions, broccoli and carrots; cook and stir 10-12 minutes or until onions are tender. Add garlic, parsley, tarragon and seasonings; cook 1 minute longer.

2. Add mushrooms and peas; cook and stir 3-5 minutes or until mushrooms are tender. Stir in turkey, broth, soup, yogurt, cream cheese and Worcestershire sauce. Bring to a boil. Reduce heat; simmer, uncovered, 10-15 minutes or until slightly thickened, stirring occasionally. Add pasta; heat through.

FREEZE OPTION *Freeze cooled pasta mixture in freezer containers. To use, partially thaw in refrigerator overnight. Heat through in a saucepan, stirring occasionally and adding a little broth or milk if necessary.*

TURKEY &
VEGETABLE PASTA

ORANGE
GINGER CHICKEN

Orange Ginger Chicken

Due to my husband's Air Force career, we move frequently and don't always have access to Chinese takeout. This dish is a a special treat, and one of his favorites. We spoon it over rice.

—**TONI SCHILZ** SAN FRANCISCO, CA

PREP: 15 MIN. • **COOK:** 20 MIN.
MAKES: 6 SERVINGS

- ⅓ **cup all-purpose flour**
- 1½ **pounds boneless skinless chicken thighs, cubed**
- ¼ **teaspoon salt**
- ¼ **teaspoon pepper**
- 2 **tablespoons canola oil**
- ½ **cup orange juice**
- ½ **cup orange marmalade**
- 2 **tablespoons reduced-sodium soy sauce**
- 2 **tablespoons honey**
- ½ **to 1 teaspoon ground ginger**
  Optional garnishes: thinly sliced green onion and sesame seeds

1. Place flour in a large resealable plastic bag. Season chicken with salt and pepper. Add to bag, a few pieces at a time, and shake to coat. In a large skillet, cook chicken in oil in batches over medium heat until chicken is no longer pink. Remove and keep warm.
2. In the same skillet, combine the remaining ingredients. Bring to a boil, stirring to loosen browned bits from pan; cook until thickened. Return chicken to the pan and heat through. Sprinkle with green onion and sesame seeds if desired.

Chicken with Mango Salsa

I like to combine sweet, tart and spicy ingredients in my tropical salsa. For the best taste, allow it to chill several hours so the flavors can blend.

—**DENISE ELDER** HANOVER, ON

PREP: 20 MIN. + CHILLING • **COOK:** 10 MIN.
MAKES: 2 SERVINGS

- ½ **cup chopped peeled mango**
- ½ **cup chopped tomato**
- 2 **tablespoons minced fresh cilantro**
- 1 **tablespoon chopped jalapeno pepper**
- 1 **tablespoon chopped red onion**
- 1½ **teaspoons chopped celery**
- 1½ **teaspoons lime juice**
- ¼ **teaspoon grated lime peel**
- 2 **boneless skinless chicken breast halves (6 ounces each)**
- ¼ **teaspoon salt**
- ⅛ **teaspoon pepper**
- 1 **tablespoon canola oil**

1. For salsa, in a small bowl, combine the mango, tomato, cilantro, jalapeno, onion, celery, lime juice and peel. Cover and refrigerate for 2-3 hours.
2. Sprinkle chicken with salt and pepper. In a large skillet, cook chicken in oil over medium-high heat for 5-6 minutes on each side or until juices run clear. Serve with salsa.
NOTE *Wear disposable gloves when cutting hot peppers; the oils can burn skin. Avoid touching your face.*
PER SERVING *1 chicken breast half with ½ cup salsa equals 285 cal., 11 g fat (2 g sat. fat), 94 mg chol., 384 mg sodium, 10 g carb., 2 g fiber, 35 g pro.* **Diabetic Exchanges:** *5 lean meat, 2 vegetable, 1 fat.*

The **sauce** for Orange Ginger Chicken is **reduced** until thickened. If you'd like a **thicker**, more saucy **texture**, mix a little **cornstarch** with **cold water or orange juice** and thicken the sauce that way.

Red Beans and Sausage

Turkey sausage makes this traditional dish more health conscious, while a zesty blend of seasonings adds some spark.

—**CATHY WEBSTER** MORRIS, IL

START TO FINISH: 20 MIN.
MAKES: 6 SERVINGS

- 1 medium green pepper, diced
- 1 medium onion, chopped
- 1 tablespoon canola oil
- 2 garlic cloves, minced
- 2 cans (16 ounces each) kidney beans, rinsed and drained
- ½ pound smoked turkey sausage, sliced
- ¾ cup water
- 1 teaspoon Cajun seasoning
- ⅛ teaspoon hot pepper sauce
  Hot cooked rice, optional

1. In a large saucepan, saute green pepper and onion in oil until tender. Add garlic; cook 1 minute longer.

2. Add the next five ingredients and bring to a boil. Reduce heat; cook for 5-7 minutes or until sausage is heated through. Serve with rice if desired.

PER SERVING *⅔ cup (calculated without rice) equals 212 cal., 4 g fat (1 g sat. fat), 24 mg chol., 706 mg sodium, 27 g carb., 8 g fiber, 16 g pro. Diabetic Exchanges: 2 lean meat, 1½ starch, ½ fat.*

Italian Chicken Sausage and Orzo

Light, quick and tasty: That's my kind of recipe. If you like a milder dish, use less crushed red pepper. Or to really bring on the heat, add more.

—**DEBRA PAQUETTE** UPTON, MA

START TO FINISH: 30 MIN.
MAKES: 5 SERVINGS

- 1 cup uncooked orzo pasta
- 1 package (12 ounces) fully cooked Italian chicken sausage links, cut into ¾-inch slices
- 3 teaspoons olive oil, divided
- 1 cup chopped onion
- 3 garlic cloves, minced
- ¼ cup white wine or chicken broth
- 1 can (28 ounces) whole tomatoes, drained and chopped
- 2 tablespoons minced fresh parsley
- 1 tablespoon capers, drained
- ½ teaspoon dried oregano
- ½ teaspoon dried basil
- ¼ teaspoon crushed red pepper flakes
- ¼ teaspoon pepper
- ½ cup crumbled feta cheese

1. Cook pasta according to the package directions.

2. Meanwhile, brown the sausage in 2 teaspoons oil in a large skillet. Remove and keep warm. In the same pan, saute onion in remaining oil until tender. Add garlic and wine; cook 1 minute longer, stirring to loosen browned bits from pan.

3. Stir in the tomatoes, parsley, capers, oregano, basil, pepper flakes and pepper. Bring to a boil. Reduce heat; simmer, uncovered, for 5 minutes. Stir in orzo and sausage; heat through. Sprinkle with cheese.

PER SERVING *1 cup equals 363 cal., 11 g fat (3 g sat. fat), 58 mg chol., 838 mg sodium, 42 g carb., 3 g fiber, 21 g pro. Diabetic Exchanges: 2 starch, 2 lean meat, 2 vegetable, 1 fat.*

RED BEANS AND SAUSAGE

**FAMILY-PLEASING
SLOPPY JOES**

Family-Pleasing Sloppy Joes

My grandma gave me this recipe long ago. I've tweaked it over the years to give the yummy sandwiches even more pizzazz.
—**JILL ZOSEL** SEATTLE, WA

START TO FINISH: 30 MIN.
MAKES: 6 SERVINGS

- 1 **pound lean ground turkey**
- 1 **small onion, chopped**
- 2 **garlic cloves, minced**
- 1 **tablespoon sugar**
- 1 **tablespoon all-purpose flour**
- ¼ **teaspoon pepper**
- 1 **cup ketchup**
- 1 **tablespoon Worcestershire sauce**
- 1 **tablespoon prepared mustard**
- 1 **tablespoon barbecue sauce**
- 6 **hamburger buns, split**

1. In a large skillet, cook turkey and onion over medium heat 6-8 minutes or until turkey is no longer pink, breaking up turkey into crumbles; drain if necessary. Add garlic; cook 1 minute longer. Stir in sugar, flour and pepper until blended.

2. Add ketchup, Worcestershire sauce, mustard and barbecue sauce. Bring to a boil. Reduce heat; simmer, covered, 10 minutes to allow flavors to blend. Spoon meat mixture onto bun bottoms; replace tops.

FREEZE OPTION *Freeze cooled meat mixture in freezer containers. To use, partially thaw in refrigerator overnight. Heat through in a saucepan, stirring occasionally and adding a little water if necessary.*

PER SERVING *1 sandwich equals 297 cal., 8 g fat (2 g sat. fat), 52 mg chol., 846 mg sodium, 38 g carb., 1 g fiber, 19 g pro. **Diabetic Exchanges:** 2½ starch, 2 lean meat.*

Soupy Chicken Noodle Supper

At least once a week my 6-year-old son, also known as Doctor John, hands me a prescription for chicken noodle soup. I'm always happy to fill it.
—**HEIDI HALL** NORTH ST. PAUL, MN

START TO FINISH: 30 MIN.
MAKES: 4 SERVINGS

- 1 **tablespoon butter**
- 1 **medium carrot, sliced**
- 1 **celery rib, sliced**
- 1 **small onion, chopped**
- 4 **cups water**
- 4 **teaspoons chicken bouillon granules**
- 1½ **teaspoons dried parsley flakes**
- ¼ **teaspoon Italian seasoning**
- ⅛ **teaspoon celery seed**
- ⅛ **teaspoon pepper**
- 3 **cups uncooked wide egg noodles**
- 1½ **cups cubed rotisserie chicken**
- 1 **can (10¾ ounces) condensed cream of chicken soup, undiluted**
- ½ **cup sour cream**
  Hot cooked stuffing, optional

1. In a large saucepan, heat butter over medium-high heat. Add carrot, celery and onion; cook and stir for 6-8 minutes or until tender.

2. Stir in water, bouillon and seasonings; bring to a boil. Add noodles; cook, uncovered, 5-7 minutes or until tender. Stir in chicken, soup and sour cream; heat through. If desired, serve with stuffing.

Farmhouse Chicken and Biscuits

My mother had two special ways of fixing chicken—browning serving-size pieces in butter, or serving up this rich homemade chicken gravy over homemade biscuits. Either way, we all loved Mother's chicken!

—**PHYLLIS KIRSLING** JUNCTION CITY, WI

PREP: 15 MIN. • **COOK:** 55 MIN.
MAKES: 6-8 SERVINGS

- 1 broiler/fryer chicken (3 to 4 pounds), cut up
- 2 carrots, sliced
- 2 celery ribs with leaves, sliced
- 1 green onion, sliced
- 5 peppercorns
- 1 teaspoon salt
- 6 cups water
- 6 tablespoons butter, cubed
- ½ cup all-purpose flour
- ¼ teaspoon pepper
  Biscuits, warmed

1. Combine the first seven ingredients in a Dutch oven; cover and simmer until the chicken is tender, about 45 minutes.
2. Remove vegetables and chicken from broth; set vegetables aside. Skin, bone and cube the chicken. Strain broth, reserving 3 cups.
3. In a large saucepan over medium heat, melt butter; stir in flour and pepper until thickened and bubbly. Gradually stir in reserved broth; bring to a boil, stirring constantly. Boil for 1 minute. Add chicken and vegetables; heat through. Serve over biscuits.

For **richer** chicken flavor, start with **broth** instead of water. Or add chicken **bouillon** and **poultry seasoning** to the cooking liquid. Decrease the **salt.**

PEAR & TURKEY SAUSAGE RIGATONI

EAT SMART
Pear & Turkey Sausage Rigatoni

The sweet pear, salty sausage and creamy blue cheese are a wonderful combination in this one-pot supper. Now we don't have to go to an expensive restaurant to get an elegant meal.

—**DEBBY HARDEN** WILLIAMSTON, MI

START TO FINISH: 30 MIN.
MAKES: 6 SERVINGS

- 8 ounces uncooked rigatoni or large tube pasta
- 2 Italian turkey sausage links (4 ounces each), casings removed
- 2 medium pears, sliced
- 2 cups fresh baby spinach
- ½ cup half-and-half cream
- ½ cup crumbled blue cheese, divided
  Toasted sliced almonds, optional

1. Cook rigatoni according to package directions. Meanwhile, in a Dutch oven, cook sausage over medium heat 6-8 minutes or until no longer pink, breaking into large crumbles. Add pears; cook and stir 3-5 minutes or until lightly browned.
2. Drain rigatoni and add to the sausage mixture. Add spinach, cream and ¼ cup cheese; cook 3-4 minutes or until spinach is wilted, stirring occasionally. Top with remaining cheese. If desired, sprinkle with sliced almonds.
NOTE *To toast nuts, bake in a shallow pan in a 350° oven for 5-10 minutes or cook in a skillet over low heat until lightly browned, stirring occasionally.*
PER SERVING *1⅓ cups (calculated without almonds) equals 273 cal., 9 g fat (4 g sat. fat), 32 mg chol., 333 mg sodium, 37 g carb., 3 g fiber, 13 g pro.*
Diabetic Exchanges: 2½ starch, 2 medium-fat meat.

Barbecue Chicken Burritos

My husband came up with this recipe, and it turned out to be a hit! Now we always keep the ingredients for these on hand.

—AMY DANDO APALACHIN, NY

START TO FINISH: 30 MIN.
MAKES: 4 SERVINGS

- ½ pound boneless skinless chicken breasts, cut into ½-inch cubes
- 1½ cups julienned green peppers
- 1 cup chopped onion
- 4 tablespoons canola oil, divided
- ½ cup barbecue sauce
- 1½ cups (6 ounces) shredded Mexican cheese blend
- 4 flour tortillas (10 inches), warmed
  Lime wedges, sour cream, shredded lettuce and chopped tomatoes, optional

1. In a large skillet, cook chicken, green peppers and onion in 2 tablespoons oil over medium heat for 6-8 minutes or until chicken is no longer pink. Stir in barbecue sauce and heat through.
2. Sprinkle cheese down the center of each tortilla; top with chicken mixture. Fold sides and ends over filling and roll up. Secure burritos with toothpicks.
3. In a large skillet, brown burritos in remaining oil on all sides over medium heat. Discard toothpicks. Serve with lime wedges, sour cream, lettuce and tomatoes if desired.

Peach Turkey Sandwiches

Here's a delicious toasted sandwich with a hint of sweetness from peaches and Vidalia dressing. Everyone raves about this recipe, especially my grandkids.

—DONIE LANGSTON WATHENA, KS

START TO FINISH: 15 MIN.
MAKES: 2 SERVINGS

- 4 slices whole wheat bread
- 2 tablespoons Vidalia onion salad dressing
- ¼ pound sliced deli turkey
- 2 slices smoked Gouda cheese
- 1 medium peach, thinly sliced
  Cooking spray

1. Spread two bread slices with salad dressing. Layer with turkey, cheese and peach slices. Top with remaining bread. Spritz outsides of sandwiches with cooking spray.
2. In a large nonstick skillet over medium heat, toast sandwiches for 2-3 minutes on each side or until cheese is melted.

Chicken Portobello Stroganoff

My chicken and portobello version of the classic beef dish is the result of having opened the fridge for dinner one night and deciding to improvise with what I had on hand.

—KATIE ROSE PEWAUKEE, WI

PREP: 15 MIN. • **COOK:** 25 MIN.
MAKES: 4 SERVINGS

- 1 pound ground chicken
- 12 ounces baby portobello mushrooms, halved
- 1 medium onion, chopped
- 1 tablespoon olive oil
- 2 garlic cloves, minced
- 3 tablespoons white wine or chicken broth
- 2 cups chicken broth
- ½ cup heavy whipping cream
- 2 tablespoons lemon juice
- ¼ teaspoon salt
- ⅛ teaspoon white pepper
- 1 cup (8 ounces) sour cream
  Hot cooked egg noodles or pasta

1. In a large skillet, cook the chicken, mushrooms and onion in oil over medium-high heat until meat is no longer pink. Add garlic; cook 1 minute longer.
2. Stir in wine. Bring to a boil; cook until liquid is almost evaporated. Add the broth, cream, lemon juice, salt and pepper. Bring to a boil; cook until liquid is reduced by half.
3. Reduce heat. Gradually stir in sour cream; heat through (do not boil). Serve with noodles.

BARBECUE CHICKEN BURRITOS

SKILLET RANCH BURGERS

Skillet Ranch Burgers

Lean ground turkey keeps these burgers light, while jalapenos and ranch dressing add plenty of zesty flavor.

—DEBRA JUSTICE MOODY, TX

START TO FINISH: 30 MIN.
MAKES: 4 SERVINGS

- ½ cup soft bread crumbs
- 1 small onion, finely chopped
- 1 small green pepper, finely chopped
- 2 jalapeno peppers, seeded and finely chopped
- ¼ cup egg substitute
- 1¼ teaspoons ranch salad dressing mix
- 1 teaspoon garlic powder
- ½ teaspoon hot pepper sauce
- 1 pound lean ground turkey
- 4 whole wheat hamburger buns, split
- 4 lettuce leaves
- 4 slices tomato
- 4 slices onion

SAUCE
- ½ cup fat-free sour cream
- 1 teaspoon ranch salad dressing mix

1. In a large bowl, combine the first eight ingredients. Crumble turkey over mixture and mix well. Shape into four patties.
2. In a large nonstick skillet coated with cooking spray, cook patties over medium heat for 6-8 minutes on each side or until a thermometer reads 165° and juices run clear.
3. Serve on buns with lettuce, tomato and onion. Combine sour cream and dressing mix; spoon over burgers.
NOTE *Wear disposable gloves when cutting hot peppers; the oils can burn skin. Avoid touching your face.*
PER SERVING *1 burger equals 373 cal., 12 g fat (3 g sat. fat), 95 mg chol., 772 mg sodium, 39 g carb., 5 g fiber, 29 g pro.* **Diabetic Exchanges:** *3 lean meat, 2 starch, 1 vegetable.*

Vietnamese Crunchy Chicken Salad

When I lived in Cleveland, I dined at a really good Vietnamese restaurant. There was a dish that I couldn't get enough of. Since I had it so frequently, I figured out the components and flavors and created my own easy-to-make version. Everyone who tastes it loves it.

—ERIN SCHILLO SAGAMORE HILLS, OH

PREP: 30 MIN. + MARINATING
COOK: 10 MIN.
MAKES: 4 SERVINGS

- 3 tablespoons olive oil
- 2 tablespoons lime juice
- 1 tablespoon minced fresh cilantro
- 1½ teaspoons grated lime peel
- ½ teaspoon salt
- ½ teaspoon pepper
- ¼ teaspoon cayenne pepper
- 1 pound boneless skinless chicken breasts, cut into thin strips

DRESSING
- ½ cup olive oil
- ¼ cup lime juice
- 2 tablespoons rice vinegar
- 2 tablespoons sugar
- 1 tablespoon grated lime peel
- ¾ teaspoon salt
- ½ teaspoon crushed red pepper flakes
- ¼ teaspoon pepper

SALAD
- 5 cups thinly sliced cabbage (about 1 pound)
- 1 cup minced fresh cilantro
- 1 cup julienned carrots
- 1 cup salted peanuts, coarsely chopped

1. In a large bowl, mix the first seven ingredients; add chicken and toss to coat. Refrigerate, covered, 30 minutes.
2. In a small bowl, whisk dressing ingredients.
3. In a large skillet over medium-high heat, stir-fry half of the chicken mixture for 4-5 minutes or until no longer pink. Remove from pan; repeat with remaining chicken. Cool slightly.
4. In a large bowl, combine cabbage, cilantro, carrots and chicken; toss to combine. Add peanuts and dressing; toss to coat. Serve immediately.

VIETNAMESE CRUNCHY
CHICKEN SALAD

Santa Fe Chicken and Rice

Cheesy chicken breasts are even more scrumptious served on a bed of Southwest-style rice. This nearly effortless meal is ready in just half an hour.

—DEBRA COOK PAMPA, TX

START TO FINISH: 30 MIN.
MAKES: 2 SERVINGS

- ½ cup chopped onion
- 2 teaspoons butter
- ⅔ cup chicken broth
- ½ cup salsa
- ½ cup uncooked long grain rice
- ⅛ teaspoon garlic powder
- 2 boneless skinless chicken breast halves (5 ounces each)
- ⅓ cup shredded cheddar cheese
  Chopped fresh cilantro, optional

1. In a small skillet, saute onion in butter until tender. Add broth and salsa; bring to a boil. Stir in the rice and garlic powder. Place chicken over rice; cover and simmer for 10 minutes.
2. Turn chicken; cook 10-15 minutes longer or until chicken juices run clear and rice is tender. Remove from the heat. Sprinkle with cheese; cover and let stand for 5 minutes. Garnish with cilantro if desired.

Quick Chicken and Dumplings

My easy chicken and dumplings recipe uses convenience items to hit the table in just 30 minutes. Onions and parsley give the simple dumplings a surprisingly homemade flavor.

—WILLIE DEWAARD CORALVILLE, IA

START TO FINISH: 30 MIN.
MAKES: 6 SERVINGS

- 1½ cups 2% milk
- 1½ cups frozen mixed vegetables, thawed
- 2½ cups cubed cooked chicken
- 1 can (10¾ ounces) condensed cream of chicken soup, undiluted
- ½ teaspoon garlic powder
- ¼ teaspoon poultry seasoning

DUMPLINGS

- 1 cup biscuit/baking mix
- ⅓ cup French-fried onions, coarsely chopped
- 7 tablespoons 2% milk
- ½ teaspoon dried parsley flakes

1. In a Dutch oven, combine the first six ingredients. Bring mixture to a boil, stirring occasionally.
2. Meanwhile, in a small bowl, combine the biscuit mix, onions, milk and parsley just until moistened. Drop by heaping teaspoonfuls onto simmering stew. Cook, uncovered, for 10 minutes.
3. Cover and simmer 10-12 minutes longer or until a toothpick inserted in a dumpling comes out clean (do not lift the cover while simmering).

QUICK CHICKEN AND DUMPLINGS

SPAGHETTI WITH
SAUSAGE AND PEPPERS

Spaghetti with Sausage and Peppers

Smoked turkey sausage with strips of fresh bell peppers is a healthy change of pace from spaghetti with Italian sausage or ground beef.

—**GINGER HARRELL** EL DORADO, AR

START TO FINISH: 30 MIN.
MAKES: 6-8 SERVINGS

- 12 **ounces uncooked spaghetti**
- 1 **package (14 ounces) smoked turkey sausage, cut into ¼-inch slices**
- 2 **medium green peppers, julienned**
- 2 **medium sweet red peppers, julienned**
- 1 **medium onion, halved and thinly sliced**
- 2 **cans (14½ ounces each) diced tomatoes, undrained**
- 3 **garlic cloves, minced**
- 6 **to 8 drops hot pepper sauce**
- 1 **teaspoon paprika**
- ½ **teaspoon salt**
- ¼ **teaspoon cayenne pepper**
- 2 **tablespoons cornstarch**
- ½ **cup chicken broth**

1. Cook spaghetti according to package directions. Meanwhile, in a Dutch oven coated with cooking spray, cook and stir sausage until lightly browned. Add peppers and onion; cook 2 minutes longer. Stir in the tomatoes, garlic, pepper sauce, paprika, salt and cayenne; cook until vegetables are tender.

2. Combine cornstarch and broth until smooth; add to sausage mixture. Bring to a boil. Cook and stir for 2 minutes or until thickened. Drain spaghetti; toss with sausage mixture.

EAT SMART

Warm Apricot Chicken Salad

This summer-fresh salad is topped with flavorful, quickly marinated chicken. It's hearty, refreshing and nutritious. Even our kids like the sweet and tangy flavor.

—**CAROLYN JOHNS** LACEY, WA

START TO FINISH: 30 MIN.
MAKES: 4 SERVINGS

- 1 **pound boneless skinless chicken breasts, cut into strips**
- 2 **tablespoons orange marmalade**
- 1 **tablespoon reduced-sodium soy sauce**
- 6 **fresh apricots, sliced**
- 2 **teaspoons grated orange peel**
- ½ **pound fresh spinach, stems removed**
- 1 **medium sweet red pepper, julienned**
- 1 **tablespoon canola oil**
- ¼ **cup ranch salad dressing**
- ¼ **cup slivered almonds, toasted**

1. In a large bowl, combine the chicken, marmalade and soy sauce. Refrigerate for 20-30 minutes.

2. Meanwhile, toss apricots and orange peel. Place spinach on a serving platter or four salad plates; top with apricots. In a skillet, saute red pepper and chicken mixture in oil until chicken is no longer pink. Remove from heat; stir in salad dressing. Spoon over spinach and apricots; sprinkle with almonds.

PER SERVING *1 serving equals 343 cal., 18 g fat (3 g sat. fat), 65 mg chol., 529 mg sodium, 19 g carb., 4 g fiber, 27 g pro.* **Diabetic Exchanges:** *3 lean meat, 2 fat, 1 vegetable, 1 fruit.*

TURKEY CURRY

TURKEY MARSALA

EAT SMART
Turkey Curry

START TO FINISH: 20 MIN.
MAKES: 4 SERVINGS

- 1 cup sliced celery
- ½ cup sliced carrots
- 1 cup fat-free milk, divided
- 2 tablespoons cornstarch
- ¾ cup reduced-sodium chicken broth
- 2 cups diced cooked turkey or chicken
- 2 tablespoons dried minced onion
- ½ teaspoon garlic powder
- 1 to 4 teaspoons curry powder
  Hot cooked rice, optional

1. Lightly coat a skillet with cooking spray; saute celery and carrots until tender. In a bowl, mix ¼ cup milk and cornstarch until smooth. Add broth and remaining milk; mix until smooth.
2. Pour over vegetables. Bring to a boil; cook and stir for 2 minutes or until thickened. Add the turkey, onion, garlic powder and curry powder; heat through, stirring occasionally. Serve with rice if desired.
PER SERVING 1 cup (calculated without rice) equals 232 cal., 6 g fat (0 sat. fat), 37 mg chol., 206 mg sodium, 15 g carb., 0 fiber, 29 g pro. **Diabetic Exchanges:** 3 lean meat, 1 starch.

EAT SMART
Turkey Marsala
This recipe originally called for beef, but I substituted turkey to make it healthier. It's easy to prepare, but the rich sauce makes it seem like you spent all day in the kitchen. I serve this with a baked sweet potato and a green vegetable.
—**DEBORAH WILLIAMS** PEORIA, AZ

PREP: 10 MIN. • **COOK:** 30 MIN.
MAKES: 4 SERVINGS

- 1 package (20 ounces) turkey breast tenderloins
- ¼ cup all-purpose flour
- ½ teaspoon salt, divided
- ½ teaspoon pepper, divided
- 1 tablespoon olive oil
- 1 tablespoon butter
- ½ pound sliced fresh mushrooms
- ½ cup reduced-sodium chicken broth
- ½ cup Marsala wine
- 1 teaspoon lemon juice

1. Cut tenderloins crosswise in half; pound with a meat mallet to ¾-in. thickness. In a shallow bowl, mix flour and ¼ teaspoon each salt and pepper. Dip turkey in flour mixture to coat both sides; shake off excess.
2. In a large nonstick skillet, heat oil over medium heat. Add turkey; cook 6-8 minutes on each side or until a thermometer reads 165°. Remove from pan; keep warm.
3. In same skillet, heat butter over medium-high heat. Add mushrooms; cook and stir 3-4 minutes or until tender. Stir in broth and wine. Bring to a boil; cook until liquid is reduced by half, about 12 minutes. Stir in lemon juice and the remaining salt and pepper. Serve with turkey.
PER SERVING 4 ounces cooked turkey with ¼ cup mushroom mixture equals 295 cal., 8 g fat (3 g sat. fat), 77 mg chol., 482 mg sodium, 12 g carb., 1 g fiber, 36 g pro. **Diabetic Exchanges:** 4 lean meat, 1½ fat, 1 starch.

Pork

135   136   147

This chapter is brimming with **tasty, family-pleasing** meals made with **pork, bacon, ham and sausage**. Toss some leftover ham into a **pretty pasta**, create the ultimate **grilled cheese** or slowly simmer **tangy barbecues** for a crowd with these **fabulous** home-cooked specialties.

SPAGHETTI WITH EGGS AND BACON

FREEZE IT
Smoked Kielbasa with Rice

With just the right blend of heat, sweet barbecue flavors and smokiness, this skillet dinner is an easy way to please a bunch. You can also omit the rice and serve the sausage as an appetizer.

—NICOLE JACKSON EL PASO, TX

START TO FINISH: 25 MIN.
MAKES: 6 SERVINGS

- 2 pounds smoked kielbasa or Polish sausage, halved lengthwise and cut into ¼-inch slices
- ¼ cup finely chopped onion
- 3 bacon strips, finely chopped
- ¾ cup honey barbecue sauce
- ¼ cup packed brown sugar
- 1 tablespoon prepared horseradish
- 2 teaspoons water
- 2 teaspoons minced garlic
- ½ teaspoon crushed red pepper flakes
- Hot cooked rice

In a Dutch oven, saute the kielbasa, onion and bacon until onion is tender; drain. Add the barbecue sauce, brown sugar, horseradish, water, garlic and pepper flakes. Bring to a boil; cook and stir for 2-3 minutes or until sauce is thickened. Serve with rice.

FREEZE OPTION *Place cooled individual portions in freezer containers without rice. Freeze for up to 3 months. To use, thaw in refrigerator overnight. Place in a saucepan; heat through, gently stirring and adding a little water if necessary. Serve with rice.*

Spaghetti with Eggs and Bacon

Most folks are surprised when they see this combination of ingredients. But I usually make a big batch because it always disappears in a hurry.

—GAIL JENNER ETNA, CA

START TO FINISH: 25 MIN.
MAKES: 4 SERVINGS

- 8 ounces uncooked spaghetti
- 4 eggs
- ¾ cup half-and-half cream
- ½ cup grated Parmesan cheese
- ½ pound bacon strips, cooked and crumbled
- Additional grated Parmesan cheese, optional

1. Cook spaghetti according to package directions in a 6-qt. stockpot. In a small saucepan, whisk eggs and cream until blended. Cook over low heat until a thermometer reads 160°, stirring constantly (do not allow to simmer). Remove from heat; stir in cheese.

2. Drain spaghetti; return to stockpot. Add sauce and bacon; toss to combine. Serve immediately. Sprinkle with additional cheese if desired.

For more **robust-tasting spaghetti,** cook **bacon** with **chopped onions** until bacon is crisp. Toss in a little minced **garlic** at the end of cooking. Drain well.

**PORK QUESADILLAS
WITH FRESH SALSA**

Pork Quesadillas with Fresh Salsa

I threw this together one night when I was in the mood for quesadillas but didn't feel like going out. The homemade salsa is so tasty and versatile, you might want to double the recipe.

—ADAM GAYLORD NATICK, MA

START TO FINISH: 30 MIN.
MAKES: 4 SERVINGS (¾ CUP SALSA)

- 1 tablespoon olive oil
- 1 each small green, sweet red and orange peppers, sliced
- 1 medium red onion, sliced
- ¾ pound thinly sliced cooked pork (about 3 cups)
- ¼ teaspoon salt
- ⅛ teaspoon pepper

SALSA
- 2 medium tomatoes, seeded and chopped
- 1 tablespoon chopped red onion
- 1 tablespoon minced fresh cilantro
- 2 teaspoons olive oil
- 1 to 2 teaspoons chopped seeded jalapeno pepper
- 1 teaspoon cider vinegar
- ⅛ teaspoon salt
- Dash pepper

QUESADILLLAS
- 4 flour tortillas (10 inches)
- 1½ cups (6 ounces) shredded part-skim mozzarella cheese

1. In a large skillet, heat oil over medium-high heat. Add peppers and onion; cook 4-5 minutes or until tender, stirring occasionally. Stir in pork, salt and pepper; heat through. Meanwhile, in a small bowl, combine salsa ingredients.

2. Place tortillas on a griddle. Layer one-half of each tortilla with ¼ cup cheese, 1 cup pork mixture and 2 tablespoons cheese; fold other half over filling.

3. Cook quesadillas over medium heat 1-2 minutes on each side or until golden brown and cheese is melted. Cut into wedges. Serve with salsa.

NOTE *Wear disposable gloves when cutting hot peppers; the oils can burn skin. Avoid touching your face.*

Pork Chops Normandy

Pears and a brandy cream sauce team up to turn ordinary pork chops into a dish that's special enough for guests. I like to sprinkle each serving with a tiny bit of finely grated lemon zest.

—GINA QUARTERMAINE ALEXANDRIA, VA

START TO FINISH: 30 MIN.
MAKES: 4 SERVINGS

- 4 boneless pork loin chops (6 ounces each)
- 3 tablespoons butter
- 3 medium pears, peeled and chopped
- 3 tablespoons chopped shallots
- 3 garlic cloves, minced
- 3 tablespoons brandy or chicken broth
- ½ cup heavy whipping cream
- ½ teaspoon salt
- ½ teaspoon rubbed sage
- ½ teaspoon dried thyme
- ½ teaspoon pepper

1. In a large skillet, brown pork chops in butter. Remove and keep warm. In the same skillet, saute pears and shallots until crisp-tender. Add the garlic; saute 1 minute longer. Remove from the heat. Stir in the brandy; cook over medium heat until the liquid is evaporated.

2. Stir in the cream and seasonings; cook for 2-3 minutes or until sauce is slightly thickened. Return the pork chops to the skillet; cover and cook for 8-10 minutes or until a thermometer reads 160°, turning once.

PORK CHOPS NORMANDY

BEST-EVER GRILLED CHEESE SANDWICHES

"I put a spin on a typical stir-fry that you would normally serve over rice. Ramen noodles are quick to sub in for the rice, and coleslaw mix gives the dish lots of fresh bite with very little work."

—BARBARA PLETZKE HERNDON, VA

Best-Ever Grilled Cheese Sandwiches

For deluxe grilled cheese, it doesn't get any better than this. You can also use your imagination for other fillings, such as a sprinkle of Parmesan cheese, Italian seasoning, chives or even a tiny spoonful of salsa.

—EDIE DESPAIN LOGAN, UT

START TO FINISH: 20 MIN.
MAKES: 2 SERVINGS

- 2 tablespoons mayonnaise
- 1 teaspoon Dijon mustard
- 4 slices sourdough bread
- 2 slices Swiss cheese
- 2 slices cheddar cheese
- 2 slices sweet onion
- 1 medium tomato, sliced
- 6 cooked bacon strips
- 2 tablespoons butter, softened

1. Combine the mayonnaise and mustard; spread over two bread slices. Layer with cheeses, onion, tomato and bacon; top with the remaining bread. Spread the outsides of sandwiches with butter.

2. In a small skillet over medium heat, toast sandwiches for 2-3 minutes on each side or until cheese is melted.

Spicy Pepper Penne

Bring a bit of Sicily to the supper table! This zesty combination of pepperoni, pasta and peppers is a delectable way to shake up your dinner routine.

—CANDACE GREENE COLUMBIANA, OH

START TO FINISH: 30 MIN.
MAKES: 8 SERVINGS

- 1 package (16 ounces) penne pasta
- ½ teaspoon minced fresh rosemary or ⅛ teaspoon dried rosemary, crushed
- 2 packages (3½ ounces each) sliced pepperoni, halved
- ½ cup pepperoncini
- 1 jar (7 ounces) roasted sweet red peppers, drained and chopped
- 3½ cups boiling water
- ½ cup heavy whipping cream
- ½ cup grated Parmesan cheese

In a large skillet, layer the pasta, rosemary, pepperoni, pepperoncini and red peppers. Add water; bring to a boil. Reduce heat; cover and simmer for 12 minutes or until pasta is tender. Add cream and Parmesan cheese; toss to coat.

NOTE *Look for pepperoncinis (pickled peppers) in the pickle and olive section of your grocery store.*

Pork & Ramen Stir-Fry

START TO FINISH: 30 MIN.
MAKES: 4 SERVINGS

- ¼ cup reduced-sodium soy sauce
- 2 tablespoons ketchup
- 2 tablespoons Worcestershire sauce
- 2 teaspoons sugar
- ¼ teaspoon crushed red pepper flakes
- 3 teaspoons canola oil, divided
- 1 pound boneless pork loin chops, cut into ½-inch strips
- 1 cup fresh broccoli florets
- 4 cups coleslaw mix
- 1 can (8 ounces) bamboo shoots, drained
- 4 garlic cloves, minced
- 2 packages (3 ounces each) ramen noodles

1. In a small bowl, whisk the first five ingredients until blended. In a large skillet, heat 2 teaspoons oil over medium-high heat. Add pork; stir-fry 2-3 minutes or until no longer pink. Remove from pan.

2. In same pan, stir-fry broccoli in remaining oil 3 minutes. Add coleslaw mix, bamboo shoots and garlic; stir-fry 3-4 minutes longer or until broccoli is crisp-tender. Stir in soy sauce mixture and pork; heat through.

3. Meanwhile, cook the noodles according to package directions, discarding or saving the seasoning packets for another use. Drain the noodles; add to pork mixture and toss to combine.

**PORK & RAMEN
STIR-FRY**

**HAM &
BROCCOLI PASTA**

Pork Tenderloin with Dried Cherries

Cherries pair beautifully with pork, and this wonderful dish takes only minutes to cook. It's fabulous both for weeknights and serving to dinner guests.
—**KATHY FOX** GOODYEAR, AZ

PREP: 20 MIN. • **COOK:** 15 MIN.
MAKES: 4 SERVINGS

- ¾ **cup chicken broth**
- ⅓ **cup dried tart cherries**
- ¼ **cup brandy**
- 1 **teaspoon minced fresh thyme or**
  ¼ **teaspoon dried thyme**
- ⅛ **teaspoon ground allspice**
- 1 **pound pork tenderloin, cut into**
  1-inch slices
- ½ **teaspoon salt, divided**
- ½ **teaspoon pepper, divided**
- 1 **tablespoon butter**
- 1 **shallot, minced**
- ¼ **cup heavy whipping cream**

1. In a small saucepan, combine the first five ingredients. Bring to a boil; cook until liquid is reduced to ½ cup. Set aside and keep warm.
2. Flatten pork to ½-in. thickness; sprinkle with ¼ teaspoon salt and ¼ teaspoon pepper. In a large skillet, brown pork in butter; remove and keep warm.
3. In the same skillet, saute shallot in drippings until tender. Add cream, the reserved cherry mixture and the remaining salt and pepper, stirring to loosen browned bits from pan. Bring to a boil; cook until liquid is reduced to sauce consistency. Return pork to the pan; cook until no longer pink.
PER SERVING *3 ounces cooked pork with 1 tablespoon sauce equals 269 cal., 12 g fat (7 g sat. fat), 92 mg chol., 551 mg sodium, 11 g carb., 1 g fiber, 24 g pro.*

Ham & Broccoli Pasta

It's hard to beat a meal that's created in one pan, takes 30 minutes to pull together, and your kids actually thank you for making. Sounds like a keeper in my book!
—**JANA CATHEY** ADA, MI

START TO FINISH: 30 MIN.
MAKES: 6 SERVINGS

- 4½ **cups uncooked bow tie pasta**
  (12 ounces)
- 1 **package (16 ounces) frozen**
  broccoli florets
- 3 **cups cubed fully cooked ham**
- 1 **carton (8 ounces) spreadable**
  chive and onion cream cheese
- ⅓ **cup milk**
- ¼ **teaspoon salt**
- ½ **teaspoon pepper**

1. In Dutch oven, cook pasta according to package directions, adding the broccoli during last 5 minutes; drain and set aside.
2. In the same pan, combine the remaining ingredients; cook and stir over medium heat until heated through and cream cheese is melted. Return pasta mixture to pan and toss to combine.

German Pizza

Crispy hash browns create the irresistible crust in this simple brunch-style pizza.
—**MARSHA BENDA** ROUND ROCK, TX

PREP: 10 MIN. • **COOK:** 25 MIN.
MAKES: 4-6 SERVINGS

- ¼ **cup butter, cubed**
- 3 **cups frozen shredded hash brown**
  potatoes
- ⅛ **teaspoon salt**
  Pinch pepper
- 4 **eggs, lightly beaten**
- ½ **pound fully cooked ham, julienned**
- ½ **cup shredded cheddar cheese**

1. In a large nonstick skillet over low heat, melt butter. Add the potatoes, salt and pepper; cover and cook for 15 minutes, stirring occasionally.
2. Pour eggs over the potatoes; sprinkle with ham. Cover and cook for 10-12 minutes or until eggs are set. Sprinkle with cheese; cook, uncovered, until melted. Cut into wedges.

Garam masala is a good substitute for **allspice** in **savory recipes**. Or, use a dash of **nutmeg** (and **cinnamon**, if you like it).

Curried Apricot Pork Chops

A fresh fruit glaze that's both sweet and savory turns these fork-tender pork chops into a main dish pretty enough to serve for a big night in.

—**TRISHA KRUSE** EAGLE, ID

START TO FINISH: 30 MIN.
MAKES: 2 SERVINGS

- 2 tablespoons apricot nectar
- 1 tablespoon plus 1½ teaspoons apricot preserves
- 1 tablespoon Dijon mustard
- 1 tablespoon reduced-sodium soy sauce
- 1 teaspoon curry powder
- 2 boneless pork loin chops (5 ounces each)
- ⅛ teaspoon salt
- ⅛ teaspoon pepper
- 1½ teaspoons canola oil
- ½ cup sliced fresh apricots
- 2 green onions, sliced

1. In a small bowl, combine the first five ingredients; set aside.

2. Sprinkle pork chops with salt and pepper. In a small nonstick skillet, cook chops in oil for 4-5 minutes on each side or until a thermometer reads 145°. Remove and keep warm.

3. Add apricots and onions to the pan; saute until onions are tender. Stir in nectar mixture. Bring to a boil; cook and stir for 2 minutes or until slightly thickened. Serve with pork chops.

PER SERVING *1 pork chop with ⅓ cup sauce equals 306 cal., 12 g fat (3 g sat. fat), 68 mg chol., 679 mg sodium, 20 g carb., 2 g fiber, 29 g pro.* **Diabetic Exchanges:** *4 lean meat, 1 starch, 1 fat.*

Ribs with Caraway Kraut and Stuffing Balls

I like to entertain frequently, serving hearty meals to my guests. Everyone compliments me on these ribs and their Old World flavor.

—**PATRICIA JOHNSON** SANTA PAULA, CA

PREP: 15 MIN. • **COOK:** 2 HOURS
MAKES: 6 SERVINGS

- 3 pounds boneless country-style pork ribs
- 1 can (14 ounces) sauerkraut, drained
- 1½ cups tomato juice
- ½ cup chicken broth
- 1 medium apple, diced
- 1 tablespoon brown sugar
- 2 to 3 teaspoons caraway seeds
- ⅛ teaspoon salt
- ⅛ teaspoon pepper

STUFFING BALLS

- 1 package (8 ounces) herb-seasoned stuffing mix
- 1⅓ cups hot water
- ½ cup butter, melted
- 2 eggs, beaten

1. In a large skillet, brown ribs; drain. Combine the sauerkraut, tomato juice, broth, apple, brown sugar, caraway, salt and pepper; pour over ribs. Cover and simmer 1½ hours or until meat is very tender.

2. For stuffing balls, combine stuffing mix, water and butter; mix lightly and let stand for 5 minutes. Stir in eggs; mix well. Shape into 2-in. balls; place over ribs and sauerkraut. Cover and simmer for 20 minutes.

"We've lived in Arizona for decades, so Mexican-style cooking has become the same as 'Arizona-style cooking' for us. Nothing tastes better than chili-spiced pork with tortillas."

—ANNE FATOUT PHOENIX, AZ

MEXICAN PORK
& PINTO BEANS

Mexican Pork & Pinto Beans

PREP: 30 MIN. • **COOK:** 4 HOURS
MAKES: 16 SERVINGS (4 QUARTS)

- 1 bone-in pork loin roast (3 pounds), trimmed
- 1 package (16 ounces) dried pinto beans, soaked overnight
- 4 to 5 cloves garlic, minced
- 2 tablespoons chili powder
- 1 to 1½ teaspoons ground cumin
- 1 teaspoon dried oregano
- 2 cans (4 ounces each) chopped green chilies
  Pepper to taste
- 5 medium carrots, sliced
- 4 celery ribs, sliced
- 1 can (14½ ounces) diced tomatoes, undrained
- 3 small zucchini, sliced
  Flour tortillas, warmed

1. In a stockpot, combine the first eight ingredients; cover with water. Bring to a boil. Reduce heat; simmer, covered, 3 to 4 hours or until meat and beans are tender.

2. Remove pork; cool slightly. Stir carrots, celery and tomatoes into bean mixture; return to a boil. Reduce heat; simmer, covered, until the vegetables are crisp-tender. Add the zucchini; cook 8-10 minutes longer or until crisp-tender.

3. Meanwhile, remove pork from bone; discard bone. Cut pork into bite-size pieces; return to pot and heat through. Serve with tortillas.

FREEZE OPTION *Freeze cooled pork mixture in freezer containers. To use, partially thaw in refrigerator overnight. Microwave, covered, on high in a microwave-safe dish until heated through, gently stirring and adding a little broth or water if necessary. Serve with tortillas.*

PER SERVING *1 cup equals 253 cal., 7 g fat (0 sat. fat), 41 mg chol., 160 mg sodium, 26 g carb., 0 fiber, 22 g pro.* **Diabetic Exchanges:** *1½ starch, 1½ meat, 1 vegetable.*

TENDER GLAZED PORK CHOPS

Tender Glazed Pork Chops

Topped with a tangy apricot glaze, these tender pork chops are a breeze to put together. My mother and I both love this recipe. It's excellent with rolls and any veggie side dish.
—**JUDITH WIEZOREK** GAINESVILLE, GA

START TO FINISH: 30 MIN.
MAKES: 4 SERVINGS

- ½ teaspoon onion powder
- ½ teaspoon garlic powder
- ½ teaspoon dried oregano
- 4 boneless pork loin chops (4 ounces each)
- 1 cup apricot preserves
- 1½ teaspoons lemon juice
- 1½ teaspoons lime juice
- 2 tablespoons olive oil

1. Combine the onion powder, garlic powder and oregano; sprinkle over pork chops. In a small saucepan, combine the apricot preserves, lemon juice and lime juice; cook and stir over low heat for 10 minutes or until the preserves are melted.

2. Meanwhile, in a large skillet, cook chops in oil over medium-low heat for 5 minutes or until lightly browned on one side. Turn chops; generously brush cooked sides with apricot glaze. Cook 8-10 minutes longer or until a thermometer reads 145°. Let stand 5 minutes before serving. Serve with remaining glaze.

FREEZE OPTION *Freeze cooled pork chops and remaining glaze in freezer containers. To use, partially thaw in refrigerator overnight. Heat through slowly in a covered skillet until a thermometer inserted in pork reads 145°, turning occasionally and adding a little broth or water if necessary.*

Polynesian Stir-Fry

Here's a restaurant-quality meal that blends the sweet taste of pineapple with crunchy veggies and tender pork. The peanuts add a special touch.
—SUSIE VAN ETTEN CHAPMANSBORO, TN

START TO FINISH: 30 MIN.
MAKES: 4 SERVINGS

- 1 can (8 ounces) unsweetened pineapple chunks
- 1 tablespoon cornstarch
- 2 tablespoons cold water
- 1 tablespoon reduced-sodium soy sauce
- 2 tablespoons reduced-sugar apricot preserves
- 1 pound pork tenderloin, thinly sliced
- 3 teaspoons canola oil, divided
- 1 medium onion, halved and sliced
- 1 small green pepper, cut into 1-inch pieces
- 1 small sweet red pepper, cut into 1-inch pieces
- 2 cups hot cooked rice
  Chopped unsalted peanuts, optional

1. Drain pineapple, reserving juice; set aside. For sauce, in a small bowl, combine cornstarch and water until smooth. Stir in soy sauce, preserves and the reserved pineapple juice; set aside.

2. In a large nonstick skillet or wok, stir-fry pork in 2 teaspoons oil until no longer pink. Remove and keep warm.

3. Stir-fry the onion and peppers in remaining oil for 3 minutes. Add the pineapple; stir-fry 2-3 minutes longer or until vegetables are crisp-tender.

4. Stir cornstarch mixture and add to the pan. Bring to a boil; cook and stir for 2 minutes or until thickened. Add pork; heat through. Serve with rice. Just before serving, sprinkle each serving with peanuts if desired.

SOUTHERN SKILLET CHOPS

Southern Skillet Chops

Creole seasoning adds just the right amount of spice to these Southern-style pork chops with black-eyed peas.
—IRENE SULLIVAN LAKE MILLS, WI

START TO FINISH: 25 MIN.
MAKES: 4 SERVINGS

- 4 bone-in pork loin chops (8 ounces each)
- 2 teaspoons plus ⅛ teaspoon Creole seasoning, divided
- 2 tablespoons canola oil
- 2 cans (14½ ounces each) diced tomatoes with mild green chilies, undrained
- 1 can (15½ ounces) black-eyed peas, rinsed and drained
  Shredded cheddar cheese, optional

1. Sprinkle the pork chops with 2 teaspoons Creole seasoning. In a large skillet, brown chops in oil. Remove and keep warm.

2. Drain one can tomatoes; discard liquid. Add tomatoes to skillet with the remaining can of undrained tomatoes, black-eyed peas and the remaining Creole seasoning, stirring to loosen browned bits from pan.

3. Bring to a boil and return pork chops to pan. Reduce heat; simmer, uncovered, for 2-4 minutes or until a thermometer reads 145°. Sprinkle with cheese if desired. Let stand for 5 minutes.

NOTE *The following spices may be substituted for 1 teaspoon Creole seasoning: ¼ teaspoon each salt, garlic powder and paprika; and a pinch each of dried thyme, ground cumin and cayenne pepper.*

Hearty Sausage 'n' Beans

Our son is a brand-new dad. He cooked this blend of sausage, beans and rice when we came to visit our newborn granddaughter, Jenna. The beauty of this recipe is its simplicity: Toss the ingredients in one pan, simmer, and you've got dinner.
—**WILL OWEN** WACO, TX

START TO FINISH: 25 MIN.
MAKES: 6 SERVINGS

- 1 pound smoked sausage, sliced
- 1 medium onion, chopped
- 2 tablespoons canola oil
- 2 cans (15 ounces each) pinto beans, rinsed and drained
- 1½ cups water
- 1 can (14½ ounces) diced tomatoes with mild green chilies, undrained
- 1 tablespoon ranch salad dressing mix
- 2 cups uncooked instant rice

In a Dutch oven, cook sausage and onion in oil over medium heat until onion is tender. Add the beans, water, tomatoes and salad dressing mix. Bring to a boil; stir in rice. Reduce heat; cover and simmer for 5 minutes or until rice is tender.

Rigatoni with Bacon and Asparagus

Wouldn't it be great to find a company-worthy dish that not only impresses with its taste, but also with its nutritional numbers? Look no further! This creamy rigatoni with bacon delivers on all counts.
—**JOANIE FUSON** INDIANAPOLIS, IN

PREP: 25 MIN. • **COOK:** 20 MIN.
MAKES: 8 SERVINGS

- 1 package (16 ounces) rigatoni
- 1 pound fresh asparagus, trimmed and coarsely chopped
- 8 bacon strips
- 1 garlic clove, minced
- 2 tablespoons butter
- 1 tablespoon olive oil
- ⅔ cup half-and-half cream
- ½ cup shredded part-skim mozzarella cheese
- ½ teaspoon salt
- ¼ cup minced fresh parsley
- ⅛ teaspoon coarsely ground pepper
- ¼ cup grated Parmigiano-Reggiano cheese

1. Cook pasta according to the package directions.
2. Meanwhile, in a Dutch oven, bring 2 cups water to a boil. Add asparagus; cover and boil for 3 minutes. Drain and immediately place asparagus in ice water. Drain and pat dry.
3. In the same pan, cook bacon over medium heat until crisp. Remove to paper towels to drain. Crumble bacon and set aside. Saute garlic in butter and oil for 1 minute. Stir in cream. Bring to a boil. Reduce heat; simmer, uncovered, for 3-4 minutes or until slightly thickened.
4. Stir in mozzarella cheese until melted. Drain pasta; add to pan. Stir in the salt, asparagus, parsley and reserved bacon. Sprinkle with pepper and Parmigiano-Reggiano cheese.
PER SERVING *1¼ cups equals 345 cal., 13 g fat (6 g sat. fat), 32 mg chol., 428 mg sodium, 44 g carb., 2 g fiber, 15 g pro.*

HEARTY SAUSAGE 'N' BEANS

PORK CHOPS WITH ONION GRAVY

Speedy Stovetop Spaghetti

PREP: 10 MIN. • **COOK:** 30 MIN.
MAKES: 4 SERVINGS

- 1 pound bulk Italian sausage
- ½ cup finely chopped onion
- 1 garlic clove, minced
- 3 ounces uncooked spaghetti, broken into 1-inch pieces
- 1 tablespoon minced fresh parsley or 1 teaspoon dried parsley flakes
- 1 teaspoon dried basil
- 1 can (28 ounces) diced tomatoes, undrained
- 1 can (15 ounces) tomato sauce
- 3 tablespoons dry red wine or beef broth
- ½ teaspoon sugar
- 3 tablespoons shredded Parmesan cheese

1. Saute the sausage, onion and garlic in a large skillet for 5-7 minutes or until the sausage is no longer pink; drain. Stir in the spaghetti, parsley, basil, tomatoes, tomato sauce, wine and sugar.
2. Bring to a boil. Reduce heat; cover and simmer for 20 minutes or until spaghetti is tender. Sprinkle with cheese. Cover and cook 2-3 minutes longer or until cheese is melted.

Serve the **spaghetti** with a **salad** of cooked **green beans**, chopped **tomatoes**, minced **basil** and cubed **mozzarella cheese**. Toss the ingredients with **balsamic vinaigrette** or Italian dressing.

EAT SMART **FREEZE IT**
Pork Chops with Onion Gravy

I created this rich onion gravy because my husband generally isn't a big fan of pork chops. These are so saucy and flavorful, he gives them a thumbs up!

—AMY RADYSHEWSKY GREAT FALLS, MT

START TO FINISH: 30 MIN.
MAKES: 4 SERVINGS

- 4 boneless pork loin chops (4 ounces each)
- ¼ teaspoon pepper
- ⅛ teaspoon salt
- 1 small onion, sliced and separated into rings
- 1 tablespoon canola oil
- ¼ cup reduced-sodium chicken broth
- 1 envelope pork gravy mix
- ⅛ teaspoon garlic powder
- ¾ cup water

1. Sprinkle pork chops with pepper and salt. In a large skillet over medium heat, cook chops with onion in oil for 2-3 minutes on each side or until lightly browned.
2. Add broth. Bring to a boil. Reduce heat; cover and simmer for 10 minutes or until a thermometer reads 160°.
3. In a small bowl, whisk the gravy mix, garlic powder and water. Pour over pork. Bring to a boil. Reduce heat; simmer, uncovered, for 3-4 minutes or until sauce is thickened, stirring occasionally.
FREEZE OPTION *Cool pork and gravy. Freeze in freezer containers. To use, partially thaw in the refrigerator overnight. Heat through slowly in a covered skillet, stirring occasionally and adding a little broth or water if necessary.*
PER SERVING *1 pork chop with 3 tablespoons gravy equals 210 cal., 10 g fat (3 g sat. fat), 55 mg chol., 528 mg sodium, 6 g carb., trace fiber, 22 g pro.* **Diabetic Exchanges:** *3 lean meat, ½ starch, ½ fat.*

"Here's a quick take on a favorite that you'll want to make again and again. This dish tastes like it cooked all day, but it's ready to eat in just 40 minutes. The pasta cooks right in the pan, and the 20-minute simmer gives me plenty of time to prepare sides or a salad to go with the meal."

—**KRISTIN NANNEY** MARBLE HILL, MO

SPEEDY STOVETOP SPAGHETTI

Apricot Ham Rolls

This is the kind of hearty dish we 10 kids would devour after doing chores on our parents' farm. Mom always had many appreciators of her wonderful cooking. When I'm short on time, I rely on this tasty recipe of hers.

—CAROLYN HANNAY ANTIOCH, TN

START TO FINISH: 30 MIN.
MAKES: 4 SERVINGS

- 1⅔ cups apricot nectar, divided
- 1 tablespoon Dijon mustard
- ½ teaspoon salt
- 1 cup uncooked instant rice
- 2 tablespoons minced fresh parsley
- 8 thin slices fully cooked ham
- 2 tablespoons maple syrup

1. In a large saucepan over medium heat, combine 1⅓ cups apricot nectar, mustard and salt; bring to a boil. Stir in rice.

2. Remove from heat; cover and let stand for 6-8 minutes or until the liquid is absorbed. Add parsley and fluff with a fork.

3. Place about ¼ cup of rice mixture on each ham slice. Overlap two opposite corners of ham over rice mixture; secure with a toothpick.

4. In a large skillet over medium-high heat, combine syrup and remaining nectar; bring to a boil. Add ham rolls; reduce heat. Cover and simmer for about 5 minutes or until heated through, basting occasionally with the sauce. Remove toothpicks.

Add a large **chopped apple** to the **kielbasa** dish for even more authentic **German** flavor.

German-Style Kielbasa and Noodles

Kielbasa, cabbage and tender, buttery noodles create a classic flavor combination. Using a bag of coleslaw mix really saves on prep time.

—LILY JULOW LAWRENCEVILLE, GA

PREP: 15 MIN. + STANDING • **COOK:** 20 MIN.
MAKES: 2 SERVINGS

- 5½ cups coleslaw mix
- 1 teaspoon salt
- 1½ cups uncooked egg noodles
- ½ pound smoked kielbasa or Polish sausage, cut into ¼-inch slices
- 1 small onion, finely chopped
- 2 tablespoons butter
- 1 teaspoon sugar
- ⅛ teaspoon pepper
- ½ teaspoon poppy seeds, optional

1. Place coleslaw mix in a colander over a plate; sprinkle with salt and toss. Let stand for 30 minutes. Rinse and drain well.

2. Cook noodles according to the package directions. Meanwhile, in a large skillet, saute kielbasa and onion in butter until onion is tender. Add the coleslaw mix, sugar and pepper; cover and cook over medium-low heat for 10-15 minutes or until mixture is heated through. Stir in poppy seeds if desired. Drain noodles; serve with cabbage mixture.

GERMAN-STYLE KIELBASA AND NOODLES

Pretty Ham Primavera

Put a fresh take on leftover ham with a creamy pasta dish that's loaded with mushrooms and peas.

—**JOAN LAURENZO** JOHNSTOWN, OH

START TO FINISH: 20 MIN.
MAKES: 4 SERVINGS

- ½ **pound sliced fresh mushrooms**
- ⅓ **cup chopped onion**
- 2 **tablespoons olive oil**
- 2 **tablespoons all-purpose flour**
- 2 **teaspoons Italian seasoning**
- 2 **teaspoons chicken bouillon granules**
- ½ **teaspoon salt**
- ⅛ **teaspoon pepper**
- 2 **cups milk**
- 1 **package (7 ounces) thin spaghetti, cooked and drained**
- 2 **cups cubed fully cooked ham**
- 1 **package (10 ounces) frozen peas, thawed**
  Grated Parmesan cheese, optional

1. In a large skillet, saute mushrooms and onion in oil until tender. Stir in the flour, Italian seasoning, bouillon, salt and pepper until smooth.
2. Gradually add the milk, stirring constantly. Bring to a boil; cook and stir for 2 minutes or until thickened. Stir in the spaghetti, ham and peas; heat through. Sprinkle with cheese if desired.

Tangy Pork Barbecue

A dear neighbor shared this zesty recipe with me long ago. She'd found it in a Marine officers' wives cookbook. The barbecue has always been a great hit with my family. We usually have it with French fries and coleslaw.

—**CARMINE WALTERS** SAN JOSE, CA

PREP: 20 MIN. • **COOK:** 3¼ HOURS
MAKES: 12 SERVINGS

- 2 **tablespoons butter**
- 3 **tablespoons all-purpose flour**
- 1 **bottle (28 ounces) ketchup**
- 2 **cups water**
- ¼ **cup white vinegar**
- ¼ **cup Worcestershire sauce**
- 1 **medium onion, chopped**
- 1 **garlic clove, minced**
- 2 **teaspoons chili powder**
- 1 **teaspoon salt, optional**
- 1 **teaspoon ground mustard**
- ⅛ **teaspoon cayenne pepper**
- 1 **boneless pork loin roast (3½ to 4 pounds)**
- 12 **sandwich buns, split**

1. In a Dutch oven, melt butter over medium heat. Stir in flour until smooth. Add ketchup, water, vinegar, Worcestershire sauce, onion, garlic and seasonings; bring to a boil. Add roast. Reduce heat; simmer, covered, 3 hours or until meat is very tender.
2. Remove roast; shred with two forks. Skim fat from cooking juices; return meat to pan and heat through. Using a slotted spoon, place mixture on buns.

Fish
& Seafood

153   156   159

With the **taste-tempting** recipes that follow, it's easy to treat the ones you love to a **healthful, delicious** fish or seafood dish. Whip up a simple red **clam sauce**, a quick-and-easy **tuna pasta**, or a time-honored entree such as **trout meuniere** or **shrimp and grits**.

**CORNMEAL CATFISH
WITH AVOCADO SAUCE**

Cod Florentine

My husband has high cholesterol and I'm always on the lookout for healthy new fish recipes for us to try. I found this one in a cookbook and hope you like it as much as we do.

—LORI BOLIN SOAP LAKE, WA

PREP: 10 MIN. • **COOK:** 25 MIN.
MAKES: 4 SERVINGS

- ¼ teaspoon salt
- ¼ teaspoon pepper
- 4 cod fillets (6 ounces each)
- 2 tablespoons lemon juice, divided
- 2 packages (6 ounces each) fresh baby spinach
- 2 tablespoons butter
- ¼ cup all-purpose flour
- 1¾ cups fat-free milk
- 2 tablespoons shredded Parmesan cheese, divided

1. In a small bowl, combine salt and pepper. Sprinkle half over the cod; set remaining salt mixture aside. In a nonstick skillet coated with cooking spray, cook fillets until fish flakes easily with a fork. Remove from the heat. Drizzle with 1 tablespoon lemon juice; keep warm.
2. In another nonstick skillet coated with cooking spray, cook spinach for 3 minutes or until wilted. Drain and keep warm. In the same skillet, melt butter. Stir in flour and reserved salt mixture until blended. Gradually stir in milk until smooth. Bring to a boil; cook and stir for 2 minutes or until thickened. Stir in 1 tablespoon Parmesan cheese and remaining lemon juice. Set aside ½ cup sauce. Stir spinach into remaining sauce; heat through.
3. Divide spinach mixture among four plates; top with fish. Drizzle with reserved sauce and sprinkle with remaining Parmesan cheese.
PER SERVING *1 serving equals 271 cal., 8 g fat (4 g sat. fat), 84 mg chol., 463 mg sodium, 15 g carb., 3 g fiber, 35 g pro.* **Diabetic Exchanges:** *5 lean meat, 1 vegetable, 1 fat, ½ fat-free milk.*

Cornmeal Catfish with Avocado Sauce

When I was growing up in California, my mother often made catfish. Now I cook it with my own twist. When only frozen catfish fillets are available, I thaw them in the refrigerator overnight, and they work just as well as fresh.

—MARY LOU COOK WELCHES, OR

START TO FINISH: 25 MIN.
MAKES: 4 SERVINGS (¾ CUP SAUCE)

- 1 medium ripe avocado, peeled and cubed
- ⅓ cup reduced-fat mayonnaise
- ¼ cup fresh cilantro leaves
- 2 tablespoons lime juice
- ½ teaspoon garlic salt
- ¼ cup cornmeal
- 1 teaspoon seafood seasoning
- 4 catfish fillets (6 ounces each)
- 3 tablespoons canola oil
- 1 medium tomato, chopped

1. Place the first five ingredients in a food processor; process until blended.
2. In a shallow bowl, mix cornmeal and seafood seasoning. Dip catfish in cornmeal mixture to coat both sides; shake off excess.
3. In a large skillet, heat oil over medium heat. Add catfish in batches; cook 4-5 minutes on each side or until fish flakes easily with a fork. Top with avocado sauce and chopped tomato.

Avocado is high in monounsaturated fat, a so-called **"good fat"** that can lower your **blood cholesterol** along with the risk of **stroke** and **heart disease.**

SPRING PILAF WITH
SALMON & ASPARAGUS

Spring Pilaf with Salmon & Asparagus

Celebrate the very best of spring in one fabulous dish! Fresh asparagus, carrots, lemon and chives perfectly complement leftover cooked salmon in this simple, sensational entree.

—STEVE WESTPHAL WIND LAKE, WI

PREP: 15 MIN. • **COOK:** 30 MIN.
MAKES: 4 SERVINGS

- 2 **medium carrots, sliced**
- 1 **medium sweet yellow pepper, chopped**
- ¼ **cup butter**
- 1½ **cups uncooked long grain rice**
- 4 **cups reduced-sodium chicken broth**
- ½ **teaspoon salt**
- ¼ **teaspoon pepper**
- 2½ **cups cut fresh asparagus (1-inch pieces)**
- 12 **ounces fully cooked salmon chunks**
- 2 **tablespoons lemon juice**
- 2 **tablespoons minced fresh chives, divided**
- 1 **teaspoon grated lemon peel**

1. Saute carrots and yellow pepper in butter in a large saucepan until crisp-tender. Add rice; cook and stir for 1 minute or until lightly toasted.
2. Stir in the broth, salt and pepper. Bring to a boil. Reduce heat; cover and simmer for 20 minutes. Stir in the asparagus. Cook, uncovered, for 3-4 minutes longer or until the rice is tender.
3. Stir in the salmon, lemon juice, 1 tablespoon chives and lemon peel; heat through. Fluff with a fork. Sprinkle with remaining chives.

Tilapia & Veggies with Red Pepper Sauce

This dish's impressive look and taste are delectably deceiving. Only the cook needs to know how quickly the saucy fish and sauteed veggies come together.

—HELEN CONWELL PORTLAND, OR

START TO FINISH: 30 MIN.
MAKES: 6 SERVINGS

- ½ **cup dry white wine or chicken broth**
- ¼ **cup water**
- 1 **tablespoon lemon juice**
- 1 **teaspoon salt, divided**
- 6 **tilapia fillets (4 ounces each)**
- 2 **small yellow summer squash, cut into ¼-inch slices**
- 1 **medium zucchini, cut into ¼-inch slices**
- 1 **medium onion, halved and sliced**
- 1 **tablespoon olive oil**
- 1 **garlic clove, minced**
- ¼ **teaspoon pepper**
- ⅓ **cup roasted sweet red peppers, drained**
- 1 **tablespoon white balsamic vinegar**

1. In a large skillet, bring wine, water, lemon juice and ½ teaspoon salt to a boil. Reduce heat; add tilapia. Poach, uncovered, for 5-10 minutes or until fish flakes easily with a fork, turning once. Remove and keep warm.
2. Bring poaching liquid to a boil; cook until reduced to about ½ cup. Meanwhile, in another skillet, saute the yellow squash, zucchini and onion in oil until tender. Add the garlic; cook 1 minute longer. Sprinkle with pepper and remaining salt.
3. In a blender, combine the reduced liquid, roasted peppers and vinegar; cover and process until smooth. Serve with fish and vegetables.

PER SERVING *1 fillet with ½ cup vegetables and 2 tablespoons sauce equals 163 cal., 3 g fat (1 g sat. fat), 55 mg chol., 490 mg sodium, 7 g carb., 2 g fiber, 23 g pro.* **Diabetic Exchanges:** *3 lean meat, 1 vegetable, ½ fat.*

Spicy Mango Scallops

Warm up your whole family with this spicy-sweet dish! If you prepare the recipe with smaller scallops, be sure to decrease the cooking time.

—NICOLE FILIZETTI STEVENS POINT, WI

START TO FINISH: 30 MIN.
MAKES: 4 SERVINGS

- 12 sea scallops (1½ pounds)
- 1 tablespoon peanut or canola oil
- 1 medium red onion, chopped
- 1 garlic clove, minced
- ¼ to ½ teaspoon crushed red pepper flakes
- ½ cup unsweetened pineapple juice
- ¼ cup mango chutney
- 2 cups hot cooked basmati rice
  Minced fresh cilantro

1. In a large skillet over medium-high heat, cook the scallops in oil for 1½-2 minutes on each side or until firm and opaque. Remove scallops and keep warm.

2. In the same skillet, saute onion until tender. Add garlic and pepper flakes; cook 1 minute longer. Stir in pineapple juice. Bring to a boil; cook until liquid is reduced by half. Remove from the heat. Add the chutney and scallops; stir to coat. Serve with rice. Sprinkle with cilantro.

PER SERVING *3 scallops with ½ cup cooked rice and 2 tablespoons sauce equals 371 cal., 5 g fat (1 g sat. fat), 56 mg chol., 447 mg sodium, 47 g carb., 1 g fiber, 31 g pro.* **Diabetic Exchanges:** *4 lean meat, 3 starch, ½ fat.*

Sesame Noodles with Shrimp & Snap Peas

Stir-fries and busy nights are a mealtime match made in heaven. For a boost of vibrant color and freshness, I sometimes stir in chopped cilantro just before I serve it from the pan.

—NEDRA SCHELL FORT WORTH, TX

START TO FINISH: 25 MIN.
MAKES: 4 SERVINGS

- 8 ounces uncooked whole wheat linguine
- 1 tablespoon canola oil
- 1 pound uncooked medium shrimp, peeled and deveined
- 2 cups fresh sugar snap peas, trimmed
- ⅛ teaspoon salt
- ⅛ teaspoon crushed red pepper flakes
- ¾ cup reduced-fat Asian toasted sesame salad dressing

1. Cook linguine according to package directions for al dente.

2. Meanwhile, in a large skillet, heat oil over medium-high heat. Add shrimp, peas, salt and pepper flakes; stir-fry 2-3 minutes or until shrimp turn pink and peas are crisp-tender. Drain linguine, reserving ¼ cup pasta water. Add pasta, pasta water and salad dressing to shrimp mixture; toss to combine.

PER SERVING *1½ cups equals 418 cal., 10 g fat (1 g sat. fat), 138 mg chol., 646 mg sodium, 60 g carb., 8 g fiber, 29 g pro.*

SESAME NOODLES WITH SHRIMP & SNAP PEAS

CAROLINA CRAB BOIL

Carolina Crab Boil

This pot is a fun way to feed a crowd for a tailgate. Drain the cooking liquid and pour the pot out on a paper-lined table so folks can dig in, or serve it as a stew in its liquid over hot rice.
—**MELISSA BIRDSONG** WALESKA, GA

PREP: 15 MIN. • **COOK:** 35 MIN.
MAKES: 4 SERVINGS

- 2 teaspoons canola oil
- 1 package (14 ounces) smoked turkey sausage, sliced
- 2 cartons (32 ounces each) reduced-sodium chicken broth
- 4 cups water
- 1 bottle (12 ounces) light beer or 1½ cups additional broth
- ¼ cup seafood seasoning
- 5 bay leaves
- 4 medium ears sweet corn, cut into 2-inch pieces
- 1 pound fingerling potatoes
- 1 medium red onion, quartered
- 2 pounds cooked snow crab legs
  Pepper to taste

1. In a stockpot, heat oil over medium-high heat; brown sausage. Stir in broth, water, beer, seafood seasoning and bay leaves. Add the vegetables; bring to a boil. Reduce the heat; simmer, uncovered, for 20-25 minutes or until potatoes are tender.
2. Add crab; heat through. Drain; remove bay leaves. Transfer to a serving bowl; season with pepper.

Snow crab are so named for their **snow-white** flesh. These small, **sweet-tasting crab** are from the northernmost fishing grounds in **Canada** and the **Bering Sea.**

GINGER-CHUTNEY SHRIMP STIR-FRY

Ginger-Chutney Shrimp Stir-Fry

I made this recipe a lot when I was juggling college, work and a growing family. It tastes like you spent a lot of time making it, yet it takes less than half an hour to toss together.
—**SALLY SIBTHORPE** SHELBY TOWNSHIP, MI

START TO FINISH: 25 MIN.
MAKES: 4 SERVINGS

- 2 tablespoons peanut or canola oil
- 1 pound uncooked medium shrimp, peeled and deveined, tails removed
- 1 tablespoon minced fresh gingerroot
- 3 cups frozen pepper and onion stir-fry blend, thawed
- ¾ cup mango chutney
- 2 tablespoons water
- ¾ teaspoon salt

In a large skillet, heat the oil over medium-high heat. Add shrimp and ginger; stir-fry 4-5 minutes or until shrimp turn pink. Stir in remaining ingredients; cook until vegetables are crisp-tender, stirring occasionally.

Trout Meuniere

A delightful dinner is ready in minutes if you pair my crispy version of the classic French dish with a simple green salad.
—**NANCY KELLEY** NASHVILLE, TN

START TO FINISH: 15 MIN.
MAKES: 4 SERVINGS

- 4 trout fillets (6 ounces each)
- 1⅓ cups crushed saltines
- 4 tablespoons butter, divided
- 1 package (2¼ ounces) sliced almonds
- 2 tablespoons lemon juice

1. Coat both sides of fillets with crushed saltines. In a large skillet, melt 3 tablespoons butter over medium-high heat. Cook fillets for 3-5 minutes on each side or until fish flakes easily with a fork. Remove and keep warm.
2. In the same skillet, cook and stir the almonds in remaining butter until lightly toasted. Stir in the lemon juice. Serve with trout.

SMOKED SALMON QUESADILLAS WITH CREAMY CHIPOTLE SAUCE

EAT SMART

Tilapia with Grapefruit Salsa

This nutritious, low-fat fish comes with a surprisingly fresh and zesty spin on salsa. Also try the salsa with fried fish, queso fresco and corn tortillas.

—**EMILY SEEFELDT** RED WING, MN

PREP: 25 MIN. + MARINATING
COOK: 10 MIN. • **MAKES:** 2 SERVINGS

- ⅓ cup unsweetened grapefruit juice
- ½ teaspoon ground cumin
- 1 garlic clove, minced
- ¼ teaspoon grated grapefruit peel
- ⅛ teaspoon salt
- ⅛ teaspoon pepper
  Dash to ⅛ teaspoon cayenne pepper
- 2 tilapia fillets (6 ounces each)
- ½ cup canned black beans, rinsed and drained
- ⅓ cup chopped pink grapefruit sections
- ¼ cup chopped red onion
- 1 tablespoon minced fresh cilantro
- 1 to 2 teaspoons chopped jalapeno pepper
- 2 teaspoons butter

1. For marinade, in a small bowl, combine the first seven ingredients. Set aside 1 tablespoon. Place tilapia in a large resealable plastic bag; add remaining marinade. Seal bag and turn to coat. Refrigerate for 1 hour.

2. For the salsa, in a small bowl, combine the beans, grapefruit, onion, cilantro, jalapeno and reserved marinade. Cover and refrigerate until serving.

3. Drain and discard marinade. In a small skillet over medium heat, cook tilapia in butter for 4-5 minutes on each side or until fish flakes easily with a fork. Serve with salsa.

NOTE *Wear disposable gloves when cutting hot peppers; the oils can burn skin. Avoid touching your face.*

PER SERVING *1 fillet with ½ cup salsa equals 264 cal., 6 g fat (3 g sat. fat), 93 mg chol., 369 mg sodium, 18 g carb., 4 g fiber, 36 g pro.* **Diabetic Exchanges:** *5 lean meat, 1 starch, 1 fat.*

Smoked Salmon Quesadillas with Creamy Chipotle Sauce

These quesadillas taste extra-special, but they take just minutes to make. A fresh burst of chopped fresh cilantro is the perfect finishing touch.

—**DANIEL SHEMTOB** IRVINE, CA

START TO FINISH: 25 MIN.
MAKES: 3 SERVINGS (⅔ CUP SAUCE)

- ½ cup creme fraiche or sour cream
- 2 tablespoons minced chipotle peppers in adobo sauce
- 2 tablespoons lime juice
- ⅛ teaspoon salt
- ⅛ teaspoon pepper

QUESADILLAS

- ¼ cup cream cheese, softened
- 2 ounces fresh goat cheese
- 3 flour tortillas (8 inches)
- 3 ounces smoked salmon or lox, chopped
- ¼ cup finely chopped shallots
- ¼ cup finely chopped roasted sweet red pepper
  Coarsely chopped fresh cilantro

1. In a small bowl, mix the first five ingredients. In another bowl, mix cream cheese and goat cheese until blended; spread over tortillas. Top half side of each with the salmon, shallots and red pepper; fold over.

2. Place quesadillas on a greased griddle. Cook over medium heat for 1-2 minutes on each side or until lightly browned and cheeses are melted. Serve with sauce; top with cilantro.

Mediterranean Tuna Linguine

It'll remind you of a good old-fashioned tuna noodle casserole, but this creamy dish comes together quickly with no bake time. Serve it with spinach salad and breadsticks for a weekday dinner.
—**TASTE OF HOME** TEST KITCHEN

START TO FINISH: 20 MIN.
MAKES: 5 SERVINGS

- 8 ounces uncooked linguine
- 2 cans (10¾ ounces each) condensed cream of celery soup, undiluted
- 1 cup 2% milk
- 1 teaspoon garlic powder
- ½ teaspoon seafood seasoning
- 3 cans (5 ounces each) light water-packed tuna, drained and flaked
- 1 jar (7½ ounces) marinated quartered artichoke hearts, drained
- 2 medium tomatoes, chopped
- 1 cup sliced ripe olives, drained

1. Cook linguine according to package directions.

2. Meanwhile, in a large saucepan, combine the soup, milk, garlic powder and seafood seasoning. Stir in the tuna, artichoke hearts, tomatoes and olives. Bring to a boil. Reduce heat; drain linguine and stir into soup mixture until blended.

MEDITERRANEAN TUNA LINGUINE

Thai Shrimp Pasta

I came up with this recipe when my son was home from the Navy. He loves Thai food and I wanted to make something special but simple. There wasn't a noodle left in the bowl!
—**JANA RIPPEE** CASA GRANDE, AZ

START TO FINISH: 30 MIN.
MAKES: 4 SERVINGS

- 8 ounces thin flat rice noodles
- 1 tablespoon curry powder
- 1 pound uncooked shrimp (31–40 per pound), peeled and deveined
- 1 can (13.66 ounces) light coconut milk
- ¼ teaspoon salt
- ¼ teaspoon pepper
- ½ cup minced fresh cilantro
  Lime wedges, optional

1. Soak noodles according to package directions. Meanwhile, in a large dry skillet over medium heat, toast the curry powder until aromatic, about 1-2 minutes. Stir in shrimp, coconut milk, salt and pepper. Bring to a boil. Reduce heat; simmer, uncovered, 5-6 minutes or until shrimp turn pink.

2. Drain noodles. Add noodles and cilantro to pan; heat through. If desired, serve with lime wedges.

PER SERVING *1 cup equals 361 cal., 9 g fat (5 g sat. fat), 138 mg chol., 284 mg sodium, 44 g carb., 2 g fiber, 22 g pro.* ***Diabetic Exchanges:*** *3 lean meat, 2½ starch, 1 fat.*

CAJUN CATFISH SANDWICHES

Cajun Catfish Sandwiches

You won't miss the fat and calories in this lightened-up version of a restaurant classic. Serve alongside your favorite veggie and enjoy.

—SHAUNIECE FRAZIER LOS ANGELES, CA

START TO FINISH: 25 MIN.
MAKES: 4 SERVINGS

- ¾ teaspoon seasoned pepper
- ½ teaspoon chili powder
- ½ teaspoon cayenne pepper
- ¼ teaspoon seasoned salt
- 4 catfish fillets (4 ounces each)
- 2 teaspoons olive oil, divided
- 2 green onions, chopped
- 3 garlic cloves, minced
- ½ cup fat-free mayonnaise
- 4 French or kaiser rolls, split and toasted
- 4 romaine leaves

1. Combine the seasoned pepper, chili powder, cayenne and seasoned salt; sprinkle over fillets.
2. In a large skillet, cook the fillets in 1 teaspoon oil for 4-6 minutes on each side or until fish flakes easily with a fork. Remove and keep warm.
3. In the same skillet, saute onions in remaining oil until tender. Add garlic; cook 1 minute longer. Remove from the heat; stir in mayonnaise. Spread over roll bottoms; top each with a romaine leaf and fillet. Replace tops.

Tuna Burgers

My family was hesitant to try out these burgers when I first prepared them. They were so accustomed to the typical beef burger. But any skepticism they had disappeared after just one bite.

—KIM STOLLER SMITHVILLE, OH

START TO FINISH: 20 MIN.
MAKES: 4 SERVINGS

- 1 egg, beaten
- ½ cup dry bread crumbs
- ½ cup finely chopped celery
- ⅓ cup mayonnaise
- ¼ cup finely chopped onion
- 2 tablespoons chili sauce
- 1 pouch (6.4 ounces) light tuna in water
- 2 tablespoons butter
- 4 hamburger buns, split and toasted
  Lettuce leaves and sliced tomato, optional

1. In a small bowl, combine the first six ingredients; fold in tuna. Shape into four patties.
2. Melt butter in a skillet; cook patties for 4-5 minutes on each side or until lightly browned. Serve on buns with lettuce and tomato if desired.

California Shrimp Tacos with Corn Salsa

START TO FINISH: 25 MIN.
MAKES: 4 SERVINGS

- 1 can (11 ounces) Mexicorn, drained
- ¾ cup chopped seeded tomatoes
- ½ cup black beans, rinsed and drained
- ¼ cup minced fresh cilantro
- 3 garlic cloves, minced
- ¼ teaspoon pepper
- ½ cup guacamole
- 3 tablespoons reduced-fat ranch salad dressing
- 16 uncooked large shrimp, peeled and deveined
- 3 teaspoons chili powder
- ½ teaspoon Cajun seasoning
- 8 taco shells, warmed

1. In a small bowl, combine the first six ingredients. In another bowl, combine guacamole and salad dressing. Toss shrimp with chili powder and Cajun seasoning. In a large nonstick skillet coated with cooking spray, saute shrimp until pink, about 5 minutes.
2. Place two shrimp in each taco shell. Top with ⅓ cup corn salsa; drizzle with 1 tablespoon guacamole mixture.

Red Clam Sauce

This sensational basil-seasoned clam sauce will shake up your dinner routine.

—LAURA VALDEZ ARLINGTON, TX

START TO FINISH: 25 MIN.
MAKES: 4 SERVINGS

- 2 teaspoons minced garlic
- 2 tablespoons butter
- 1½ teaspoons olive oil
- 1 can (15 ounces) tomato sauce
- 1 can (6½ ounces) chopped clams, drained
- 1 tablespoon dried parsley flakes
- 1 tablespoon dried basil
- ⅛ teaspoon pepper
  Hot cooked linguine

In a large saucepan, saute garlic in butter and oil for 30 seconds. Add tomato sauce, clams and seasonings. Bring to a boil. Reduce heat; cover and simmer for 15 minutes, stirring sauce occasionally. Serve with linguine.

> "After trying fish tacos, I fell in love. I wanted to recreate them at home and thought, 'Why not use shrimp?' It's an affordable, healthy way to feed my seafood-loving family."
> —**KAYLA DOUTHITT** ELIZABETHTOWN, KY

CALIFORNIA SHRIMP TACOS WITH CORN SALSA

Creole Shrimp & Rice

Running out of time to make dinner? Turn to this light, simple weekday recipe with lots of Creole flavor.

—**ELSIE EPP** NEWTON, KS

PREP: 25 MIN. • **COOK:** 20 MIN.
MAKES: 4 SERVINGS

- 1 celery rib, chopped
- 1 small onion, chopped
- 1 small green pepper, chopped
- 1 tablespoon canola oil
- 1 garlic clove, minced
- 1 can (14½ ounces) diced tomatoes, undrained
- 2 tablespoons savory herb with garlic soup mix
- 1 teaspoon Worcestershire sauce
- 1 bay leaf
- ⅛ teaspoon cayenne pepper
- 1 pound cooked medium shrimp, peeled and deveined
- 2 cups hot cooked rice

1. In a large skillet, saute the celery, onion and green pepper in oil until tender. Add garlic; cook 1 minute longer. Add the tomatoes, soup mix, Worcestershire sauce, bay leaf and cayenne. Bring to a boil. Reduce heat; cover and simmer for 15 minutes.

2. Add shrimp; heat through. Discard bay leaf. Serve with rice.

FREEZE OPTION *Stir in shrimp but do not heat through. Cool mixture; freeze in freezer containers for up to 3 months. To use, partially thaw in refrigerator overnight. Heat through in a covered saucepan, gently stirring and adding a little water if necessary. Serve with rice.*

PER SERVING *¾ cup shrimp mixture with ½ cup rice equals 304 cal., 6 g fat (1 g sat. fat), 172 mg chol., 622 mg sodium, 34 g carb., 3 g fiber, 27 g pro.*
Diabetic Exchanges: 3 lean meat, 2 vegetable, 1½ starch.

Blackened Halibut

Try serving the spicy fillets with garlic mashed potatoes, hot, crusty bread and a crisp salad. This is what my family eats when we want to celebrate.

—**BRENDA WILLIAMS** SANTA MARIA, CA

START TO FINISH: 25 MIN.
MAKES: 4 SERVINGS

- 2 tablespoons garlic powder
- 1 tablespoon salt
- 1 tablespoon onion powder
- 1 tablespoon dried oregano
- 1 tablespoon dried thyme
- 1 tablespoon cayenne pepper
- 1 tablespoon pepper
- 2½ teaspoons paprika
- 4 halibut fillets (4 ounces each)
- 2 tablespoons butter

1. In a large resealable plastic bag, combine the first eight ingredients. Add halibut fillets, two at a time, and shake to coat.

2. In a large cast-iron skillet, cook fillets in butter over medium heat for 3-4 minutes on each side or until fish flakes easily with a fork.

PER SERVING *1 fillet equals 189 cal., 8 g fat (4 g sat. fat), 51 mg chol., 758 mg sodium, 3 g carb., 1 g fiber, 24 g pro.*
Diabetic Exchanges: 3 lean meat, 1 fat.

> Celery, **onion** and **green pepper** is a classic Creole combination called **holy trinity** or **Cajun mirepoix. Standard** mirepoix uses **carrots instead** of green pepper.

BLACKENED HALIBUT

SHRIMP & CHICKEN SAUSAGE WITH GRITS

EAT SMART

Shrimp & Chicken Sausage with Grits

START TO FINISH: 30 MIN.
MAKES: 5 SERVINGS

- 3 cups water
- 1 cup quick-cooking grits
- 4 ounces reduced-fat cream cheese, cubed
- 3 fully cooked spicy chicken sausage links (3 ounces each), cut into ½-inch slices
- 2 teaspoons canola oil, divided
- 2 garlic cloves, minced
- 2 green onions, chopped, divided
- 4 teaspoons whole wheat flour
- 1½ cups chicken broth
- ¼ cup fat-free evaporated milk
- 1 pound uncooked medium shrimp, peeled and deveined
- 1 medium tomato, chopped

1. In a large saucepan, bring the water to a boil. Slowly stir in grits. Reduce heat; cook and stir for 5-7 minutes or until thickened. Stir in cream cheese until melted.

2. Meanwhile, in a large skillet, brown sausage in 1 teaspoon oil. Remove and keep warm.

3. In the same pan, heat remaining oil over medium-high heat. Add garlic and half of the green onions; cook and stir for 1 minute. Stir in flour until blended; gradually whisk in broth and milk. Bring to a boil, stirring constantly; cook and stir 2 minutes or until thickened.

4. Stir in shrimp and sausage; cook for 3-5 minutes or until shrimp turn pink. Serve with grits; top with tomato and remaining green onion.

PER SERVING ¾ cup shrimp mixture with ¾ cup grits equals 367 cal., 13 g fat (5 g sat. fat), 161 mg chol., 810 mg sodium, 30 g carb., 2 g fiber, 31 g pro. **Diabetic Exchanges:** 4 lean meat, 2 starch, ½ fat.

**CHICKEN CORDON BLEU
PASTA, PAGE 192**

" Facebook fans of my blog, *Chef in Training,* inspired me to create this creamy pasta casserole out of ingredients I had on hand. Success! I took the dish for another flavorful spin and added a bit of smoky bacon and toasted bread crumbs. "

—**NIKKI BARTON** PROVIDENCE, UT
about her recipe, Chicken Cordon Bleu Pasta, on page 192

Oven Entrees

Beef & Ground Beef

169   172   180

Turn here for **cozy casseroles**, potpies, **zesty broiled sandwiches** and easy yet **elegant** baked entrees such as **veal cordon bleu** and **beef tenderloin** wrapped in a **savory** horseradish crust. These dishes prove you don't have to sacrifice **good taste** for **ease of preparation**.

Sauerbraten

Here's my simplified take on traditional German fare. The beef roast's definitive pickled flavor is sure to delight fans of Bavarian cuisine.

—**PATRICIA RUTHERFORD** WINCHESTER, IL

PREP: 25 MIN. + MARINATING
BAKE: 3 HOURS • **MAKES:** 6 SERVINGS

- 4 **cups water**
- 2 **cups red wine vinegar**
- 12 **whole cloves**
- 2 **bay leaves**
- 3 **teaspoons salt**
- 3 **teaspoons brown sugar**
- 1 **boneless beef chuck roast or rump roast (4 pounds)**
- ¼ **cup all-purpose flour**
- 2 **tablespoons canola oil**
- 1 **large onion, cut into wedges**
- 5 **medium carrots, cut into 1½-inch pieces**
- 2 **celery ribs, cut into 1½-inch pieces**

1. In a large bowl, combine the water, vinegar, cloves, bay leaves, salt and brown sugar. Remove 2 cups to a small bowl; cover and refrigerate. Pour remaining marinade into a 2-gal. resealable plastic bag. Add roast; seal bag and turn to coat. Refrigerate for 1-2 days, turning twice each day.
2. Discard marinade and spices. Pat roast dry; dredge in flour. In a large skillet over medium-high heat, brown roast in oil on all sides. Transfer to a small roasting pan. Add the onion, carrots, celery and reserved marinade.
3. Cover pan and bake at 325° for 3-3½ hours or until meat is tender. With a slotted spoon, remove meat and vegetables to a serving platter. Strain cooking juices; thicken if desired.

Old-Fashioned Pot Roast

Every time I serve this flavorful beef to friends, I get requests for the recipe. Some people I've shared the recipe with have prepared it with brisket instead of the round roast that I use.

—**GEORGIA EDGINGTON** CRYSTAL, MN

PREP: 15 MIN. • **BAKE:** 3 HOURS
MAKES: 8 SERVINGS

- 1 **beef eye round roast (3 to 4 pounds)**
- 1 **bottle (12 ounces) chili sauce**
- 1 **cup water**
- 1 **envelope onion soup mix**
- 4 **medium potatoes, cut into 1-inch pieces**
- 5 **medium carrots, cut into 1-inch pieces**
- 2 **celery ribs, cut into 1-inch pieces**

1. Place the roast in an ungreased roasting pan. Combine the chili sauce, water and soup mix; pour over roast. Cover and bake at 350° for 2 hours.
2. Cut roast into ½-in. slices; return to pan. Top with the potatoes, carrots and celery. Cover and bake 1 hour longer or until meat and vegetables are tender, stirring vegetables once.

Serve the **sauerbraten** with a **starchy side dish** to soak up the flavorful liquid. **Potatoes, noodles, spaetzle or dumplings** would all make **tasty** accompaniments.

HORSERADISH-ENCRUSTED BEEF TENDERLOIN

FREEZE IT
BBQ Meat Loaf Minis

START TO FINISH: 30 MIN.
MAKES: 6 SERVINGS

- 1 package (6 ounces) stuffing mix
- 1 cup water
- 2 tablespoons hickory smoke-flavored barbecue sauce
- 1 pound ground beef
- 1 cup (4 ounces) shredded cheddar cheese
  Additional hickory smoke-flavored barbecue sauce, optional

1. Preheat oven to 375°. In a large bowl, combine stuffing mix, water and 2 tablespoons barbecue sauce. Add beef; mix lightly but thoroughly. Place ⅓ cup mixture into each of 12 ungreased muffin cups, pressing lightly into cups.
2. Bake, uncovered, 18-22 minutes or until a thermometer reads 160°. Sprinkle tops with cheese; bake 2-4 minutes longer or until cheese is melted. If desired, serve with additional barbecue sauce.
FREEZE OPTION *Securely wrap and freeze cooled meat loaves in plastic wrap and foil. To use, partially thaw in refrigerator overnight. Unwrap meat loaves; reheat on a greased shallow baking pan in a preheated 350° oven until heated through and a thermometer inserted in center reads 165°.*

Use herb-seasoned **stuffing mix** in the meatballs or, for a **piquant** touch, prepare them with **cranberry** stuffing (available during the **holidays**).

Horseradish-Encrusted Beef Tenderloin

Wow friends and family with this tender beef in a golden horseradish crust. Roasted garlic boosts the robust flavor even more.
—LAURA BAGOZZI DUBLIN, OH

PREP: 30 MIN. + COOLING
BAKE: 45 MIN. + STANDING
MAKES: 8 SERVINGS

- 1 whole garlic bulb
- 1 teaspoon olive oil
- ⅓ cup prepared horseradish
- ¼ teaspoon salt
- ¼ teaspoon dried basil
- ¼ teaspoon dried thyme
- ¼ teaspoon pepper
- ⅓ cup soft bread crumbs
- 1 beef tenderloin roast (3 pounds)

1. Remove papery outer skin from garlic (do not peel or separate cloves). Cut top off garlic bulb; brush with oil. Wrap in heavy-duty foil. Bake at 425° for 30-35 minutes or until softened. Cool for 10-15 minutes.
2. Squeeze softened garlic into a small bowl; stir in the horseradish, salt, basil, thyme and pepper. Add bread crumbs; toss to coat. Spread over top of tenderloin. Place on a rack in a large shallow roasting pan.
3. Bake at 400° for 45-55 minutes or until meat reaches desired doneness (for medium-rare, a thermometer should read 145°; medium, 160°; well-done, 170°). Let meat stand for 10 minutes before slicing.
PER SERVING *about 5 ounces cooked beef equals 268 cal., 11 g fat (4 g sat. fat), 75 mg chol., 119 mg sodium, 4 g carb., 1 g fiber, 37 g pro.* **Diabetic Exchange:** *5 lean meat.*

"Kids can have fun helping to prepare these mini meat loaves in muffin cups. For extra spice, we sometimes add 2 teaspoons chili powder and 1 cup of salsa."

—LINDA CALL FALUN, KS

BBQ MEAT LOAF MINIS

**COUNTRY CHUCK ROAST
WITH MUSHROOM GRAVY**

Country Chuck Roast with Mushroom Gravy

This tender, savory roast practically melts in your mouth. It looks a bit more complex, but the hands-free oven time makes it my go-to company recipe on a cold day.

—MARY KAY LABRIE CLERMONT, FL

PREP: 20 MIN. • **COOK:** 2¼ HOURS
MAKES: 8 SERVINGS

- 1 **boneless beef chuck roast (2½ to 3 pounds)**
- 3 **garlic cloves, halved**
- 1 **tablespoon brown sugar**
- 1½ **teaspoons kosher salt**
- ½ **teaspoon pepper**
- 2 **tablespoons olive oil**
- 1 **large sweet onion, quartered**
- 1 **can (10½ ounces) condensed beef consomme, undiluted**
- 2 **tablespoons Worcestershire sauce**
- 1 **tablespoon stone-ground mustard**
- 1 **bay leaf**
- 3 **to 4 drops browning sauce, optional**
- ½ **pound sliced fresh mushrooms**
- 1 **bottle (12 ounces) light beer or nonalcoholic beer**
- 1 **teaspoon dried thyme**
- 3 **tablespoons cornstarch**
- 3 **tablespoons cold water**

1. With a sharp knife, cut six 1-in.-long slits in meat; insert a garlic clove half into each slit. Combine the brown sugar, salt and pepper; rub over roast.
2. In an ovenproof Dutch oven, brown roast in oil on all sides. Add the onion, consomme, Worcestershire sauce, mustard, bay leaf and, if desired, browning sauce.
3. Cover and bake at 350° for 1¾ to 2¼ hours or until meat is tender. Remove roast to a serving platter; keep warm.
4. Discard bay leaf. Add the mushrooms, beer and thyme to the pan. Bring to a boil. Cook until liquid is reduced by half. Combine cornstarch and water until smooth; gradually stir into pan. Bring to a boil; cook and stir for 2 minutes or until thickened. Serve with roast.

Reunion Meatballs

Whenever we attend a picnic or family get-together, people expect me to bring these saucy meatballs along with copies of the recipe. My aunt shared the recipe with me years ago.

—TONI KING LONDON, KY

PREP: 20 MIN. • **BAKE:** 1½ HOURS
MAKES: 8 SERVINGS

- ½ **cup milk**
- 1 **egg**
- 1 **medium onion, chopped**
- 3 **bacon strips, cooked and crumbled**
- ½ **cup crushed saltines (about 15 crackers)**
- 1½ **teaspoons salt**
- 1½ **pounds lean ground beef (90% lean)**
- ½ **pound bulk pork sausage**

SAUCE
- 1 **bottle (14 ounces) ketchup**
- 1¼ **cups water**
- ½ **cup white vinegar**
- ½ **cup packed brown sugar**
- 1 **medium onion, chopped**
- 1 **tablespoon chili powder**
- 1½ **teaspoon Worcestershire sauce**
   Dash salt

1. In a large bowl, combine the first six ingredients. Crumble beef and sausage over mixture and mix well. Shape into 1½-in. balls. Place in a greased 13x9-in. baking dish.
2. In a large saucepan, combine the sauce ingredients. Bring to a boil; reduce heat. Simmer, uncovered, for 5 minutes.
3. Pour over meatballs. Bake, uncovered, at 350° for 1½ hours or until a thermometer reads 160°.

Easy Zucchini Lasagna

No-cook lasagna noodles can save you prep and cleanup time. Since the noodles expand during baking, be sure not to overlap them. The noodles will touch the sides of the dish when finished baking.

—*TASTE OF HOME* TEST KITCHEN

PREP: 25 MIN. • **BAKE:** 40 MIN.
MAKES: 6 SERVINGS

- 1 **pound ground beef**
- ½ **cup chopped onion**
- 2 **jars (24 ounces, one 14 ounces) spaghetti sauce**
- 1 **can (15 ounces) crushed tomatoes**
- 1 **teaspoon dried basil**
- 1 **teaspoon dried oregano**
- 1 **teaspoon fennel seed, crushed**
- 1 **teaspoon minced garlic**
- 9 **no-cook lasagna noodles**
- 2 **cups sliced zucchini**
- 1 **cup ricotta cheese**
- 1 **carton (5 ounces) shredded Asiago cheese**

1. In a large skillet, cook beef and onion over medium heat until meat is no longer pink; drain. Stir in the spaghetti sauce, tomatoes, basil, oregano, fennel and garlic. Bring to a boil. Reduce heat; cover and simmer for 10 minutes.

2. Spread 1½ cups meat sauce in a greased 13x9-in. baking dish. Top with three noodles. Spread 1½ cups sauce to edges of noodles. Top with half of the zucchini, ½ cup ricotta cheese and ½ cup Asiago cheese. Repeat layers. Top with remaining noodles, sauce and Asiago cheese.

3. Cover dish and bake at 375° for 30 minutes. Uncover; bake 10-15 minutes longer or until bubbly. Let stand 5 minutes before cutting.

Hot Italian Wraps

The kids will love these pepperoni and beef wraps. They're easy to assemble because each tortilla is simply wrapped around a portion of hearty meat filling with a piece of string cheese.

—*TASTE OF HOME* TEST KITCHEN

START TO FINISH: 30 MIN.
MAKES: 6 SERVINGS

- 1 **pound ground beef**
- 1 **medium green pepper, chopped**
- ⅓ **cup chopped onion**
- 1 **can (8 ounces) pizza sauce**
- 30 **slices pepperoni**
- ½ **teaspoon dried oregano**
- 6 **flour tortillas (10 inches), warmed**
- 6 **pieces (1 ounce each) string cheese**

1. In a large skillet, cook the beef, green pepper and onion over medium heat until meat is no longer pink; drain. Stir in the pizza sauce, pepperoni and oregano.

2. Spoon about ½ cup beef mixture off-center on a tortilla; top with a piece of string cheese. Fold one side of tortilla over filling and roll up from the opposite side. Repeat.

3. Place seam side down on an ungreased baking sheet. Bake at 350° for 10 minutes or until cheese is melted.

FREEZE OPTION *Cool filling before making wraps. Individually wrap in foil and freeze in a resealable plastic freezer bag. To use, partially thaw overnight in refrigerator. Reheat foil-wrapped wraps on a baking sheet in a preheated 350° oven until heated through. Or, to reheat one wrap, remove foil and rewrap in paper towel; place on a microwave-safe plate. Microwave on high until heated through, turning once. Let stand 15 seconds.*

HOT ITALIAN WRAPS

BEEF NOODLE
CASSEROLE

Beef Noodle Casserole

This casserole is perfect when there's a busy day coming up, because you can prepare it ahead of time. The flavors blend together to create a delicious combination.

—GRACE LEMA WINTON, CA

PREP: 20 MIN. • **BAKE:** 45 MIN.
MAKES: 8-10 SERVINGS

- 1 package (8 ounces) egg noodles
- 2 pounds ground beef
- 1 large onion, chopped
- 1 medium green pepper, chopped
- 1 can (14¾ ounces) cream-style corn
- 1 can (10¾ ounces) condensed tomato soup, undiluted
- 1 can (8 ounces) tomato sauce
- 1 jar (2 ounces) sliced pimientos, drained
- 2 tablespoons chopped jalapeno pepper
- 1½ teaspoons salt
- ½ teaspoon chili powder
- ¼ teaspoon ground mustard
- ¼ teaspoon pepper
- 1 jar (4½ ounces) sliced mushrooms, drained
- 1½ cups (6 ounces) shredded cheddar cheese

1. Cook noodles according to package directions.
2. Meanwhile, in a large skillet, cook the beef, onion and green pepper over medium heat until the meat is no longer pink and vegetables are tender; drain. Add the next 10 ingredients. Drain noodles; stir into mixture.
3. Transfer to a greased 13x9-in. baking dish. Sprinkle with cheese. Bake casserole, uncovered, at 350° for 45 minutes or until heated through.
NOTE *Wear disposable gloves when cutting hot peppers; the oils can burn skin. Avoid touching your face.*

OPEN-FACED CHEESESTEAK SANDWICHES

Open-Faced Cheesesteak Sandwiches

You might need a fork and knife to tackle this big sandwich. Hot pepper sauce and pepper jack cheese add spicy heat to the roast beef and veggies.

—MICHAEL KLOTZ SCOTTSDALE, AZ

START TO FINISH: 30 MIN.
MAKES: 2 SERVINGS

- 1 French roll, split
- 2 teaspoons butter
- ¼ teaspoon garlic powder
- ½ cup julienned green pepper
- ¼ cup sliced onion
- ¼ teaspoon salt
- ¼ teaspoon pepper
- 2 tablespoons canola oil, divided
- ⅓ pound sliced deli roast beef
- ½ teaspoon hot pepper sauce
- 4 slices pepper jack cheese

1. Spread roll halves with butter; sprinkle with garlic powder. Set aside.
2. In a small skillet, saute the green pepper, onion, salt and pepper in 1 tablespoon oil until tender. Remove and keep warm. In the same skillet, saute beef and hot sauce in remaining oil until heated through. Spoon beef onto buns; top with pepper mixture and cheese.
3. Place on a baking sheet. Broil 2-3 in. from the heat 2-4 minutes or until cheese is melted.

Church Supper Hot Dish

This recipe was in my mother's church cookbook, and now it's in my church cookbook! Apparently is was too good to miss a generation. I often make this dish to take along to potlucks.

—**NORMA TURNER** HASLETT, MI

PREP: 40 MIN. • **BAKE:** 30 MIN.
MAKES: 8 SERVINGS

- 1 **pound ground beef**
- 2 **cups sliced peeled potatoes**
- 2 **cups finely chopped celery**
- ¾ **cup finely chopped carrots**
- ¼ **cup finely chopped green pepper**
- ¼ **cup finely chopped onion**
- 2 **tablespoons butter**
- 1 **cup water**
- 2 **cans (10¾ ounces each) condensed cream of mushroom soup, undiluted**
- 1 **can (5 ounces) chow mein noodles, divided**
- 1 **cup (4 ounces) shredded cheddar cheese**

1. In a large skillet, cook beef over medium heat until no longer pink; drain and set aside.

2. In same pan, saute potatoes, celery, carrots, green pepper and onion in butter 5 minutes. Add water; cover and simmer 10 minutes or until vegetables are tender. Stir in soup and cooked ground beef until blended.

3. Sprinkle half of the chow mein noodles into a greased shallow 2-qt. baking dish. Spoon meat mixture over top. Cover and bake at 350° for 20 minutes. Top with cheese and remaining noodles. Bake, uncovered, 10 minutes or until heated through.

CHURCH SUPPER HOT DISH

Chilies Rellenos Casserole

I love green chilies and cook with them often when I entertain. This easy version of the classic Mexican dish gives you big pepper taste in every meaty bite.

—**NADINE ESTES** ALTO, NM

PREP: 15 MIN. • **BAKE:** 45 MIN.
MAKES: 6 SERVINGS

- 1 **can (7 ounces) whole green chilies**
- 1½ **cups (6 ounces) shredded Colby-Monterey Jack cheese**
- ¾ **pound ground beef**
- ¼ **cup chopped onion**
- 1 **cup milk**
- 4 **eggs**
- ¼ **cup all-purpose flour**
- ¼ **teaspoon salt**
- ⅛ **teaspoon pepper**

1. Split chilies and remove seeds; dry on paper towels. Arrange chilies on the bottom of a greased 2-qt. baking dish. Top with cheese. In a skillet, cook beef and onion over medium heat until meat is no longer pink; drain. Spoon over the cheese.

2. In a bowl, beat milk, eggs, flour, salt and pepper until smooth; pour over beef mixture. Bake, uncovered, at 350° for 45-50 minutes or until a knife inserted near the center comes out clean. Let casserole stand 5 minutes before serving.

If you like **spicy** foods, substitute **chorizo** for the ground beef in the **chilies rellenos** casserole. Or **zip things up** with a sprinkling of **cumin**, chili powder or **taco seasoning**.

TACO BUBBLE PIZZA

EAT SMART
Marinated Beef Kabobs
A zesty marinade gives tongue-tingling orange flavor to these satisfying kabobs. Best of all, you can enjoy them year-round because they're made in the oven!

—**SUSIE FREEMAN** IRONS, MI

PREP: 15 MIN. + MARINATING
BROIL: 15 MIN.
MAKES: 2 SERVINGS

- 1 **small navel orange**
- ¾ **cup orange juice**
- 2 **tablespoons teriyaki sauce**
- 1 **tablespoon Dijon mustard**
- 2 **teaspoons honey**
- 2 **garlic cloves, minced**
- ⅛ **teaspoon pepper**
- ½ **pound beef top sirloin steak (1 inch thick)**
- 8 **large fresh mushrooms**
- 8 **medium green onions, cut into 2-inch pieces**
- 1 **teaspoon cornstarch**
- 2 **teaspoons cold water**
- 2 **cups hot cooked rice**

1. Grate orange peel; remove remaining peel and pith. Separate orange into segments. In a bowl, combine grated peel, orange juice, teriyaki sauce, mustard, honey, garlic and pepper. Cut beef into 1-in. cubes; place in a resealable plastic bag. Add oranges, mushrooms, onions and half of marinade. Seal bag; refrigerate overnight. Refrigerate remaining marinade for sauce.
2. Drain and discard marinade. On four metal or soaked wooden skewers, alternately thread beef, oranges and vegetables. Broil 3 in. from the heat for 15-20 minutes or until the meat reaches desired doneness and the vegetables are tender, turning often.
3. In a saucepan, combine cornstarch and water until smooth. Stir in the reserved marinade. Bring to a boil; cook and stir for 2 minutes. Serve over kabobs and rice.

PER SERVING *2 kabobs with ¼ cup sauce and 1 cup rice equals 503 cal., 8 g fat (3 g sat. fat), 67 mg chol., 631 mg sodium, 75 g carb., 5 g fiber, 34 g pro.*

Taco Bubble Pizza
Your entire family's going to be requesting this meal! Luckily for you, it's a cinch with tomato soup, refrigerated biscuits and taco seasoning. Set up a taco bar and let everyone add their favorite toppings.
—**DAWN SCHUTTER** TITONKA, IA

PREP: 20 MIN. • **BAKE:** 30 MIN.
MAKES: 8 SERVINGS

- 1½ **pounds lean ground beef (90% lean)**
- 1 **can (10¾ ounces) condensed tomato soup, undiluted**
- ¾ **cup water**
- 1 **envelope taco seasoning**
- 1 **can (12 ounces) refrigerated buttermilk biscuits**
- 2 **cups (8 ounces) shredded cheddar cheese**

TOPPINGS
- 2 **cups torn leaf lettuce**
- 2 **medium tomatoes, seeded and chopped**
- 1 **cup salsa**
- 1 **cup (8 ounces) sour cream**
- 1 **can (2¼ ounces) sliced ripe olives, drained**
  Green onions, optional

1. Cook the beef in a large skillet over medium heat until no longer pink; drain. Stir in the soup, water and taco seasoning; bring to a boil. Reduce heat; simmer, uncovered, for 3 minutes.
2. Meanwhile, cut each biscuit into 8 pieces. Remove beef mixture from heat and gently stir in the biscuits. Transfer to an ungreased 13x9-in. baking dish.
3. Bake, uncovered, at 375° for 20-25 minutes or until biscuits are golden brown. Sprinkle with cheese; bake 8-10 minutes longer or until cheese is melted. Serve with toppings.

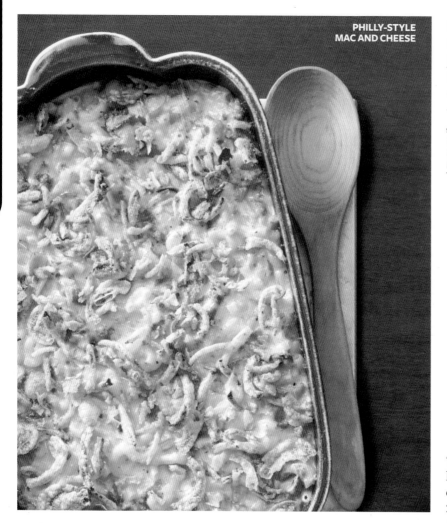

PHILLY-STYLE MAC AND CHEESE

Philly-Style Mac and Cheese

My son loves macaroni and cheese, and I'm always looking for ways to sneak in some veggies. This version is a huge hit with us both!

—JENNIFER BERRY LEXINGTON, OH

PREP: 30 MIN. • **BAKE:** 25 MIN.
MAKES: 6 SERVINGS

- 2 **cups uncooked elbow macaroni**
- ½ **pound sliced fresh mushrooms**
- 1 **medium onion, chopped**
- 1 **medium green pepper, chopped**
- ¼ **cup butter, cubed**
- ¼ **cup all-purpose flour**
- 1 **cup 2% milk**
- 1 **cup beef broth**
- 2 **cups (8 ounces) shredded provolone cheese**
- 2 **cups (8 ounces) shredded part-skim mozzarella cheese**
- 1 **teaspoon garlic powder**
- 1 **teaspoon Montreal steak seasoning**
- ½ **teaspoon onion powder**
- 1 **package (10½ ounces) frozen Steak-umm sliced steaks, browned**
- ½ **cup French-fried onions**

1. Cook macaroni according to package directions.
2. Meanwhile, in a large skillet, saute the mushrooms, onion and green pepper in butter until tender. Stir in flour until blended; gradually add milk and broth. Bring to a boil; cook and stir for 2 minutes or until thickened. Reduce heat. Stir in the cheeses, garlic powder, Montreal steak seasoning and onion powder.
3. Drain macaroni; add to the sauce mixture. Stir in steak. Transfer to an ungreased 13x9-in. baking dish; sprinkle fried onions over top. Bake, uncovered, at 350° for 25-30 minutes or until bubbly.

Onion Beef au Jus

Garlic and sweet onions make a flavorful juice for dipping these savory open-faced sandwiches. Any leftover beef makes delicious cold sandwiches, too.

—MARILYN BROWN WEST UNION, IA

PREP: 20 MIN.
BAKE: 2½ HOURS + STANDING
MAKES: 12 SERVINGS

- 1 **beef rump roast or bottom round roast (4 pounds)**
- 2 **tablespoons canola oil**
- 2 **large sweet onions, cut into ¼-inch slices**
- 6 **tablespoons butter, softened, divided**
- 5 **cups water**
- ½ **cup reduced-sodium soy sauce**
- 1 **envelope onion soup mix**
- 1 **garlic clove, minced**
- 1 **teaspoon browning sauce, optional**
- 1 **loaf (1 pound) French bread**
- 1 **cup (4 ounces) shredded Swiss cheese**

1. In a Dutch oven over medium-high heat, brown roast on all sides in oil; drain. In a large skillet, saute onions in 2 tablespoons of butter until tender. Add the water, soy sauce, soup mix, garlic and, if desired, browning sauce. Pour over roast.
2. Cover and bake at 325° for 2½ hours or until meat is tender.
3. Let meat stand for 10 minutes, then thinly slice. Return meat to pan juices. Split bread lengthwise; cut into 3-in. sections. Spread with remaining butter. Place on a baking sheet.
4. Broil bread 4-6 in. from the heat for 2-3 minutes or until golden brown. Top with beef and onions; sprinkle with cheese. Broil for 1-2 minutes or until cheese is melted. Serve with the cooking juices.

Quick Shepherd's Pie

Shepherd's pie is great with leftover homemade mashed potatoes, but it's tasty with ready-made spuds from the grocery store, too.

—**JENNIFER EARLY** EAST LANSING, MI

START TO FINISH: 25 MIN.
MAKES: 4 SERVINGS

- 1 tub (24 ounces) refrigerated cheddar mashed potatoes
- 1 pound lean ground beef (90% lean)
- 1 envelope mushroom gravy mix
- 1½ cups frozen mixed vegetables
- 1 cup water
- ⅛ teaspoon pepper

1. Heat potatoes according to the package directions.
2. Meanwhile, in a large skillet, cook beef over medium heat 6-8 minutes or until no longer pink, breaking into crumbles; drain. Stir in the gravy mix. Add vegetables and water; bring to boil. Reduce heat; cook until heated through, stirring occasionally.
3. Transfer to a 9-in.-square baking pan. Spread the potatoes over top; sprinkle with pepper. Broil 4-6 in. from the heat for 10-15 minutes or until golden brown.

Herb-Stuffed Red Peppers

We love to cook and experiment with new dishes in our house. We found this recipe online but were missing a few of the ingredients, so we improvised. Here's the tasty result!

—**BRENDA JOYNER** PATEROS, WA

PREP: 25 MIN. • **BAKE:** 35 MIN.
MAKES: 2 SERVINGS

- 2 large sweet red peppers
- 2 tablespoons water
- ½ pound ground beef
- ½ cup chopped onion
- 1½ cups cooked brown rice
- 1 tablespoon dried parsley flakes
- ¾ teaspoon salt
- ⅛ to ¼ teaspoon cayenne pepper
- ⅛ teaspoon ground allspice
- 1 can (8 ounces) tomato sauce
- ¼ cup chicken broth
- 2 teaspoons balsamic vinegar
- 1½ teaspoons dried basil
- 4 tablespoons grated Parmesan or Romano cheese, divided

1. Cut tops off peppers; remove the seeds. Place peppers and water in a microwave-safe bowl. Cover and microwave on high for 2-3 minutes or until crisp-tender; set aside.
2. In a small skillet, cook beef and onion over medium heat until meat is no longer pink; drain. Remove from the heat; stir in the rice, parsley, salt, cayenne and allspice.
3. In a small saucepan, bring tomato sauce and broth to a boil. Stir in the vinegar, basil and 3 tablespoons Parmesan cheese; stir about ½ cup sauce into rice mixture. Spoon into peppers. Place in a greased shallow 1-qt. baking dish.
4. Cover dish and bake at 350° for 30 minutes. Sprinkle with remaining Parmesan cheese. Bake, uncovered, for 5-10 minutes or until peppers are tender. Serve with remaining sauce.

HERB-STUFFED RED PEPPERS

Veal Cordon Bleu

I try to make varied meals for two that are appetizing and interesting. I sometimes double this recipe so we can have the leftovers for lunch.

—JEANNE MOLLOY FEEDING HILLS, MA

START TO FINISH: 30 MIN.
MAKES: 2 SERVINGS

- 8 **fresh asparagus spears, trimmed**
- 2 **tablespoons water**
- 2 **veal cutlets (6 ounces each)**
- ¼ **teaspoon salt**
- ⅛ **teaspoon pepper**
- 2 **garlic cloves, minced**
- 1 **tablespoon olive oil**
- 4 **large fresh mushrooms, sliced**
- 2 **thin slices prosciutto or deli ham**
- ½ **cup shredded Italian cheese blend**

1. Place asparagus and water in an 11x7-in. microwave-safe dish. Cover and microwave on high 2-3 minutes or until asparagus is crisp-tender; drain and set aside.

2. Flatten veal to ¼-in. thickness; sprinkle with salt and pepper. In a small skillet, saute garlic in oil. Add the veal; brown for 2-3 minutes on each side.

3. Transfer to an ungreased 11x7-in. baking dish. In the pan drippings, saute mushrooms until tender; spoon over veal. Top each cutlet with four asparagus spears and a slice of prosciutto. Sprinkle with cheese. Bake veal, uncovered, at 350° for 5-10 minutes or until juices run clear.

Pure olive oil works better for cooking than **virgin** or **extra-virgin** oil. These **higher grades** have a delicate flavor ideal for **cold foods**, but don't work as well for **cooking**.

CRANBERRY SHORT RIBS

Cranberry Short Ribs

This recipe originally came from my mother-in-law. Living in the bush in the Yukon, I sometimes substitute moose for the beef, and I pick wild cranberries in the fall. I prepare this comfort food often during the long winter months, and we never tire of it.

—CATHY WYLIE DAWSON CITY, YT

PREP: 20 MIN. • **BAKE:** 1½ HOURS
MAKES: 2 SERVINGS

- 1½ **pounds bone-in beef short ribs**
- ½ **teaspoon salt, divided**
- ¼ **teaspoon pepper**
- 1 **tablespoon all-purpose flour**
- 1 **tablespoon brown sugar**
- ⅛ **teaspoon ground mustard**
  Dash ground cloves
- ¾ **cup water**
- 2 **teaspoons cider vinegar**
- ½ **cup fresh or frozen cranberries**
- 1½ **to 2 teaspoons grated lemon peel**
- ½ **teaspoon browning sauce, optional**

1. Preheat oven to 350°. Place ribs in a greased 8-in.-square baking dish; sprinkle with ¼ teaspoon salt and pepper. Bake, covered, 1¼-1½ hours or until tender.

2. In a small saucepan, combine flour, brown sugar, mustard, cloves and remaining salt; gradually whisk in water and vinegar until smooth. Stir in cranberries, lemon peel and, if desired, browning sauce; bring to a boil. Cook and stir for 2 minutes or until thickened.

3. Drain ribs. Pour cranberry mixture over ribs and bake, uncovered, for 15 minutes.

"This recipe was inspired by my family's love of two things—beef stew and biscuits. After years of making the two separately, I put the biscuits on top of the stew like a cobbler. This dinner is as down-home as it gets."
—**JANINE TALLEY** ORLANDO, FL

SHORT RIB COBBLER

Short Rib Cobbler

PREP: 45 MIN. • **BAKE:** 3 HOURS
MAKES: 8 SERVINGS

- ½ cup plus 3 tablespoons all-purpose flour, divided
- 1¼ teaspoons salt, divided
- ½ teaspoon pepper
- 2 pounds well-trimmed boneless beef short ribs, cut into 1½-in. pieces
- 5 tablespoons olive oil, divided
- 1 large onion, chopped
- 1 medium carrot, chopped
- 1 celery rib, chopped
- 1 garlic clove, minced
- 2 tablespoons tomato paste
- 5 cups beef stock
- 1 cup dry red wine or additional beef stock
- 1 teaspoon poultry seasoning
- 1 bay leaf
- 1 package (14 ounces) frozen pearl onions, thawed
- 4 medium carrots, cut into 2-inch pieces

COBBLER TOPPING

- 2 cups biscuit/baking mix
- ⅔ cup 2% milk
  Fresh thyme leaves

1. Preheat oven to 350°. In a shallow bowl, mix ½ cup flour, ¾ teaspoon salt and pepper. Dip short ribs in the flour mixture to coat all sides; shake off excess.

2. In an ovenproof Dutch oven, heat 3 tablespoons oil over medium heat. Brown the beef in batches. Remove from pan.

3. In same pan, heat remaining oil over medium heat. Add onion, chopped carrot and celery; cook and stir 2-3 minutes or until tender. Add garlic; cook 1 minute longer. Stir in tomato paste and remaining flour until blended. Gradually stir in stock and wine until blended. Return beef to pan; stir in poultry seasoning, bay leaf and remaining salt. Bring to a boil.

4. Bake, covered, 1¾ hours. Stir in pearl onions and carrot pieces. Bake, covered, 30-45 minutes longer or until beef and onions are tender. Skim fat and remove bay leaf.

5. In a small bowl, mix biscuit mix and milk just until a soft dough forms.

Drop by scant ¼ cupfuls over beef mixture. Bake, uncovered, 40-45 minutes longer or until topping is golden brown. Sprinkle with thyme.

EAT SMART
Light Mexican Casserole

Here's a must-try dinner—a healthy layered casserole using whole wheat tortillas, lean beef and more veggies than traditional recipes.
—*TASTE OF HOME* **TEST KITCHEN**

PREP: 30 MIN. • **BAKE:** 25 MIN.
MAKES: 6 SERVINGS

- 1 pound extra-lean ground beef (95% lean)
- 1 medium onion, chopped
- 1 medium green pepper, chopped
- ¾ cup water
- 1 tablespoon all-purpose flour
- 1 tablespoon hot chili powder
- 1 teaspoon garlic powder
- ½ teaspoon ground cumin
- ½ teaspoon ground coriander
- ¼ teaspoon salt
- 1 can (16 ounces) refried beans
- ½ cup salsa
- 4 whole wheat tortillas (8 inches)
- 1 cup frozen corn
- ¾ cup shredded sharp cheddar cheese
  Shredded lettuce and chopped tomatoes, optional

1. In a large nonstick skillet, cook the beef, onion and green pepper over medium heat until meat is no longer pink. Stir in the water, flour, chili powder, garlic powder, cumin, coriander and salt. Bring to a boil. Reduce heat; simmer, uncovered, for 5-6 minutes or until thickened.

2. In a small bowl, combine beans and salsa. Place two tortillas in a round 2½-qt. baking dish coated with cooking spray. Layer with half of the beef mixture, bean mixture and corn; repeat layers. Top with cheese.

3. Bake, uncovered, at 350° for 25-30 minutes or until heated through. Let stand for 5 minutes before cutting. Serve with lettuce and tomatoes if desired.

PER SERVING *1 piece (calculated without lettuce and tomatoes) equals 367 cal., 11 g fat (5 g sat. fat), 64 mg chol., 657 mg sodium, 39 g carb., 8 g fiber, 26 g pro.* **Diabetic Exchanges:** *3 lean meat, 2½ starch, 1 vegetable, ½ fat.*

LIGHT MEXICAN CASSEROLE

**CORNED BEEF AND
COLESLAW SANDWICHES**

Corned Beef and Coleslaw Sandwiches

These open-faced sandwiches with layers of savory beef, creamy slaw and melted Swiss take only 15 minutes to create.

—**MARILOU ROBINSON** PORTLAND, OR

START TO FINISH: 15 MIN.
MAKES: 4 SERVINGS

- 2 cups coleslaw mix
- 3 tablespoons sour cream
- 4 teaspoons mayonnaise
- 1 tablespoon horseradish sauce
- 1 teaspoon prepared mustard
- ⅛ teaspoon salt
- 4 slices rye bread
- ½ pound thinly sliced corned beef
- 8 slices Swiss cheese

1. Place coleslaw mix in a small bowl. Combine sour cream, mayonnaise, horseradish sauce, mustard and salt. Pour over the coleslaw mix and toss to coat.

2. Place the bread on an ungreased baking sheet. Broil 4 in. from the heat for 2-3 minutes on each side or until toasted. Layer with the corned beef, coleslaw mixture and cheese. Broil for 2-3 minutes or until cheese is melted.

Ribeyes with Mushrooms

Here's an easy entree you can make for a special occasion—hearty ribeye steak with a quick, flavorful marinade and a hearty mushroom sauce.

—**LISSA HUTSON** PHELAN, CA

PREP: 5 MIN. + MARINATING
COOK: 10 MIN.
MAKES: 2 SERVINGS

- 8 green onions, sliced
- 2 garlic cloves, minced
- 1 cup beef broth
- 2 tablespoons balsamic vinegar
- ½ teaspoon dried thyme
- ½ teaspoon pepper
- 2 beef ribeye steaks (8 ounces each)
- 1 cup sliced fresh mushrooms

1. In a small bowl, combine the first six ingredients. Place the steaks in a large resealable plastic bag; add half of the marinade. Seal bag and turn to coat; refrigerate for 1-2 hours. Cover and refrigerate remaining marinade.
2. Drain and discard marinade from steaks. Broil steaks 4-6 in. from the heat for 5-6 minutes on each side or until meat reaches desired doneness (for medium-rare, a thermometer should read 145°; medium, 160°; well-done, 170°).
3. Meanwhile, place remaining marinade and the mushrooms in a small saucepan. Cook, stirring occasionally, over medium heat until mushrooms are tender. Serve with steaks.

Penne Beef Bake

EAT SMART

I had ground beef and veggies on hand, so I came up with this pizza-flavored casserole. I never expected my family to love it so much. It's a good way to sneak in some extra veggies for the kids.

—JENNIFER WISE SELINSGROVE, PA

PREP: 35 MIN. • **BAKE:** 25 MIN.
MAKES: 8 SERVINGS

- 1 package (12 ounces) whole wheat penne pasta
- 1 pound lean ground beef (90% lean)
- 2 medium zucchini, finely chopped
- 1 large green pepper, finely chopped
- 1 small onion, finely chopped
- 1 jar (24 ounces) spaghetti sauce
- 1½ cups reduced-fat Alfredo sauce
- 1 cup (4 ounces) shredded part-skim mozzarella cheese, divided
- ¼ teaspoon garlic powder

1. Cook penne according to package directions. Meanwhile, in a Dutch oven, cook the beef, zucchini, pepper and onion over medium heat until meat is no longer pink; drain. Stir in the spaghetti sauce, Alfredo sauce, ½ cup mozzarella cheese and garlic powder. Drain penne; stir into the meat mixture.

2. Transfer to a 13x9-in. baking dish coated with cooking spray. Cover and bake at 375° for 20 minutes. Sprinkle with remaining mozzarella cheese. Bake, uncovered, 3-5 minutes longer or until cheese is melted.

PER SERVING *1⅓ cups equals 395 cal., 12 g fat (6 g sat. fat), 62 mg chol., 805 mg sodium, 45 g carb., 7 g fiber, 25 g pro.* **Diabetic Exchanges:** *3 starch, 2 lean meat, 1 fat.*

Ground Beef 'n' Biscuits

A good friend gave me this recipe when I got married, and I have used it many times since. The family-pleasing dinner is quick to prepare and easy on the budget.

—LOIS HILL TRINITY, NC

PREP: 20 MIN. • **BAKE:** 20 MIN.
MAKES: 6 SERVINGS

- 1½ pounds ground beef
- ½ cup chopped celery
- ½ cup chopped onion
- 2 tablespoons all-purpose flour
- 1 teaspoon salt
- ¼ teaspoon dried oregano
- ⅛ teaspoon pepper
- 2 cans (8 ounces each) tomato sauce
- 1 package (10 ounces) frozen peas
- 1 tube (12 ounces) refrigerated buttermilk biscuits
- 1 cup (4 ounces) shredded cheddar cheese

1. In a large skillet, cook the beef, celery and onion over medium heat, until meat is no longer pink; drain. Stir in the flour, salt, oregano and pepper until blended. Add tomato sauce and peas; simmer for 5 minutes.

2. Place in a greased 13x9-in. baking dish. Separate biscuits; arrange over top. Sprinkle with cheese.

3. Bake, uncovered, at 350° for 20 minutes or until biscuits are golden brown and cheese is melted.

Bacon Cheeseburger Roll-Ups

My husband and I both love these roll-ups. I often serve them with broccoli and cheese. They must be good, because the recipe won a first-place prize at the Iowa State Fair!

—JESSICA CAIN DES MOINES, IA

PREP: 25 MIN. • **BAKE:** 20 MIN.
MAKES: 8 SERVINGS

- 1 pound ground beef
- 6 bacon strips, diced
- ½ cup chopped onion
- 1 package (8 ounces) process cheese (Velveeta), cubed
- 1 tube (16.3 ounces) large refrigerated buttermilk biscuits
- ½ cup ketchup
- ¼ cup yellow mustard

1. In a large skillet, cook the beef, bacon and onion over medium heat until meat is no longer pink; drain. Add cheese; cook and stir until melted. Remove from the heat.

2. Flatten biscuits into 5-in. circles; top each with ⅓ cup beef mixture. Fold sides and ends over filling and roll up. Place seam side down on a greased baking sheet. Bake at 400° for 18-20 minutes or until golden brown.

3. Combine ketchup and mustard; serve with roll-ups.

PENNE BEEF BAKE

Bavarian Beef Pie

I found this recipe in an old church cookbook of my grandmother's when I was in 4-H. With its unique combination of ingredients, it has an Old World flavor that folks always appreciate. I get rave reviews whenever I serve it.

—CINDY SECOR GRAHAM, WA

PREP: 45 MIN. • **BAKE:** 30 MIN.
MAKES: 3 SERVINGS

- 1 cup all-purpose flour
- ¼ teaspoon salt
- ⅓ cup shortening
- 2 egg yolks, divided
- ¼ teaspoon white vinegar
- 1 tablespoon plus 2 to 3 teaspoons cold water

FILLING

- 1 beef top sirloin steak (¾ pound), cut into ½-inch cubes
- 2 teaspoons canola oil
- 1 small potato, peeled and cut into ½-inch cubes
- 1 small onion, chopped
- ½ cup shredded peeled tart apple
- 1 tablespoon butter
- 1 garlic clove, minced
- 2 teaspoons all-purpose flour
- 1½ teaspoons beef bouillon granules
- 1 teaspoon minced fresh parsley
- ⅛ teaspoon celery seed
- ⅛ teaspoon dill weed
- ⅛ teaspoon dried thyme
- ⅛ teaspoon pepper
- ½ cup plus 2 teaspoons water, divided

1. In a small bowl, combine flour and salt; cut in the shortening until crumbly. Stir in 1 egg yolk and vinegar. Gradually add water, tossing with a fork until dough forms a ball.
2. Divide dough in half so one portion is slightly larger than the other. Cover and refrigerate for 30 minutes or until easy to handle.

3. Meanwhile, in a small skillet, brown beef in oil. Remove with a slotted spoon; set aside. In the same skillet, saute the potato, onion and apple in butter for 2-3 minutes or until onion is tender. Add garlic; cook 1 minute longer. Stir in flour until blended. Add the bouillon, seasonings, beef and ½ cup water. Bring to a boil; cook and stir for 2 minutes or until thickened.
4. On a lightly floured surface, roll out larger portion of dough to fit a 7-in. pie plate. Transfer pastry to pie plate; trim even with edge. Fill with beef mixture. Roll out remaining pastry to fit top of pie. Place over filling. Trim, seal and flute edges. Cut slits in pastry.
5. Beat remaining egg yolk and water; brush over pastry. Bake at 375° for 30-35 minutes or until golden brown.

FREEZE IT

Phyllo-Layered Pastichio

PREP: 1 HOUR • **BAKE:** 35 MIN. + STANDING
MAKES: 2 CASSEROLES (6 SERVINGS EACH)

- 1½ pounds ground beef
- 1 medium onion, chopped
- 1 garlic clove, minced
- 1 can (15 ounces) tomato sauce
- ¼ cup white wine or beef broth
- 1 cinnamon stick (3 inches)
- 1 bay leaf
- 1 teaspoon sugar
- ½ teaspoon salt
- ¼ teaspoon pepper

ASSEMBLY

- 1 pound ziti or other small tube pasta
- 1⅓ cups grated Romano cheese
- 4 eggs, lightly beaten
- ¾ cup butter, melted, divided
- 20 sheets phyllo dough (14x9 inches)

1. Preheat oven to 350°. In a large skillet, cook beef, onion and garlic over medium heat 6-8 minutes or until meat is no longer pink, breaking up beef into crumbles; drain.
2. Stir in tomato sauce, wine, cinnamon stick, bay leaf, sugar, salt and pepper. Bring to a boil; reduce heat and simmer 20-25 minutes or until thickened, stirring occasionally. Discard cinnamon stick and bay leaf.
3. Meanwhile, cook ziti according to package directions for al dente. Drain and return to pan. Stir in cheese, eggs and ¼ cup butter.
4. Place one sheet of phyllo dough on a work surface; brush with butter. Layer with nine additional phyllo sheets, brushing each layer. (Keep remaining phyllo covered with plastic wrap and a damp towel to prevent it from drying out.) Cut phyllo stack crosswise in half; place one stack in each of two greased 8-in.-square baking dishes.
5. In each dish, layer 2 cups pasta mixture and 1 cup sauce. Repeat layers. Prepare a second stack of 10 phyllo sheets, brushing each with butter; cut in half and place one stack over each dish.
6. Bake, uncovered, 35-40 minutes or until golden brown. Let stand for 15 minutes before cutting.
FREEZE OPTION *Cool unbaked casseroles; cover and freeze. To use, partially thaw in the refrigerator overnight. Remove from refrigerator 30 minutes before baking. Preheat oven to 350°. Bake casseroles as directed, increasing the baking time to 60-70 minutes or until golden brown and a thermometer inserted in center reads 165°.*

Also spelled **pastitsio**, pastichio is a **Greek** version of **lasagna**. The layered dish generally consists of cooked **ziti** or macaroni, ground **beef** or lamb, **cinnamon** and a **white sauce**. This **simplified version** doesn't use a white sauce and adds a **flaky** phyllo top.

"My grandfather always made pastichio on special occasions or when we had guests coming for dinner. I cherish the happy memories I have of him teaching me how to cook one of his signature dishes."
—TINA WAISMAN SAFETY HARBOR, FL

PHYLLO-LAYERED PASTICHIO

Poultry

184   190   197

When you're craving **down-home flavor**, turn to the **heartwarming** dishes on these pages. From old-fashioned favorites like **roasted chicken** and **turkey tetrazzini** to **fresh twists** such as tropical **game hens** and good-for-you **"fried" chicken**, you'll find a dish to suit every occasion.

APPLE-SAGE ROASTED TURKEY

Chicken Parmigiana

My family loves Italian food, and chicken parmigiana is one of our favorites. Since most of the recipes I found for it were time-consuming, I came up with this version that bakes in about half an hour.
—**ROBIN STEVENS** CADIZ, KY

PREP: 15 MIN. • **BAKE:** 25 MIN.
MAKES: 4 SERVINGS

   4 **boneless skinless chicken breast halves (4 ounces each)**
   1 **can (6 ounces) tomato paste**
   ¾ **cup water**
   2 **garlic cloves, minced**
   1 **tablespoon dried parsley flakes**
   1 **teaspoon salt**
   ¼ **teaspoon pepper**
   ½ **teaspoon Italian seasoning**
   ½ **teaspoon dried oregano**
   ¼ **teaspoon crushed red pepper flakes, optional**
   2 **cups (8 ounces) shredded part-skim mozzarella cheese**
   ¼ **cup grated Parmesan cheese**

1. Place the chicken in a greased 8-in.-square baking dish. In a small saucepan, bring the tomato paste, water, garlic and seasonings to a boil. Pour over chicken.
2. Bake, uncovered, at 400° for 15 minutes. Sprinkle with cheeses; bake 10-15 minutes longer or until a thermometer reads 165°.

This **version** of chicken parmigiana is **quick** because you **don't bread or brown** the chicken first. Serve it with **hot cooked spaghetti** for a classic accompaniment.

FREEZE IT
Apple-Sage Roasted Turkey

A hint of sweet apple flavor gives this classic recipe a new spin that will appeal to even your pickiest eaters. As this moist and beautiful turkey cooked, the lovely aroma had everybody talking.
—**SUZY HORVATH** MILWAUKIE, OR

PREP: 20 MIN.
BAKE: 3½ HOURS + STANDING
MAKES: 14 SERVINGS

   ½ **cup apple cider or juice**
   ½ **cup apple jelly**
   ⅓ **cup butter, cubed**
TURKEY
   ⅓ **cup minced fresh sage**
   ¼ **cup butter, softened**
   1 **turkey (14 to 16 pounds)**
   2 **tablespoons apple cider or juice**
   1½ **teaspoons salt**
   1½ **teaspoons pepper**
   2 **large apples, cut into wedges**
   1 **large onion, cut into wedges**
   8 **fresh sage leaves**

1. Preheat oven to 325°. In a small saucepan, combine the apple cider, jelly and butter. Cook and stir until butter is melted. Remove from heat and set aside.

2. In a small bowl, combine minced sage and butter. With your fingers, carefully loosen skin from the turkey breast; rub butter mixture under the skin. Brush turkey with apple cider. Sprinkle salt and pepper over turkey and inside cavity.
3. Place apples, onion and sage leaves inside the cavity. Tuck wings under the turkey; tie drumsticks together. Place breast side up on a rack in a roasting pan.
4. Bake, uncovered, 3½-4 hours or until a thermometer reads 180°, basting occasionally with cider mixture. Cover loosely with foil if turkey browns too quickly. Cover and let stand 20 minutes before slicing.
FREEZE OPTION *Place sliced turkey in freezer containers; top with any cooking juices. Cool and freeze. To use, partially thaw in the refrigerator overnight. Heat through in a covered saucepan, gently stirring and adding a little broth or water if necessary.*

PIZZA CHICKEN ROLL-UPS

3. Bake, uncovered, at 400° for 20-25 minutes or until heated through and cheese is melted. Let stand for 10 minutes before serving. Serve with salsa and sour cream if desired.

FREEZE OPTION *Cover and freeze unbaked casserole for up to 3 months. Thaw in the refrigerator overnight. Remove from refrigerator 30 minutes before baking. Bake as directed or until lasagna is heated through and a thermometer inserted in center reads 165°.*

PER SERVING *1 piece (calculated without salsa and sour cream) equals 282 cal., 11 g fat (3 g sat. fat), 57 mg chol., 697 mg sodium, 27 g carb., 2 g fiber, 22 g pro.* **Diabetic Exchanges:** *2 lean meat, 1½ starch, 1 fat.*

Pizza Chicken Roll-Ups

I love the spinach and cream cheese chicken roll-ups that my mom used to make for special occasions. My own kids wouldn't eat those, so I came up with a pizza-flavored version that they absolutely go crazy for.

—TANJA PENQUITE OREGON, OH

PREP: 10 MIN. • **BAKE:** 40 MIN.
MAKES: 4 SERVINGS

- 4 boneless skinless chicken breast halves (4 ounces each)
- 12 pepperoni slices
- 8 slices slices part-skim mozzarella cheese
- 1 can (15 ounces) pizza sauce

1. Flatten chicken to ¼-in. thickness. Place three slices of pepperoni and one slice of cheese on each. Roll up tightly; secure with toothpicks. Place in a greased 11x7-in. baking dish. Spoon pizza sauce over top.
2. Cover dish and bake at 350° for 35-40 minutes or until chicken is no longer pink. Uncover; top with the remaining cheese. Bake 5 minutes longer or until cheese is melted.

EAT SMART **FREEZE IT**
Turkey Enchilada Lasagna

The whole family will love the familiar Southwestern flavors in this tasty dish.
—JULIE CACKLER WEST DES MOINES, IA

PREP: 25 MIN. • **BAKE:** 20 MIN. + STANDING
MAKES: 8 SERVINGS

- 1 pound lean ground turkey
- 1 large onion, chopped
- 1 large green pepper, chopped
- 1 small sweet red pepper, chopped
- 1 package (8 ounces) fat-free cream cheese
- 1 teaspoon chili powder
- 1 can (10 ounces) enchilada sauce
- 6 whole wheat flour tortillas (8 inches)
- 1 cup (4 ounces) shredded reduced-fat Mexican cheese blend
  Salsa and sour cream, optional

1. In a large skillet, cook the turkey, onion and peppers over medium heat until meat is no longer pink; drain. Stir in cream cheese and chili powder.
2. Pour enchilada sauce into a shallow bowl. Dip the tortillas in sauce to coat. Place two tortillas in a 13x9-in. baking dish coated with cooking spray; spread with half of the turkey mixture. Sprinkle with ⅓ cup cheese. Repeat layers. Top with remaining tortillas and cheese.

EAT SMART
Oven-Fried Chicken Drumsticks

PREP: 20 MIN. + MARINATING
BAKE: 40 MIN. • **MAKES:** 4 SERVINGS

- 1 cup fat-free plain Greek yogurt
- 1 tablespoon Dijon mustard
- 2 garlic cloves, minced
- 8 chicken drumsticks (4 ounces each), skin removed
- ½ cup whole wheat flour
- 1½ teaspoons paprika
- 1 teaspoon baking powder
- 1 teaspoon salt
- 1 teaspoon pepper
  Olive oil-flavored cooking spray

1. In a large resealable plastic bag, combine the yogurt, mustard and garlic. Add chicken; seal bag and turn to coat. Refrigerate for 8 hours or overnight.
2. Preheat oven to 425°. In another plastic bag, mix flour, paprika, baking powder, salt and pepper. Remove chicken from marinade and add, one piece at a time, to flour mixture; close bag and shake to coat. Place on a wire rack over a baking sheet; spritz with cooking spray. Bake 40-45 minutes or until a thermometer reads 180°.

PER SERVING *2 chicken drumsticks equals 227 cal., 7 g fat (1 g sat. fat), 81 mg chol., 498 mg sodium, 9 g carb., 1 g fiber, 31 g pro.* **Diabetic Exchanges:** *4 lean meat, ½ starch.*

"This fabulous recipe uses an easy Greek yogurt marinade that makes the chicken incredibly moist. No one will guess this lightened-up version wasn't fried!"

—**KIMBERLY WALLACE** DENNISON, OH

OVEN-FRIED CHICKEN DRUMSTICKS

Turkey Spaghetti Casserole

My mom often made this creamy spaghetti when I was growing up. Whenever I have any leftover chicken or turkey, I look forward to preparing this simple, tasty dinner.

—**CASANDRA HETRICK** LINDSEY, OH

PREP: 30 MIN. • **BAKE:** 1¼ HOURS
MAKES: 6 SERVINGS

- 1 medium onion, chopped
- 1 medium carrot, chopped
- 1 celery rib, chopped
- ⅓ cup sliced fresh mushrooms
- 1 tablespoon butter
- 2½ cups reduced-sodium chicken broth
- 1 can (10¾ ounces) reduced-fat reduced-sodium condensed cream of mushroom soup, undiluted
- ¼ teaspoon salt
- ¼ teaspoon pepper
- 2½ cups cubed cooked turkey breast
- 6 ounces uncooked spaghetti, broken into 2-inch pieces
- ½ cup shredded reduced-fat Colby-Monterey Jack cheese
- ½ teaspoon paprika

1. In a small skillet, saute vegetables in butter until tender. In a large bowl, combine the chicken broth, soup, salt and pepper.

2. In a 2½-qt. baking dish coated with cooking spray, layer the turkey, spaghetti and vegetable mixture. Pour broth mixture over the top.

3. Cover dish and bake at 350° for 70-80 minutes or until the spaghetti is tender, stirring once. Uncover; sprinkle with cheese and paprika. Bake 5-10 minutes longer or until cheese is melted.

PER SERVING *1 cup equals 284 cal., 6 g fat (3 g sat. fat), 62 mg chol., 702 mg sodium, 30 g carb., 3 g fiber, 26 g pro.* **Diabetic Exchanges:** *3 lean meat, 1½ starch, 1 vegetable, ½ fat.*

Baked Caesar Chicken

This chicken has a cult following among my friends. One friend ran it in her child's fundraising cookbook as a dish that's so simple, children will enjoy helping to make it. I even prepared it once on a tugboat!

—**KIRSTEN NORGAARD** ASTORIA, OR

PREP: 10 MIN. • **BAKE:** 30 MIN.
MAKES: 4 SERVINGS

- 4 boneless skinless chicken breast halves (6 ounces each)
- ½ cup fat-free creamy Caesar salad dressing
- 1 medium ripe avocado, peeled and cubed
- ¼ cup shredded Parmesan cheese, divided

1. Place chicken in an 11x7-in. baking dish coated with cooking spray.

2. In a small bowl, combine the salad dressing, avocado and 2 tablespoons cheese; spoon over chicken. Bake, uncovered, at 375° for 30-35 minutes or until a thermometer reads 170°. Sprinkle with remaining cheese.

PER SERVING *1 chicken breast half equals 320 cal., 12 g fat (3 g sat. fat), 98 mg chol., 530 mg sodium, 15 g carb., 4 g fiber, 38 g pro.* **Diabetic Exchanges:** *5 lean meat, 1 starch, 1 fat.*

BAKED CAESAR CHICKEN

Turkey-Stuffed Bell Peppers

This lactose-free meal is so tasty, you won't even miss having real cheddar cheese. Round out the dinner with a salad or a side of rice.

—**JUDY HAND-TRUITT** BIRMINGHAM, AL

PREP: 30 MIN. • **BAKE:** 20 MIN.
MAKES: 5 SERVINGS

- 5 **medium green peppers**
- 1 **large onion, chopped**
- 2 **teaspoons olive oil**
- 1¼ **pounds extra-lean ground turkey**
- 2 **teaspoons ground cumin**
- 1 **teaspoon Italian seasoning**
- 1 **garlic clove, minced**
- ½ **teaspoon salt**
- ½ **teaspoon pepper**
- 1 **package (7 ounces) shredded cheddar-flavored soy cheese**
- 2 **medium tomatoes, finely chopped**
- 1½ **cups soft bread crumbs**
- ¼ **teaspoon paprika**

1. Cut peppers in half lengthwise; discard seeds. In a Dutch oven, cook peppers in boiling water 3-5 minutes or until crisp-tender. Drain and rinse in cold water; set aside.

2. In a large skillet, saute onion in oil until tender. Add the turkey, cumin, Italian seasoning, garlic, salt and pepper; cook and stir over medium heat until meat is no longer pink.

3. Transfer to a large bowl; stir in the soy cheese, tomatoes and bread crumbs. Spoon into pepper halves. Place in a 15x10x1-in. baking pan coated with cooking spray. Sprinkle with paprika.

4. Bake peppers, uncovered, at 325° for 20-25 minutes or until heated through and peppers are tender.

PER SERVING *2 filled pepper halves equals 323 cal., 10 g fat (trace sat. fat), 45 mg chol., 771 mg sodium, 20 g carb., 4 g fiber, 40 g pro.* **Diabetic Exchanges:** *5 lean meat, 2 vegetable, 1 starch, ½ fat.*

Chicken and Shells Dinner

Like most kids, mine love macaroni and cheese. The addition of chicken and peas turns it into a satisfying one-dish meal they never refuse.

—**LEEANN MCCUE** CHARLOTTE, NC

PREP: 15 MIN. • **BAKE:** 20 MIN.
MAKES: 4-6 SERVINGS

- 1 **package (12 ounces) shells and cheese dinner mix**
- ¼ **cup chopped onion**
- 4 **tablespoons butter, divided**
- 2 **cups cubed cooked chicken**
- 1 **package (10 ounces) frozen peas, thawed**
- ⅔ **cup mayonnaise**
- ⅓ **cup seasoned bread crumbs**

1. Prepare dinner mix according to package directions. Meanwhile, in a small skillet, saute the onion in 2 tablespoons butter until tender.

2. Stir the chicken, peas, mayonnaise and sauteed onion into dinner mix.

3. Transfer to a greased 1½-qt. baking dish. Melt remaining butter; toss with bread crumbs. Sprinkle over top. Bake, uncovered, at 350° for 20-25 minutes or until bubbly.

Green peppers are unripened versions of red, yellow or orange peppers. They are less expensive because they're quicker to get to market. Use colored peppers in recipes for more sweetness.

PIZZA ON A STICK

Pizza on a Stick

My daughter and her friends had fun turning sausage, pepperoni, veggies and pizza dough into these cute kabobs.

—**CHARLENE WOODS** NORFOLK, VA

START TO FINISH: 30 MIN.
MAKES: 5 SERVINGS

- 8 **ounces Italian turkey sausage links**
- 2 **cups whole fresh mushrooms**
- 2 **cups cherry tomatoes**
- 1 **medium onion, cut into 1-inch pieces**
- 1 **large green pepper, cut into 1-inch pieces**
- 30 **slices turkey pepperoni (2 ounces)**
- 1 **tube (13.8 ounces) refrigerated pizza crust**
- 1½ **cups (6 ounces) shredded part-skim mozzarella cheese**
- 1¼ **cups pizza sauce, warmed**

1. Preheat oven to 400°. In a large nonstick skillet, cook sausage over medium heat until no longer pink; drain. When cool enough to handle, cut sausage into 20 pieces. On 10 metal or wooden skewers, alternately thread the sausage, vegetables and pepperoni.

2. Unroll pizza dough onto a lightly floured surface; cut widthwise into 1-in.-wide strips. Starting at the pointed end of a prepared skewer, pierce skewer through one end of dough strip. Spiral-wrap dough strip around skewer, allowing vegetables and meats to peek through. Wrap the remaining end of dough strip around skewer above the first ingredient. Repeat with remaining dough strips and prepared skewers.

3. Arrange kabobs on a baking sheet coated with cooking spray. Bake for 10-12 minutes or until vegetables are tender and pizza crust is golden. Immediately sprinkle with cheese. Serve with pizza sauce.

PER SERVING *2 kabobs with ¼ cup sauce equals 400 cal., 13 g fat (5 g sat. fat), 58 mg chol., 1,208 mg sodium, 42 g carb., 4 g fiber, 28 g pro.* **Diabetic Exchanges:** *3 lean meat, 2 starch, 2 vegetable, 1 fat.*

Savory Rubbed Roast Chicken

A blend of paprika, onion powder, garlic and cayenne go on the skin and inside the cavity to create a delicious, slightly spicy roast chicken. The aroma of this dish while it's cooking drives my family nuts.

—**MARGARET COLE** IMPERIAL, MO

PREP: 20 MIN.
BAKE: 2 HOURS + STANDING
MAKES: 8 SERVINGS

- 2 **teaspoons paprika**
- 1 **teaspoon salt**
- 1 **teaspoon onion powder**
- 1 **teaspoon dried thyme**
- 1 **teaspoon white pepper**
- 1 **teaspoon cayenne pepper**
- ¾ **teaspoon garlic powder**
- ½ **teaspoon pepper**
- 1 **roasting chicken (6 to 7 pounds)**
- 1 **large onion, peeled and quartered**

1. In a small bowl, combine the seasonings; set aside. Place chicken breast side up on a rack in a shallow roasting pan; pat dry. Rub seasoning mixture over the outside and inside of chicken. Place onion inside cavity. Tuck wings under chicken; tie drumsticks together.

2. Bake, uncovered, at 350° for 2-2½ hours or until a thermometer inserted in thickest part of thigh reads 170°-175°, basting occasionally with pan drippings. (Cover loosely with foil if chicken browns too quickly.) Cover chicken and let stand for 15 minutes before carving.

SAVORY RUBBED ROAST CHICKEN

MEXICAN SMOTHERED
CHICKEN THIGHS

Turkey Tetrazzini

This recipe turns our leftover turkey into a whole new meal! We look forward to having it after Christmas and Thanksgiving and other times when I roast a bird for a family gathering.

—SUSAN PAYNE CORNER BROOK, NL

PREP: 25 MIN. • **BAKE:** 25 MIN.
MAKES: 4-6 SERVINGS

- 1 **package (7 ounces) thin spaghetti, broken in half**
- 2 **cups cubed cooked turkey**
- 1 **cup sliced fresh mushrooms**
- 1 **small onion, chopped**
- 3 **tablespoons butter**
- 1 **can (10¾ ounces) condensed cream of mushroom soup, undiluted**
- 1 **cup milk**
- ½ **teaspoon poultry seasoning**
- ⅛ **teaspoon ground mustard**
- 1 **cup (4 ounces) shredded cheddar cheese**
- 1 **cup (4 ounces) shredded part-skim mozzarella cheese**
- 1 **tablespoon shredded Parmesan cheese**
  Minced fresh parsley

1. Cook the spaghetti according to package directions. Drain and place in a greased 11x7-in. baking dish. Top with turkey; set aside.

2. In a large skillet, saute mushrooms and onion in butter until tender. Whisk in the soup, milk, poultry seasoning and mustard until blended. Add cheddar cheese; cook and stir over medium heat until melted. Pour over turkey.

3. Sprinkle with mozzarella and Parmesan cheeses (baking dish will be full). Bake, uncovered, at 350° for 25-30 minutes or until heated through. Sprinkle with parsley.

FREEZE IT

Mexican Smothered Chicken Thighs

Chicken thighs are a juicier, less expensive alternative to boneless skinless chicken breasts. They're used to perfection in this Mexican-inspired dish.

—JEANNIE TRUDELL DEL NORTE, CO

PREP: 20 MIN. • **BAKE:** 30 MIN.
MAKES: 8 SERVINGS

- 1 **cup all-purpose flour**
- 1 **tablespoon seasoned salt**
- 1 **teaspoon salt**
- 1 **teaspoon pepper**
- ¾ **cup 2% milk**
- 8 **bone-in chicken thighs (about 3 pounds), skin removed**
- 3 **tablespoons olive oil**
- 1 **medium onion, chopped**
- 2 **jalapeno peppers, seeded and chopped**
- 2 **cans (8 ounces each) tomato sauce**
- 1 **cup water**
- 1 **tablespoon chili powder**
- 2 **teaspoons garlic powder**
- 2 **teaspoons ground cumin**

1. In a shallow bowl, combine the flour, seasoned salt, salt and pepper. Place milk in a separate shallow bowl. Coat the chicken with flour mixture, then dip in milk and coat again with flour mixture.

2. In a large skillet, brown chicken in oil in batches. Transfer to a greased 13x9-in. baking dish.

3. In the same skillet, saute the onion and jalapenos until tender. Add the tomato sauce, water and spices. Bring to a boil. Reduce the heat; simmer, uncovered, for 5 minutes or until thickened, stirring occasionally. Pour over chicken.

4. Cover and bake chicken at 350° for 30-35 minutes or until a thermometer reads 170°-175°.

FREEZE OPTION *Place cooled chicken with sauce in freezer containers. To use, partially thaw in refrigerator overnight. Heat through in a covered skillet, gently stirring and adding a little broth or water if necessary.*

NOTE *Wear disposable gloves when cutting hot peppers; the oils can burn skin. Avoid touching your face.*

Just-Like-Thanksgiving Turkey Meat Loaf

For a holiday-esque meal any time of year, this tender turkey meat loaf is perfect. Complemented with a cranberry glaze, it's a mouthwatering dish.

—**MOLLIE BROWN** LOS ANGELES, CA

PREP: 30 MIN. + STANDING • **BAKE:** 45 MIN.
MAKES: 6 SERVINGS

- 1 cup seasoned stuffing cubes
- ½ cup milk
- 1 egg, beaten
- 1 celery rib, finely chopped
- 1 small onion, grated
- 1 small carrot, grated
- ¼ cup dried cranberries
- ½ teaspoon salt
- ¼ teaspoon pepper
- 3 to 4½ teaspoons minced fresh sage
- 3 teaspoons minced fresh rosemary
- 1½ pounds lean ground turkey
- ½ cup whole-berry cranberry sauce
- ½ cup ketchup
- ⅛ teaspoon hot pepper sauce

1. Preheat oven to 375°. In a large bowl, combine stuffing cubes and milk. Let stand 10 minutes; break up stuffing cubes with a fork. Stir in egg, celery, onion, carrot, cranberries, salt and pepper. Combine sage and rosemary; add half to the mixture. Crumble turkey over mixture and mix well. Pat into an ungreased 9x5-in. loaf pan.

2. Bake, uncovered, 25 minutes; drain if necessary. Combine cranberry sauce, ketchup, pepper sauce and remaining herbs; spread over meat loaf. Bake 20-25 minutes or until no pink remains and a thermometer reads 165°.

FREEZE OPTION *Shape meat loaf in plastic wrap-lined loaf pan; cover and freeze until firm. Remove from pan and wrap securely in foil; return to freezer. To use, unwrap meat loaf and bake in pan as directed, increasing time as necessary for a thermometer inserted in center to read 165°.*

JUST-LIKE-THANKSGIVING TURKEY MEAT LOAF

Home-Style Chicken Potpie

I served this potpie along with chili for a bowl game. No one ate the chili. In fact, one of my husband's friends called the next day and asked for the leftover pie.

—**DARLENE CLAXTON** BRIGHTON, MI

PREP: 1 HOUR + CHILLING
BAKE: 25 MIN. + STANDING
MAKES: 10-12 SERVINGS

- ¾ cup cold butter, cubed
- 2 cups all-purpose flour
- 1 cup (4 ounces) shredded cheddar cheese
- ¼ cup cold water

FILLING

- 2½ cups halved baby carrots
- 3 celery ribs, sliced
- 6 tablespoons butter, cubed
- 7 tablespoons all-purpose flour
- 1 teaspoon salt
- ¼ teaspoon coarsely ground pepper
- 2½ cups chicken broth
- 1 cup heavy whipping cream
- 4 cups cubed cooked chicken
- 1 cup frozen pearl onions, thawed
- 1 cup frozen peas, thawed
- 3 tablespoons minced chives
- 3 tablespoons minced fresh parsley
- 2 teaspoons minced fresh thyme or ½ teaspoon dried thyme
- 1 egg, lightly beaten

1. In a large bowl, cut butter into flour until crumbly. Stir in cheese. Gradually add water, tossing with a fork until dough forms a ball. Cover and refrigerate for at least 1 hour.

2. In a large saucepan, cook carrots and celery in a small amount of water until crisp-tender; drain and set aside.

3. In another pan, melt butter. Whisk in the flour, salt and pepper until smooth. Gradually whisk in broth and cream. Bring to a boil; cook and stir for 2 minutes or until thickened. Stir in the carrot mixture, chicken, onions, peas and herbs; heat through. Place in a greased 13x9-in. baking dish.

4. On a floured surface, roll out dough to fit top of dish; cut out vents. Place dough over filling; trim and flute edges. Brush with egg. Bake at 400° for 25-30 minutes or until bubbly and crust is golden brown. Let stand for 10 minutes before serving.

PESTO-TURKEY LAYERED LOAF

Pesto-Turkey Layered Loaf

This yummy sandwich is easy to make and travels well to picnics and potlucks. Use any meat, veggies and cheese you like.

—**MARION SUNDBERG** YORBA LINDA, CA

PREP: 20 MIN. • **BAKE:** 25 MIN. + STANDING
MAKES: 6 SERVINGS

- 1 loaf (1 pound) French bread
- 1 cup prepared pesto
- 1 pound thinly sliced deli turkey
- ½ pound provolone cheese, thinly sliced
- 2 small zucchini, thinly sliced
- 2 medium tomatoes, thinly sliced
- 1 medium red onion, thinly sliced

1. Preheat oven to 350°. Cut the top fourth off loaf of bread. Carefully hollow out the bottom, leaving a ½-in. shell. (Discard removed bread or save for another use.) Spread pesto on the inside of top and bottom of bread. Set top aside.
2. In bottom of bread, layer the turkey, cheese, zucchini, tomatoes and onion. Gently press the layers together. Replace bread top and wrap tightly in foil.
3. Place on a baking sheet. Bake for 25-30 minutes or until heated through. Let stand 10 minutes before cutting.

Thanksgiving Turkey for Two

One of the hardest meals to plan is a holiday meal for two. You want all the smells and feelings of the season, but you don't want leftovers that last until June! This recipe is the tasty answer.

—**JOYCE KRAMER** DONALSONVILLE, GA

PREP: 10 MIN. • **BAKE:** 30 MIN.
MAKES: 2 SERVINGS

- 2 turkey breast tenderloins (6 ounces each)
- ¼ cup white wine or chicken broth
- 1 tablespoon butter, melted
- ¼ teaspoon salt
- ¼ teaspoon dried tarragon
- ¼ teaspoon paprika
- ½ cup sliced fresh mushrooms

1. Place turkey in an 11x7-in. baking dish coated with cooking spray. In a small bowl, combine the wine, butter, salt, tarragon and paprika. Spoon over turkey. Arrange mushrooms around tenderloins.
2. Bake turkey, uncovered, at 375° for 30-35 minutes or until a thermometer reads 170°, basting occasionally with pan drippings. Let stand 5 minutes before slicing. Serve with remaining pan drippings.

Chicken Cordon Bleu Pasta

Facebook fans of my blog, *Chef in Training*, inspired me to create this creamy pasta casserole out of ingredients I had on hand. Success! I took the dish for another flavorful spin and added a bit of smoky bacon and toasted bread crumbs.

—**NIKKI BARTON** PROVIDENCE, UT

PREP: 25 MIN. • **BAKE:** 20 MIN.
MAKES: 6 SERVINGS

- 3 cups uncooked penne pasta
- 2 cups heavy whipping cream
- 1 package (8 ounces) cream cheese, softened and cubed
- 1½ cups (6 ounces) shredded Swiss cheese, divided
- ½ teaspoon onion powder
- ½ teaspoon garlic salt
- ¼ teaspoon pepper
- 3 cups sliced cooked chicken breast
- ¾ cup crumbled cooked bacon
- ¾ cup cubed fully cooked ham
- 3 tablespoons dry bread crumbs

1. Preheat oven to 350°. Cook the pasta according to package directions for al dente.
2. Meanwhile, in a large saucepan, heat cream and cream cheese over medium heat until smooth, stirring occasionally. Stir in 1 cup of the Swiss cheese, onion powder, garlic salt and pepper until blended.
3. Drain pasta; stir in chicken, bacon and ham. Add the sauce; toss to coat. Transfer to a greased 13x9-in. baking dish. Sprinkle with the remaining cheese and the bread crumbs. Bake, uncovered, 18-22 minutes or until heated through.

CHICKEN CORDON
BLEU PASTA

Baked Cornish Hens

Make that special dinner easy on yourself—bake these Cornish hens atop a simple wild rice stuffing and you'll have lots of hands-free cook time.
—*TASTE OF HOME* TEST KITCHEN

PREP: 70 MIN. • **BAKE:** 1 HOUR
MAKES: 4 SERVINGS

- 2¼ cups reduced-sodium chicken broth
- ⅔ cup uncooked wild rice
- ¼ cup chopped onion
- ¼ cup chopped celery
- 1 teaspoon olive oil
- 1 garlic clove, minced
- ½ cup chopped dried apricots
- 2 tablespoons chopped almonds
- 1 cup apricot nectar, divided
- ½ cup sweet white wine or apple juice, divided
- ¼ teaspoon plus ⅛ teaspoon salt, divided
- ¼ teaspoon poultry seasoning
- ¼ teaspoon pepper, divided
- 2 Cornish game hens (20 to 24 ounces each), cut in half
- 1 teaspoon white balsamic vinegar
  Dash ground cinnamon

1. In a saucepan, bring broth and rice to a boil. Reduce heat; cover and simmer for 60-70 minutes or until rice is tender and liquid is absorbed.
2. Meanwhile, in a nonstick skillet, saute onion and celery in oil until tender. Add garlic; cook 1 minute longer. Stir in the apricots, almonds, ⅓ cup apricot nectar, ¼ cup wine, ¼ teaspoon salt, poultry seasoning and ⅛ teaspoon pepper. Stir into cooked rice.
3. Spoon mixture into four mounds in a shallow roasting pan coated with cooking spray; top each with a hen half. Cover hens and bake at 375° for 45 minutes. Uncover hens and bake for 15-20 minutes longer or until a thermometer reads 180°.
4. In a large saucepan, combine the remaining nectar and wine. Bring to a boil; cook for 5-7 minutes or until reduced to ½ cup. Add the vinegar, cinnamon and remaining salt and pepper. Reduce heat; cook and stir over medium-low heat for 1 minute. Serve with hens and rice.

BISCUIT NUGGET CHICKEN BAKE

Biscuit Nugget Chicken Bake

Topped with seasoned biscuits, this yummy casserole is a fun, easy way to please everyone in the family. It's one of my favorite recipes for a quick dinner.
—**KAYLA DEMPSEY** O'FALLON, IL

START TO FINISH: 30 MIN.
MAKES: 4-6 SERVINGS

- 3 cups cubed cooked chicken
- 1 can (10¾ ounces) condensed cream of chicken soup, undiluted
- 1 cup milk
- 1 jar (4½ ounces) sliced mushrooms, drained
- ½ teaspoon dill weed
- ½ teaspoon paprika

TOPPING
- ¼ cup grated Parmesan cheese
- 1 tablespoon dried minced onion
- 1 teaspoon dried parsley flakes
- ½ teaspoon paprika
- 1 tube (12 ounces) refrigerated buttermilk biscuits

1. In a large saucepan, combine the first six ingredients. Cook and stir over medium heat for 5-7 minutes or until heated through; keep warm.
2. In a large resealable plastic bag, combine the cheese, onion, parsley and paprika. Separate biscuits and cut into quarters; add to bag and shake to coat. Place on an ungreased baking sheet. Bake at 400° for 5 minutes.
3. Transfer chicken mixture to a greased 8-in.-square baking dish; top with biscuits. Bake, uncovered, for 10-13 minutes or until bubbly and biscuits are golden brown.

Harvest Turkey Bread Salad

One year when we were trying to use up our Thanksgiving dinner leftovers, we came up with this delicious take on Italian panzanella. It's now a family favorite.

—MARY BETH HARRIS-MURPHREE TYLER, TX

PREP: 25 MIN. • **BAKE:** 45 MIN.
MAKES: 8 SERVINGS

- 8 cups cubed day-old Italian bread
- ¼ cup whole-berry cranberry sauce or chutney of your choice
- 6 tablespoons olive oil, divided
- 6 tablespoons balsamic vinegar, divided
- 2 teaspoons salt, divided
- 1 large sweet potato, peeled and cubed
- 1 large sweet onion, peeled and cut into wedges
- 2 tablespoons minced fresh thyme
- ½ teaspoon coarsely ground pepper
- 5 cups cubed cooked turkey breast
- ¼ cup minced fresh parsley
- ⅓ cup dried cranberries
- ⅓ cup chopped pecans or hazelnuts, toasted

1. Place bread cubes in an ungreased 15x10x1-in. baking pan. Bake at 250° for 12-15 minutes or until lightly browned. Set aside. Increase heat to 400°.

2. In a large bowl, combine the cranberry sauce, 2 tablespoons oil, 2 tablespoons vinegar and 1 teaspoon salt. Add sweet potato and onion; toss to coat. Place mixture in a foil-lined 15x10x1-in. baking pan. Bake for 30-40 minutes or until tender, stirring once.

3. In a small bowl, combine thyme and pepper with the remaining oil, vinegar and salt. In a large bowl, combine the bread cubes, roasted vegetables, turkey and parsley. Drizzle with the dressing and toss to coat. Sprinkle with cranberries and pecans.

Turkey Meatballs in Garlic Sauce

This is a pared-down recipe that my husband and I enjoy. It makes a satisfying dinner over hot rice or noodles. I also like to accompany it with baked acorn squash.

—AUDREY THIBODEAU GILBERT, AZ

PREP: 10 MIN. • **BAKE:** 30 MIN.
MAKES: 2 SERVINGS

- 2 tablespoons milk
- ½ teaspoon Worcestershire sauce
- 2 to 3 drops hot pepper sauce
- ½ cup finely crushed Ritz crackers (about 10 crackers)
- 1 tablespoon minced fresh parsley
- ¼ teaspoon salt
- ⅛ teaspoon pepper
- ½ pound lean ground turkey
- 1 cup V8 juice
- ¼ cup chicken broth
- 2 garlic cloves, minced
  Hot cooked rice

1. In a large bowl, combine the first seven ingredients. Crumble turkey over mixture and mix well. Shape into six meatballs. Place in a greased 9-in. pie plate. Bake, uncovered, at 400° for 10 minutes.

2. Meanwhile, in a small bowl, combine the V8 juice, broth and garlic. Turn meatballs; spoon sauce over top. Reduce heat to 350°. Bake 20 minutes longer, basting every 5 minutes. Serve over rice.

For a **zesty variation**, add ⅛ teaspoon granulated **garlic** to the meatballs and replace half the salt with **celery salt**. Serve over **pasta**.

HARVEST TURKEY BREAD SALAD

**PINEAPPLE-STUFFED
CORNISH HENS**

Pineapple-Stuffed Cornish Hens

PREP: 20 MIN. • **BAKE:** 55 MIN.
MAKES: 2 SERVINGS

- ½ teaspoon salt, divided
- 2 Cornish game hens (20 to 24 ounces each)
- 1 can (8 ounces) crushed pineapple
- 3 cups cubed day-old bread (½-inch cubes), crusts removed
- 1 celery rib, chopped
- ½ cup flaked coconut
- ⅔ cup butter, melted, divided
- ¼ teaspoon poultry seasoning
- 2 tablespoons steak sauce
- 2 tablespoons cornstarch
- 2 tablespoons brown sugar
- 1 cup cold water
- 1 tablespoon lemon juice

1. Sprinkle ¼ teaspoon salt inside hens; set aside. Drain pineapple, reserving juice. In a large bowl, combine the pineapple, bread cubes, celery and coconut. Add 6 tablespoons butter; toss to coat. Loosely stuff hens with mixture.

2. Tuck wings under hens; tie legs together. Place on a rack in a greased shallow roasting pan. Place remaining stuffing in a greased 1½-cup baking dish; cover and set aside.

3. Add the poultry seasoning and remaining salt to remaining butter. Spoon some of the mixture over hens. Bake, uncovered, at 350° for 40 minutes, basting twice with the butter mixture.

4. Add steak sauce and reserved pineapple juice to any remaining butter mixture; baste hens. Bake reserved stuffing with hens for 30 minutes, basting the hens occasionally with pineapple mixture.

5. Uncover the stuffing; bake for 15-20 minutes longer or until a thermometer reads 185° for hens and 165° for stuffing in hens, basting hens occasionally. Remove hens from pan; keep warm.

6. Pour drippings into a saucepan; skim fat. Combine cornstarch, brown sugar, water and lemon juice; add to the drippings. Bring to a boil; cook and stir 1-2 minutes or until thickened. Serve with hens and stuffing.

Pecan-Crusted Chicken Salad with Fig Vinaigrette

Here's a delicious way to get greens into your diet. The salad is so flavorful, great for family dinners and casual summertime entertaining. Pecan-crusted chicken and homemade fig vinaigrette make it just as good as any restaurant salad.
—**KELLY BOE** WHITELAND, IN

PREP: 35 MIN. • **BAKE:** 20 MIN.
MAKES: 6 SERVINGS

- 1 cup chopped pecans
- ½ cup panko (Japanese) bread crumbs
- 1 teaspoon dried rosemary, crushed
- ½ teaspoon salt
- ½ teaspoon dried sage leaves, crushed
- ¼ teaspoon dried basil
- ⅛ teaspoon cayenne pepper
- 1½ pounds boneless skinless chicken breasts, cut into 1-inch strips

FIG VINAIGRETTE
- 6 tablespoons fig preserves
- 3 tablespoons balsamic vinegar
- 1 small garlic clove, minced
- 6 tablespoons olive oil

SALAD
- 9 cups torn mixed salad greens
- ¾ cup crumbled goat cheese
- 3 tablespoons dried blueberries

1. Place pecans in a food processor; cover and process until finely chopped. Add the bread crumbs, rosemary, salt, sage, basil and cayenne; process until combined. Transfer to a shallow bowl.

2. Coat chicken strips with pecan mixture. Place in a greased 15x10x1-in. baking pan. Bake, uncovered, at 375° for 20-25 minutes or until no longer pink, turning once.

3. For vinaigrette, in a small saucepan over low heat, melt the fig preserves. Transfer to a small bowl; add vinegar and garlic. Gradually whisk in oil.

4. Divide salad greens among six plates; sprinkle with cheese and blueberries. Top with chicken. Drizzle with vinaigrette. Serve immediately.

PER SERVING *1 salad equals 452 cal., 27 g fat (6 g sat. fat), 80 mg chol., 314 mg sodium, 26 g carb., 4 g fiber, 28 g pro.*

PECAN-CRUSTED CHICKEN SALAD WITH FIG VINAIGRETTE

Pork

200   205   213

Dazzle family and friends with **fabulous** home-cooked **roast, pizza, chops, stromboli** and more. Wow them with **smoky** bacon sliders, **saucy** baby back ribs and **cheesy** pork enchiladas. **They'll cheer** when you serve up one of these **winning dishes** at the next meal!

TOASTY DELI HOAGIE

Roast Pork with Apple Topping

I enjoy cooking and am constantly on the lookout for new recipes to try. I feel very fortunate when I find a dish like this that instantly becomes a family favorite.

—**VIRGINA BARRETT** ROCHESTER, NY

PREP: 15 MIN. + STANDING
BAKE: 1¼ HOURS + STANDING
MAKES: 8-10 SERVINGS

- 2 **tablespoon all-purpose flour**
- 1¾ **teaspoons salt, divided**
- 1 **teaspoon ground mustard**
- 1 **teaspoon caraway seeds**
- ½ **teaspoon sugar**
- ¼ **teaspoon pepper**
- ¼ **teaspoon rubbed sage**
- 1 **boneless pork loin roast (4 to 5 pounds)**
- 1½ **cups applesauce**
- ½ **cup packed brown sugar**
- ¼ **teaspoon ground mace**

1. In a small bowl, combine the flour, 1½ teaspoons salt, ground mustard, caraway, sugar, pepper and sage; rub over roast. Cover and let stand for 30 minutes.
2. Preheat oven to 350°. Place roast on a rack in a shallow roasting pan, fat side up. Roast, uncovered, 40 minutes. In a small bowl, mix the applesauce, brown sugar, mace and remaining salt; spread over the roast. Roast for 35-40 minutes longer or until a thermometer reads 145°. Let stand 10 minutes before slicing.
PER SERVING *5 ounces cooked pork equals 291 cal., 9 g fat (3 g sat. fat), 90 mg chol., 470 mg sodium, 16 g carb., 1 g fiber, 35 g pro.* **Diabetic Exchanges:** *5 lean meat, 1 starch.*

Toasty Deli Hoagie

This deluxe sub sandwich is stacked with yummy ingredients and then broiled, so it's perfect for a picnic in the backyard. For an even fresher taste, whip up a batch of homemade guacamole.
—**STACI HOARD** BRONSTON, KY

PREP: 35 MIN. • **BROIL:** 5 MIN.
MAKES: 6 SERVINGS

- 1 **loaf (1 pound) French bread**
- 2 **tablespoons mayonnaise**
- 1 **tablespoon lemon juice**
- 2 **garlic cloves, minced**
- ½ **pound thinly sliced deli smoked turkey**
- ½ **pound thinly sliced deli ham**
- 6 **slices hard salami**
- 1 **medium sweet yellow pepper, julienned**
- 1 **small red onion, thinly sliced**
- ½ **pound sliced provolone cheese**
- 1½ **cups guacamole**

1. Cut the French bread loaf in half lengthwise; place cut side up on a baking sheet. Bake at 350° for 4-5 minutes or until toasted.
2. In a small bowl, combine the mayonnaise, lemon juice and garlic; spread over bread bottom. Layer with turkey, ham, salami, pepper, onion and cheese. Bake for 7-8 minutes or until meat is heated through; broil 3-4 in. from the heat for 3 minutes or until cheese is lightly browned.
3. Spread guacamole over bread top; place over cheese. Cut into six slices.

For best results, let **large cuts** of meat **stand** before cutting. This allows the **meat juices** to settle after cooking. Cut in too soon, and the juices **will escape**, resulting in **a drier cut**. Standing also finishes the **cooking**. Large cuts typically **rise a few degrees** as they stand.

ROASTED KIELBASA
& VEGETABLES

Italian Sausage Rigatoni Bake

This casserole combines all of our favorite Italian flavors, but the mozzarella really steals the show!

—**BLAIR LONERGAN** ROCHELLE, VA

PREP: 30 MIN. • **BAKE:** 25 MIN.
MAKES: 2 CASSEROLES (4 SERVINGS EACH)

- 1 package (16 ounces) rigatoni
- 1 pound bulk Italian sausage
- 8 ounces sliced fresh mushrooms
- 1 medium sweet red pepper, chopped
- 5 cups marinara sauce
- ¼ cup grated Parmesan cheese
- 2 tablespoons half-and-half cream
- 16 ounces sliced part-skim mozzarella cheese

1. Preheat oven to 375°. Cook rigatoni according to package directions; drain.
2. In a large skillet, cook sausage, mushrooms and pepper over medium-high heat 8-10 minutes or until meat is no longer pink and vegetables are tender, breaking up sausage into crumbles; drain. Stir in marinara sauce, Parmesan cheese and the cream. Add rigatoni; toss to coat.
3. In each of two greased 8-in.-square baking dishes, layer one-fourth of the rigatoni mixture and one-fourth of the mozzarella cheese. Repeat layers. Bake, uncovered, 25-35 minutes or until heated through and cheese is melted. (Cover loosely with foil if tops brown too quickly.)
FREEZE OPTION *Cool unbaked casseroles; cover and freeze. To use, partially thaw in the refrigerator overnight. Remove from refrigerator 30 minutes before baking. Preheat oven to 375°. Bake casseroles as directed, increasing time as necessary to heat through and for a thermometer inserted in center to read 165°.*

Roasted Kielbasa & Vegetables

The top reason I like this blend of kielbasa and veggies is that it's more healthy than typical kielbasa dishes. Second, it's a one-pan meal—a win-win dinner.

—**MARIETTA SLATER** JUSTIN, TX

PREP: 20 MIN. • **BAKE:** 40 MIN.
MAKES: 6 SERVINGS

- 3 medium sweet potatoes, peeled and cut into 1-inch pieces
- 1 large sweet onion, cut into 1-inch pieces
- 4 medium carrots, cut into 1-inch pieces
- 2 tablespoons olive oil
- 1 pound smoked kielbasa or Polish sausage, halved and cut into 1-inch pieces
- 1 medium yellow summer squash, cut into 1-inch pieces
- 1 medium zucchini, cut into 1-inch pieces
- ¼ teaspoon salt
- ¼ teaspoon pepper
  Dijon mustard, optional

1. Preheat oven to 400°. Divide sweet potatoes, onion and carrots between two greased 15x10x1-in. baking pans. Drizzle with oil; toss to coat. Roast 25 minutes, stirring occasionally.
2. Add kielbasa, squash and zucchini to pans; sprinkle with salt and pepper. Roast 15-20 minutes longer or until vegetables are tender. Transfer to a serving bowl; toss to combine. If desired, serve with mustard.

ITALIAN SAUSAGE
RIGATONI BAKE

Stuffed Banana Peppers

Here's a delightful change from traditional stuffed green peppers. Banana peppers and chili powder give this recipe a little kick. As a bonus, any leftovers reheat nicely in the microwave.

—LOUISE MENZIES ROSSVILLE, GA

PREP: 15 MIN. • **BAKE:** 30 MIN.
MAKES: 4 SERVINGS

- 8 mild banana peppers
- 1 pound bulk pork sausage
- ½ cup cooked rice
- ⅓ cup thinly sliced green onions
- 3 garlic cloves, minced
- 1 teaspoon salt
- ½ teaspoon pepper
- 1 can (8 ounces) tomato sauce
- 1 tablespoon water
- 1 teaspoon chili powder, optional
- ½ cup shredded part-skim mozzarella cheese, optional

1. Remove pepper stems; cut peppers in half lengthwise. Carefully remove seeds and membranes; set aside. Combine the sausage, rice, onions, garlic, salt and pepper; stuff into pepper halves. Place in a greased 13x9-in. baking dish. Combine tomato sauce, water and, if desired, chili powder; pour over peppers.

2. Cover dish and bake at 350° for 30 minutes or until filling is cooked and set. Sprinkle with cheese if desired; return dish to the oven for 5-10 minutes or until cheese is melted.

For a **creamier texture**, stir some softened **cream cheese** into the sausage mixture before **filling** the peppers.

Pork Chops with Corn Bread Stuffing

In our family, we love stuffing instead of potatoes. Add a vegetable and you have a fantastic meal.

—JO GROTH PLAINFIELD, IA

PREP: 20 MIN. • **BAKE:** 20 MIN.
MAKES: 6 SERVINGS

- 1 can (14½ ounces) chicken broth
- 1 can (7 ounces) Mexicorn, drained
- 1 celery rib, chopped
- ¼ cup chopped onion
- 1 egg, lightly beaten
- ¼ teaspoon dried sage leaves, crushed
- 4 cups corn bread stuffing mix
- 6 bone-in pork loin chops (6 ounces each)
- 1½ teaspoons Montreal steak seasoning
- 1 tablespoon canola oil

1. In a large bowl, combine the first six ingredients; stir in the stuffing mix. Transfer to a greased 13x9-in. baking dish.

2. Sprinkle pork chops with steak seasoning. In a large skillet, heat oil over medium heat; brown chops on both sides. Place over stuffing. Bake, uncovered, at 400° for 18-22 minutes or until a thermometer inserted in pork reads 145°. Let stand 5 minutes before serving.

PORK CHOPS WITH CORN BREAD STUFFING

HAM AND BROCCOLI BISCUIT BAKE

Ham and Broccoli Biscuit Bake

Whenever I cook this creamy dish, I'm on alert to make sure my husband doesn't nibble before I carry it to the table. I understand, though; who can resist the rich ham filling and golden biscuit crust?
—**AMY WHEELER** BALTIMORE, MD

PREP: 20 MIN. • **BAKE:** 25 MIN.
MAKES: 6 SERVINGS

- 2½ cups frozen chopped broccoli
- 1 can (10¾ ounces) condensed cream of potato soup, undiluted
- 1¼ cups 2% milk, divided
- 1 teaspoon garlic pepper blend
- ½ teaspoon crushed red pepper flakes
- ¼ teaspoon pepper
- 2 cups cubed fully cooked ham
- 1 cup (4 ounces) shredded cheddar-Monterey Jack cheese
- 1½ cups biscuit/baking mix
- 1 egg

1. Preheat oven to 350°. Combine broccoli, soup, ¾ cup milk and seasonings in a large saucepan; bring to a boil. Reduce heat; add the ham and cheese. Cook and stir until cheese is melted. Pour into a greased 11x7-in. baking dish.
2. Combine biscuit mix, egg and remaining milk in a small bowl just until moistened. Drop dough by tablespoonfuls over ham mixture; spread gently.
3. Bake, uncovered, 25-30 minutes or until golden brown.

Sausage Potato Lasagna

I decided to pair up two of my favorites—lasagna and potatoes—in this absolutely scrumptious dish. Sliced potatoes take the place of noodles. The enticing blend of traditional Italian flavors is sure to please anyone with a hearty appetite.
—**MELISSA POKORNY** ABBOTSFORD, BC

PREP: 1 HOUR • **BAKE:** 35 MIN. + STANDING
MAKES: 6-8 SERVINGS

- ½ pound bulk Italian sausage
- 2 cups sliced fresh mushrooms
- 4 medium potatoes, peeled and thinly sliced
- 1 package (10 ounces) frozen chopped spinach, thawed and well drained
- 1½ cups ricotta cheese
- ¼ cup grated Parmesan cheese
- 1 egg, beaten
- 1 medium onion, chopped
- 2 garlic cloves, minced
- 2 tablespoons butter
- 2 tablespoons all-purpose flour
  Salt and pepper to taste
- ¼ teaspoon ground nutmeg
- 1½ cups milk
- 1 cup (4 ounces) shredded part-skim mozzarella cheese, divided
  Additional nutmeg, optional

1. In a skillet, cook sausage and mushrooms over medium heat until the meat is no longer pink; drain and set aside.
2. Place potatoes in a saucepan; cover with water. Bring to a boil. Reduce heat; cover and cook for 5 minutes or until crisp-tender. Drain and set aside.
3. In a bowl, combine the spinach, ricotta, Parmesan and egg; set aside. In a saucepan, saute onion and garlic in butter until tender. Stir in flour, salt, pepper and nutmeg until blended. Gradually add milk. Bring to a boil; cook and stir for 2 minutes. Remove from the heat.
4. Layer half of the potatoes in a greased 11x7-in. baking dish. Top with half of the spinach mixture, sausage mixture, white sauce and mozzarella. Layer with the remaining potatoes, spinach mixture, sausage mixture and white sauce.
5. Cover dish and bake at 350° for 30-35 minutes or until potatoes are tender. Sprinkle with remaining mozzarella. Bake, uncovered, 5 minutes longer or until cheese is melted. Let stand for 15 minutes before cutting.

HAM &
COLLARDS QUICHE

Ham & Collards Quiche

I love quiche and wanted to make something that incorporates my Southern roots, so I came up with this version. With eggs, cheese, ham and nutritious collard greens in a flaky crust, it's a complete meal. Enjoy!

—BILLIE WILLIAMS-HENDERSON BOWIE, MD

PREP: 20 MIN. • **BAKE:** 35 MIN. + STANDING
MAKES: 6 SERVINGS

- 1 sheet refrigerated pie pastry
- 2 cups (8 ounces) shredded Colby-Monterey Jack cheese, divided
- ¾ cup cubed fully cooked ham
- 2 tablespoons olive oil
- 1 cup frozen chopped collard greens, thawed and drained
- 1 small onion, chopped
- 1 garlic clove, minced
- ¼ teaspoon salt
- ¼ teaspoon pepper
- 6 eggs
- 1 cup 2% milk

1. Preheat oven to 375°. Unroll pastry sheet into a 9-in. pie plate; flute edge. Sprinkle 1 cup cheese onto bottom of pastry-lined pie plate. Top with ham.
2. In a large skillet, heat oil over medium-high heat. Add collard greens and onion; cook and stir for 5-7 minutes or until onion is tender. Add garlic; cook 1 minute longer. Stir in the salt and pepper. Place greens mixture over ham.
3. In a large bowl, whisk eggs and milk until blended. Pour over top. Sprinkle with remaining cheese.
4. Bake quiche on lower oven rack 35-40 minutes or until a knife inserted in center comes out clean. Let stand 10 minutes before cutting.
FREEZE OPTION *Cover and freeze unbaked quiche. To use, remove from freezer 30 minutes before baking (do not thaw). Preheat oven to 375°. Place quiche on a baking sheet. Bake as directed, increasing the time as needed to 50-60 minutes.*

QUESO PORK ENCHILADAS

Queso Pork Enchiladas

My husband took these restaurant-style enchiladas to work, and now the guys always ask for them. They're rich and spicy, and you can prepare them with cooked chicken or beef, too.

—ANNA RODRIGUEZ BETHPAGE, NY

PREP: 30 MIN. • **BAKE:** 30 MIN.
MAKES: 6 SERVINGS

- 1 jar (15½ ounces) salsa con queso dip, divided
- 1 can (10 ounces) enchilada sauce, divided
- 1 can (4 ounces) chopped green chilies
- ⅓ cup water
- 2 tablespoons reduced-sodium taco seasoning
- 4 cups cubed cooked boneless country-style pork ribs (from 2 pounds boneless ribs)
- 12 flour tortillas (6 inches), warmed
- 2½ cups (10 ounces) shredded Mexican cheese blend, divided
  Shredded lettuce and chopped tomatoes, optional

1. In a large skillet, combine ¾ cup queso dip, ½ cup enchilada sauce, chopped green chilies, water and the taco seasoning. Bring to a boil. Reduce heat; simmer, uncovered, for 3 minutes.
2. Spread ⅔ cup sauce mixture into a greased 13x9-in. baking dish. Stir pork into remaining sauce mixture. Place ⅓ cup pork mixture down the center of each tortilla; top with 2 tablespoons cheese. Roll up and place seam side down in prepared dish. Combine remaining queso dip and enchilada sauce; pour over enchiladas.
3. Cover and bake at 350° for 20 minutes. Uncover; sprinkle with remaining cheese. Bake 10-15 minutes longer or until heated through. Serve with lettuce and tomatoes if desired.

SENSATIONAL STUFFED PORK CHOPS

Pepperoni Pan Pizzas

I've spent years trying to come up with the perfect pizza crust and sauce, and they're paired up in this recipe. I fix this crispy pizza for my family often, and it really satisfies my husband and three sons.

—**SUSAN LINDAHL** ALFORD, FL

PREP: 30 MIN. • **BAKE:** 10 MIN.
MAKES: 2 PIZZAS (9 PIECES EACH)

- 2¾ to 3 cups all-purpose flour
- 1 package (¼ ounce) active dry yeast
- ¼ teaspoon salt
- 1 cup warm water (120° to 130°)
- 1 tablespoon canola oil

SAUCE
- 1 can (14½ ounces) diced tomatoes, undrained
- 1 can (6 ounces) tomato paste
- 1 tablespoon canola oil
- 1 teaspoon salt
- ½ teaspoon each dried basil, oregano, marjoram and thyme
- ¼ teaspoon garlic powder
- ¼ teaspoon pepper

PIZZAS
- 1 package (3½ ounces) sliced pepperoni
- 5 cups (20 ounces) shredded part-skim mozzarella cheese
- ¼ cup grated Parmesan cheese
- ¼ cup grated Romano cheese

1. In a large bowl, combine 2 cups flour, yeast and salt. Add water and oil; beat until smooth. Add enough remaining flour to form a soft dough.
2. Turn onto a floured surface; knead until smooth and elastic, about 5-7 minutes. Cover and let stand for 10 minutes. Meanwhile, in a small bowl, combine sauce ingredients.
3. Divide dough in half; press into two 15x10x1-in. baking pans coated with cooking spray. Prick dough generously with a fork. Bake crusts at 425° for 12-16 minutes or until lightly browned.
4. Spread sauce over crusts; top with the pepperoni and cheeses. Bake for 8-10 minutes or until cheese is melted.
FREEZE OPTION *Bake crusts and assemble pizzas as directed. Securely wrap and freeze unbaked pizzas. To use, unwrap pizzas; bake as directed, increasing time as necessary.*

Sensational Stuffed Pork Chops

You'll want to make stuffing more often once you try these savory pork chops. Just a few ingredients combine to give them such fabulous flavor!

—*TASTE OF HOME* TEST KITCHEN

PREP: 30 MIN. • **BAKE:** 25 MIN.
MAKES: 4 SERVINGS

- 4 bone-in pork loin chops (8 ounces each)
- 2 cups cooked stuffing
- ¼ teaspoon pepper
- 1 tablespoon canola oil
- 2 garlic cloves, minced
- ¼ teaspoon dried thyme
- ½ cup white wine or chicken broth
- 2 tablespoons all-purpose flour
- ¾ cup chicken broth

1. Cut a pocket in each pork chop by slicing almost to the bone. Fill each chop with ½ cup stuffing; secure with toothpicks if necessary. Sprinkle with pepper.
2. In a large ovenproof skillet, brown the chops in oil. Bake, uncovered, at 350° for 25-30 minutes or until a thermometer reads 160°. Remove pork chops and set aside. Keep warm.
3. In the same skillet, cook garlic and thyme in pan drippings over medium heat for 1 minute. Add wine, stirring to loosen browned bits from pan. In a small bowl, combine flour and broth until smooth. Gradually add to pan. Bring to a boil; cook and stir for 2 minutes or until thickened.
4. Remove toothpicks from pork chops; serve chops with gravy.

Glazed BBQ Ribs

After trying a fruit salad at a backyard barbecue, I wanted to make a rib sauce that tasted as sweet. Everyone loves the raspberry-red wine combo in the sauce.

—STEVE MARINO NUTLEY, NJ

PREP: 2 HOURS • **BROIL:** 10 MIN.
MAKES: 4 SERVINGS

- 4 **pounds pork baby back ribs**
- ½ **cup olive oil**
- 2 **teaspoons salt**
- 2 **teaspoons pepper**
- 1 **bottle (18 ounces) barbecue sauce**
- 1 **cup seedless raspberry preserves**
- ¼ **cup dry red wine**
- ½ **teaspoon onion powder**
- ½ **teaspoon cayenne pepper**

1. Preheat oven to 325°. Place ribs in a shallow roasting pan, bone side down. In a small bowl, mix oil, salt and pepper; rub over ribs. Bake, covered, 1½ to 2 hours or until tender; drain.

2. In another bowl, mix remaining ingredients; reserve ¾ cup for serving with the ribs. Brush some of the remaining sauce over ribs. Bake, uncovered, 25-30 minutes or until ribs are glazed, basting occasionally with additional sauce.

3. Preheat broiler. Transfer ribs to a broiler pan, bone side down. Broil 4-5 in. from heat 8-10 minutes or until browned. Serve with reserved sauce.

Spiral Stromboli

Two types of deli meat and three kinds of cheese make this stromboli the perfect filler-upper! I frequently make this speedy bite when we return from our cabin and it's suppertime when we get home.

—JEAN GRUENERT BURLINGTON, WI

PREP: 10 MIN. • **BAKE:** 25 MIN.
MAKES: 4 SERVINGS

- 1 **tube (11 ounces) refrigerated crusty French loaf**
- ¾ **cup shredded part-skim mozzarella cheese**
- ¾ **cup shredded cheddar cheese**
- ¼ **pound each thinly sliced deli salami and ham**
- ¼ **cup chopped roasted red peppers or 1 jar (2 ounces) pimientos, drained**
- 1 **tablespoon butter, melted**
- 2 **tablespoons shredded Parmesan cheese**

1. Unroll the dough and pat into a 14x12-in. rectangle. Sprinkle with mozzarella and cheddar cheeses to within ½ in. of edges; top with meat and red peppers. Roll up jelly-roll style, starting with a short side; seal seam and tuck ends under.

2. Place seam side down on a greased baking sheet. Brush with butter; sprinkle with Parmesan cheese.

3. Bake at 375° for 25-30 minutes or until golden brown. Slice with a serrated knife.

GLAZED
BBQ RIBS

HAM & CHEESE ZITI

Pork Chops with Blue Cheese Sauce

Sometimes a sauce is just a sauce—but with these juicy chops, it really makes the dish. If you like a little spice, mix a small pinch of nutmeg with the black pepper before you sprinkle it onto the pork chops.

—**KATHLEEN SPECHT** CLINTON, MT

START TO FINISH: 25 MIN.
MAKES: 4 SERVINGS

- 4 **bone-in pork loin chops (7 ounces each)**
- 1 **teaspoon coarsely ground pepper**
- 1 **teaspoon butter**
- 1 **green onion, finely chopped**
- 1 **garlic clove, minced**
- 1 **tablespoon all-purpose flour**
- ⅔ **cup fat-free milk**
- 3 **tablespoons crumbled blue cheese**
- 1 **tablespoon white wine or reduced-sodium chicken broth**

1. Preheat broiler. Sprinkle pork chops on both sides with pepper; place on a broiler pan coated with cooking spray. Broil 4-5 in. from the heat 4-5 minutes on each side or until a thermometer reads 145°. Let stand 5 minutes before serving.
2. Meanwhile, in a small saucepan, heat butter over medium-high heat. Add green onion and garlic; cook and stir until tender. Stir in flour until blended; gradually whisk in milk. Bring to a boil, stirring constantly; cook and stir 1-2 minutes or until thickened. Add cheese and wine; heat through. Serve with chops.
PER SERVING *1 pork chop with 3 tablespoons sauce equals 263 cal., 11 g fat (5 g sat. fat), 94 mg chol., 176 mg sodium, 5 g carb., trace fiber, 33 g pro. **Diabetic Exchanges:** 5 lean meat, ½ fat.*

Ham & Cheese Ziti

You can easily make this recipe your own by changing up the cheeses and using other veggies. My family loves it!

—**DONNA BAILEY** ORELAND, PA

PREP: 25 MIN. • **BAKE:** 20 MIN.
MAKES: 6 SERVINGS

- 1 **package (16 ounces) ziti**
- ¼ **cup butter, cubed**
- ¼ **cup all-purpose flour**
- 2 **cups 2% milk**
- 2 **cups (8 ounces) shredded white cheddar cheese**
- ¼ **cup grated Parmesan cheese**
- 1 **teaspoon garlic powder**
- ½ **teaspoon pepper**
- 3 **cups cubed fully cooked ham**
- 1 **package (10 ounces) frozen chopped spinach, thawed and squeezed dry**

1. Prepare ziti according to package directions. Meanwhile, in a Dutch oven, melt butter. Stir in flour until smooth; gradually add milk. Bring to a boil; cook and stir for 2 minutes or until thickened. Reduce heat; stir in cheeses, garlic powder and pepper until cheese is melted.

2. Drain ziti; add to sauce. Stir in ham and spinach. Transfer to a greased 13x9-in. baking dish.
3. Bake, uncovered, at 375° for 20-25 minutes or until the casserole is heated through.

Sausage 'n' Sweet Potatoes

With just four ingredients and a short preparation time, a satisfying dinner is ready in almost no time flat.

—**JOAN HOCH** BOYERTOWN, PA

PREP: 10 MIN. • **BAKE:** 30 MIN.
MAKES: 6 SERVINGS

- 2 **cans (15 ounces each) sweet potatoes, drained**
- 5 **medium apples, peeled and quartered**
- 2 **tablespoons brown sugar**
- 1 **pound smoked sausage, cut into 1-inch slices**

In a greased 2½-qt. baking dish, layer sweet potatoes and apples. Sprinkle with sugar. Top with sausage. Cover and bake at 375° for 30 minutes or until the apples are tender.

**PORK CHOPS WITH
BLUE CHEESE SAUCE**

Simple Sweet Pork Chops

These tender pork chops have the perfect balance of sweet, juicy pineapple and spicy jalapeno pepper. The whole family will enjoy them.

—**SHERRI MELOTIK** OAK CREEK, WI

PREP: 10 MIN. • **BAKE:** 40 MIN.
MAKES: 6 SERVINGS

- 6 boneless pork loin chops (6 ounces each)
- 1 can (20 ounces) unsweetened pineapple chunks, undrained
- 3 tablespoons brown sugar
- 1 jalapeno pepper, seeded and finely chopped
- 1 tablespoon reduced-sodium soy sauce
- ½ teaspoon chili powder
- ¼ teaspoon garlic powder

Place the pork chops in a 13x9-in. baking dish coated with cooking spray. Combine the remaining ingredients; pour over the pork chops. Cover and bake at 350° for 30 minutes. Uncover; bake 10-15 minutes longer or until a thermometer reads 160°.

NOTE *Wear disposable gloves when cutting hot peppers; the oils can burn skin. Avoid touching your face.*

PER SERVING *1 pork chop with about ⅓ cup sauce equals 303 cal., 10 g fat (4 g sat. fat), 82 mg chol., 161 mg sodium, 19 g carb., 1 g fiber, 33 g pro. Diabetic Exchanges: 5 lean meat, 1 fruit.*

Pizza-Syle Manicotti

Ham, pepperoni and string cheese make little bundles that are stuffed into manicotti shells. It's a fun, hands-on recipe that children can help prepare.

—**JUDY ARMSTRONG** PRAIRIEVILLE, LA

PREP: 20 MIN. • **BAKE:** 25 MIN.
MAKES: 4 SERVINGS

- 8 uncooked manicotti shells
- 1 jar (24 ounces) spaghetti sauce
- 8 slices deli ham (about 6 ounces)
- 8 fresh basil leaves
- 8 pieces string cheese
- 24 slices pepperoni
- 1 can (2¼ ounces) sliced ripe olives, drained
- 1 cup shredded Parmesan cheese

1. Cook manicotti according to package directions for al dente; drain.
2. Pour 1 cup sauce into a 13x9-in. baking dish. On a short side of each ham slice, layer one basil leaf, one piece string cheese and three slices pepperoni; roll up. Insert in manicotti shells; arrange in a single layer in baking dish.
3. Pour remaining sauce over top. Sprinkle with olives and Parmesan cheese. Bake, uncovered, at 350° for 25-30 minutes or until the filling is heated through.

FREEZE OPTION *Cover unbaked casserole and freeze up to 3 months. Thaw in refrigerator overnight. Remove casserole from refrigerator 30 minutes before baking. Cover and bake at 375° for 25-30 minutes or until pasta is tender. Let stand for 10 minutes before serving.*

Balsamic Roasted Sausage and Grapes with Linguine

Pasta doesn't have to wear coats of cream and cheese, especially when red grapes and sausage give it sweetness and spice.

—LAUREN WYLER DRIPPING SPRINGS, TX

PREP: 15 MIN. • **BAKE:** 35 MIN.
MAKES: 8 SERVINGS

- ¾ pound sweet Italian sausage links
- ¾ pound hot Italian sausage links
- 3 cups seedless red grapes
- ¼ cup balsamic vinegar
- 2 tablespoons olive oil
- 2 tablespoons water
- ½ teaspoon salt
- ½ teaspoon pepper
- 1 package (12 ounces) whole wheat linguine
- ½ cup prepared pesto
- 2 cups fresh baby spinach
- 2 cups spring mix salad greens

1. Preheat oven to 425°. Place sausage links and grapes in a greased 13x9-in. baking dish. In a small bowl, combine vinegar, oil and water; pour over sausages. Sprinkle with the salt and pepper.

2. Bake 20 minutes. Turn sausages; bake 15-20 minutes longer or until a thermometer inserted in sausages reads 160°.

3. Meanwhile, cook the linguine according to package directions. Drain, reserving ½ cup pasta water.

4. Cut sausages into ½-in. slices. In a large bowl, combine the linguine, reserved pasta water and pesto; toss to coat. Add the sausage, spinach, salad greens and grapes with pan juices; toss to combine. Serve immediately.

Best-Ever Asparagus 'n' Ham Rolls

PREP: 20 MIN. • **BAKE:** 20 MIN.
MAKES: 8 SERVINGS

- 1½ pounds fresh asparagus, trimmed
- 16 slices sandwich-type ham
  Prepared mustard
- 6 tablespoons butter, cubed
- 6 tablespoons all-purpose flour
- 2 cups milk
  Salt and pepper to taste
- 1½ cups (6 ounces) shredded cheddar cheese
- 6 green onions, thinly sliced, optional

1. Cook asparagus until crisp-tender. Spread one side of each ham slice with mustard. Roll ham around two or three asparagus spears. Layer rolls, seam side down, in an 11x7-in. baking dish. Set aside.

2. In a saucepan, melt butter over medium heat. Blend in flour until smooth. Slowly stir in milk, salt and pepper. Bring to a boil. Cook and stir for 2 minutes or until thickened. Stir in cheese and, if desired, onions. Pour over ham rolls.

3. Cover dish and bake at 350° for 20 minutes or until heated through.

BALSAMIC ROASTED SAUSAGE AND GRAPES WITH LINGUINE

"I've had this recipe for several years and I really don't remember where I first got it. I have a large family and am always looking for easy recipes that will please everybody. This is definitely one of them."
—**BETTY SPARKS** WINDSOR, CT

GOLDEN PORK CHOPS

Golden Pork Chops

PREP: 10 MIN. • **BAKE:** 35 MIN.
MAKES: 4 SERVINGS

- 1 can (14¾ ounces) cream-style corn
- ½ cup finely chopped onion
- ½ cup finely chopped celery
- ½ teaspoon paprika
- 1½ cups crushed corn bread stuffing
- 4 boneless pork loin chops (6 ounces each)
- 1 tablespoon brown sugar
- 1 tablespoon spicy brown mustard

1. In a large bowl, combine the corn, onion, celery and paprika. Stir in stuffing. Transfer to a greased 11x7-in. baking dish.

2. Arrange pork chops over stuffing. Combine brown sugar and mustard; spread over chops. Bake, uncovered, at 400° for 35-40 minutes or until meat juices run clear.

Glazed Ham Steaks

Here's an easy way to serve classic fruit-sweetened ham for just a small group of people. Your family will be so impressed with this delicious dish, they will ask for it often.

—ERNESTINE BEOUGHTER AWRENCEVILLE, IL

START TO FINISH: 30 MIN.
MAKES: 4 SERVINGS

- 1 can (8 ounces) sliced pineapple
- 2 boneless fully cooked ham steaks (about 2 pounds)
- ¼ cup packed brown sugar
- ½ teaspoon Dijon mustard
- 4 maraschino cherries

Drain the pineapple, reserving 1 tablespoon juice; set pineapple aside (discard remaining juice or save for another use). Cut each ham steak in half; place in an ungreased baking pan. Combine brown sugar, mustard and reserved juice; spread over ham. Top with pineapple and cherries. Bake, uncovered, at 350° for 20-25 minutes or until heated through.

BLT MEATBALL SLIDERS

BLT Meatball Sliders

Take sliders to a whole new level with the addition of bacon, ground pork and zesty ranch mayo. Your guests will surely make these disappear fast.

—DAMALI CAMPBELL NEW YORK, NY

PREP: 25 MIN. • **BAKE:** 30 MIN.
MAKES: 1½ DOZEN

- 1 pound uncooked bacon strips
- 1 cup 2% milk
- 1 egg, beaten
- 1 cup dry bread crumbs
- 1 small onion, finely chopped
- 1 tablespoon fennel seed, crushed
- 1 teaspoon salt
- 1 teaspoon pepper
- ½ teaspoon crushed red pepper flakes
- ¾ pound ground pork
- ½ pound lean ground beef (90% lean)
- ⅔ cup mayonnaise
- 1½ teaspoons ranch dip mix
- 18 dinner rolls, split
- 3 cups spring mix salad greens
- 3 plum tomatoes, sliced

1. Place bacon in a food processor; cover and process until finely chopped. In a large bowl, combine the milk, egg, bread crumbs, onion and seasonings. Crumble the bacon, pork and beef over mixture and mix well. Shape into 2-in. meatballs.

2. Place meatballs in an ungreased 15x10x 1-in. baking pan. Bake at 425° for 30-35 minutes or until a thermometer reads 160°.

3. Combine mayonnaise and dip mix; spread over rolls. Layer each roll bottom with salad greens, a tomato slice and a meatball; replace tops.

Fish & Seafood

225 222 227

Satisfy a healthy appetite with **fresh-caught favorites** such as zesty **crab melts** or lightened-up **fish 'n' chips**. Discover easy, **indulgent potpies** for two, crunchy **fish cakes** and fabulous new ways to prepare **salmon, tilapia** and a comforting **tuna casserole** in this chapter.

TILAPIA TACOS

Sole Thermidor

My twin sister shared this recipe with me several years ago. It's both impressive and delicious, making it perfect for company.

—**NELLA PARKER** HERSEY, MI

PREP: 20 MIN. • **BAKE:** 30 MIN.
MAKES: 8 SERVINGS

- 8 sole fillets (4 ounces each)
- 2 tablespoons butter, melted
- 1½ teaspoons seasoned salt
- ⅛ teaspoon pepper
- 1¼ cups milk, divided
- 3 tablespoons butter
- 3 tablespoons all-purpose flour
- 1 cup (4 ounces) shredded cheddar cheese
- 3 tablespoons sherry or chicken broth
- 1 teaspoon dried tarragon
- ⅛ teaspoon paprika

1. Brush fillets with melted butter; sprinkle with seasoned salt and pepper. Starting with a short side, roll up. Place seam side down in a greased 9-in.-square baking pan. Pour ½ cup milk over fillets. Bake, uncovered, at 350° for 25-30 minutes or until fish flakes easily with a fork.
2. Meanwhile, in a small saucepan, melt butter. Stir in flour until smooth; gradually add remaining milk. Bring to a boil; cook and stir for 1 minute or until thickened. Reduce heat; stir in the cheese, sherry and tarragon.
3. Drain pan juices from the fish, reserving ¼ cup; stir into cheese mixture. Pour over fish; sprinkle with paprika. Broil 4 in. from the heat for 3-4 minutes or until lightly browned.

Flounder, another type of **delicately flavored flatfish,** is an **excellent substitute** if sole is not available or too expensive.

Tilapia Tacos

I absolutely love fish tacos and wanted to create a slimmed-down recipe so I could enjoy them anytime without the guilt. I never get complaints when I serve these for dinner.

—**JADE PETERSON** PORTLAND, OR

START TO FINISH: 30 MIN.
MAKES: 4 SERVINGS

- 1 egg
- 1 tablespoon fat-free milk
- ½ teaspoon green hot pepper sauce
- ½ cup cornmeal
- 2 tablespoons all-purpose flour
- ¼ teaspoon ground cumin
- ¼ teaspoon pepper
- 4 tilapia fillets (4 ounces each), cut lengthwise in half
- 4 teaspoons olive oil
- 1 can (15 ounces) Southwestern black beans
- 8 corn tortillas (6 inches), warmed
- 3 plum tomatoes, chopped
- 2 cups shredded cabbage
- ½ cup salsa verde
- ¼ cup minced fresh cilantro
   Lime wedges

1. Preheat oven to 375°. In a shallow bowl, whisk egg, milk and pepper sauce. In another shallow bowl, mix cornmeal, flour, cumin and pepper. Dip tilapia in egg mixture, then in cornmeal mixture, patting to help coating adhere. Place on a baking sheet coated with cooking spray. Drizzle the tops with oil. Bake for 15-20 minutes or until fish flakes easily with a fork.
2. Meanwhile, place beans in a small saucepan; heat through over medium-low heat, stirring occasionally. Serve tilapia in tortillas; top with beans, tomatoes, cabbage, salsa verde and cilantro. Serve with lime wedges.
PER SERVING *2 tacos equals 438 cal., 9 g fat (2 g sat. fat), 87 mg chol., 567 mg sodium, 57 g carb., 12 g fiber, 34 g pro.*

CAPTAIN RUSSELL'S JAMBALAYA

EAT SMART

Walnut-Crusted Salmon

Whenever I can get salmon for a good price, I turn to this simple and delicious recipe. The fish is good served with mashed potatoes and fresh green beans.
—**EDIE DESPAIN** LOGAN, UT

START TO FINISH: 25 MIN.
MAKES: 4 SERVINGS

- 4 **salmon fillets (4 ounces each)**
- 4 **teaspoons Dijon mustard**
- 4 **teaspoons honey**
- 2 **slices whole wheat bread, torn into pieces**
- 3 **tablespoons finely chopped walnuts**
- 2 **teaspoons canola oil**
- ½ **teaspoon dried thyme**

1. Preheat oven to 400°. Place salmon on a baking sheet coated with cooking spray. Mix mustard and honey; brush over salmon. Place bread in a food processor; pulse until coarse crumbs form. Transfer to a small bowl. Stir in walnuts, oil and thyme; press onto the salmon.
2. Bake 12-15 minutes or until topping is lightly browned and fish just begins to flake easily with a fork.
PER SERVING *1 fillet equals 295 cal., 17 g fat (3 g sat. fat), 57 mg chol., 243 mg sodium, 13 g carb., 1 g fiber, 22 g pro.* **Diabetic Exchanges:** *3 lean meat, 1 starch, ½ fat.*

You can **freeze** salmon and other **oily types of fish**, such as whitefish, mackerel and lake trout, for **up to 3 months**. Wrap fish in **freezer paper**, freezer **bags** or heavy-duty **foil** before freezing.

Captain Russell's Jambalaya

A tour guide in New Orleans gave me this recipe. It's so easy to prepare, and the deliciously authentic Cajun flavors make it one of my favorites.
—**DONNA LAMANO** OLATHE, KS

PREP: 15 MIN. • **BAKE:** 40 MIN.
MAKES: 6 SERVINGS

- 1 **can (10½ ounces) condensed French onion soup**
- 1¼ **cups reduced-sodium beef broth**
- 1 **can (8 ounces) tomato sauce**
- ½ **cup butter, cubed**
- 1 **small green pepper, chopped**
- 1 **small onion, chopped**
- 1½ **teaspoons Creole seasoning**
- 1 **teaspoon hot pepper sauce**
- 1 **pound uncooked medium shrimp, peeled and deveined**
- ½ **pound fully cooked andouille sausage links, halved lengthwise and cut into ½-inch slices**
- 2 **cups uncooked long grain rice**

1. Preheat oven to 375°. In a large saucepan, combine the first eight ingredients. Bring to a boil. Remove from heat; stir in shrimp, sausage and rice. Transfer to a greased 13x9-in. baking dish.
2. Cover and bake for 30 minutes. Remove foil and stir; cover and bake 10-15 minutes longer or until the rice is tender.
NOTE *The following spices may be substituted for 1 teaspoon Creole seasoning: ¼ teaspoon each salt, garlic powder and paprika; and a pinch each of dried thyme, ground cumin and cayenne pepper.*

WALNUT-CRUSTED SALMON

Broccoli Tuna Casserole

When I was in the Navy, a co-worker's wife shared this recipe with me. I've made adjustments over the years, but it still brings back memories of my "family" away from home.

—YVONNE COOK HASKINS, OH

PREP: 35 MIN. • **BAKE:** 1 HOUR
MAKES: 8 SERVINGS

- 5 **cups uncooked whole wheat egg noodles**
- 1 **teaspoon butter**
- ¼ **cup chopped onion**
- ¼ **cup cornstarch**
- 2 **cups fat-free milk**
- 1 **teaspoon dried basil**
- 1 **teaspoon dried thyme**
- ¾ **teaspoon salt**
- ½ **teaspoon pepper**
- 1 **cup reduced-sodium chicken broth**
- 1 **cup (4 ounces) shredded Monterey Jack cheese, divided**
- 4 **cups frozen broccoli florets, thawed**
- 2 **pouches (6.4 ounces each) albacore white tuna in water**
- ⅓ **cup panko (Japanese) bread crumbs**
- 1 **tablespoon butter, melted**

1. Preheat oven to 350°. Cook the noodles according to the package directions; drain. Transfer to a shallow 3-qt. or 13x9-in. baking dish coated with cooking spray.

2. In a large nonstick skillet coated with cooking spray, heat butter over medium-high heat. Add onion; cook and stir until tender. In a small bowl, whisk the cornstarch, milk and seasonings until smooth; stir into pan. Add broth. Bring to a boil; cook and stir 2 minutes or until thickened. Stir in ¾ cup cheese, broccoli and tuna.

3. Spoon over noodles; mix well. Sprinkle with remaining cheese. Toss bread crumbs with melted butter; sprinkle over the top. Bake, covered, for 45 minutes. Uncover and bake 15-20 minutes longer or until cheese is melted.

FREEZE OPTION *Cool unbaked casserole; cover and freeze. To use, partially thaw in the refrigerator overnight. Remove from refrigerator 30 minutes before baking. Preheat oven to 350°. Bake the casserole as directed, increasing time as necessary to heat through and for a thermometer inserted in center to read 165°.*

PER SERVING *1¼ cups equals 271 cal., 8 g fat (4 g sat. fat), 38 mg chol., 601 mg sodium, 30 g carb., 4 g fiber, 22 g pro.* **Diabetic Exchanges:** *2 starch, 2 lean meat, ½ fat.*

Fish Po'boys

You can use your favorite brand of frozen breaded fish in this classic sandwich recipe. The quick sauce makes it taste homemade.

—*TASTE OF HOME* TEST KITCHEN

START TO FINISH: 30 MIN.
MAKES: 6 SERVINGS

- 2 **packages (11.4 ounces each) frozen crunchy breaded fish fillets**
- ½ **cup mayonnaise**
- 1 **tablespoon minced fresh parsley**
- 1 **tablespoon ketchup**
- 2 **teaspoons stone-ground mustard**
- 1 **teaspoon horseradish sauce**
- 2 **to 4 drops hot pepper sauce**
- 1½ **cups deli coleslaw**
- 6 **hamburger buns, split**

1. Bake fish according to the package directions. Meanwhile, in a small bowl, combine the mayonnaise, parsley, ketchup, mustard, horseradish sauce and pepper sauce until blended.

2. Spoon ¼ cup coleslaw onto the bottom of each bun; top with two pieces of fish. Spread with sauce; replace bun tops.

Red Snapper for Two

Here's a fast and easy recipe that's healthy, too. Add a tossed salad and some bakery bread, and you have a gourmet meal with very little cleanup.

—JOY ADCOCK AMARILLO, TX

PREP: 20 MIN. • **BAKE:** 15 MIN.
MAKES: 2 SERVINGS

- ¼ cup chopped onion
- 1 garlic clove, minced
- 2 teaspoons olive oil
- ½ cup chopped fresh mushrooms
- 1 medium tomato, chopped
- ¼ cup white wine or chicken broth
- ¼ teaspoon salt
- ¼ teaspoon dried basil
- ¼ teaspoon dried oregano
  Dash pepper
- 2 red snapper fillets (8 ounces each)
- 2 teaspoons grated Parmesan cheese
- 1 tablespoon minced fresh parsley

1. In a small saucepan, saute onion and garlic in oil for 1 minute. Stir in mushrooms and tomato; cook 3 minutes longer. Stir in the wine, salt, basil, oregano and pepper. Bring to a boil. Reduce heat and simmer, uncovered, for 7-11 minutes or until sauce is thickened.

2. Place fish in a greased 13x9-in. baking dish; top with sauce. Sprinkle with cheese. Bake, uncovered, at 400° for 12-18 minutes or until fish flakes easily with a fork. Sprinkle with the minced parsley.

PER SERVING *1 fillet equals 297 cal., 8 g fat (2 g sat. fat), 73 mg chol., 416 mg sodium, 7 g carb., 2 g fiber, 43 g pro.* **Diabetic Exchanges:** *6 lean meat, 1 vegetable, 1 fat.*

"My family loves fish, and this superfast entree is popular in our house. It cooks in minutes under the broiler while you whip up the hearty salsa to serve alongside. We like it with couscous and plenty of lemon wedges."

—BRENDA COFFEY SINGER ISLAND, FL

Tilapia with Corn Salsa

START TO FINISH: 10 MIN.
MAKES: 4 SERVINGS

- 4 tilapia fillets (6 ounces each)
- 1 tablespoon olive oil
- ¼ teaspoon salt
- ¼ teaspoon pepper
- 1 can (15 ounces) black beans, rinsed and drained
- 1 can (11 ounces) whole kernel corn, drained
- ¾ cup Italian salad dressing
- 2 tablespoons chopped green onion
- 2 tablespoons chopped sweet red pepper

1. Drizzle both sides of fillets with oil; sprinkle with salt and pepper.

2. Broil 4-6 in. from the heat for 5-7 minutes or until fish flakes easily with a fork. Meanwhile, in a small bowl, combine the remaining ingredients. Serve with the fish.

RED SNAPPER FOR TWO

**BAKED COD PICCATA
WITH ASPARAGUS**

Baked Cod Piccata with Asparagus

It takes longer for the oven to preheat than it does to assemble this delicious dish. While it's baking, I throw together a simple salad.

—**BARBARA LENTO** HOUSTON, PA

START TO FINISH: 30 MIN.
MAKES: 4 SERVINGS

- 1 **pound fresh asparagus, trimmed**
- ¼ **cup water**
- 1 **pound cod fillet, cut into four pieces**
- 2 **tablespoons lemon juice**
- 1 **teaspoon salt-free lemon-pepper seasoning**
- ½ **teaspoon garlic powder**
- 2 **tablespoons butter, cubed**
- 2 **teaspoons capers**
  Minced fresh parsley, optional

1. Place asparagus in an ungreased 11x7-in. baking dish; add water. Arrange cod over asparagus. Sprinkle with the lemon juice, lemon pepper and garlic powder. Dot with butter; sprinkle with capers.

2. Bake, uncovered, at 400° for 12-15 minutes or until fish flakes easily with a fork and asparagus is tender. If desired, sprinkle with minced parsley.

PER SERVING *1 serving equals 150 cal., 7 g fat (4 g sat. fat), 58 mg chol., 265 mg sodium, 3 g carb., 1 g fiber, 20 g pro. Diabetic Exchanges: 3 lean meat, 1 fat.*

Capers are the **flower buds** of a small bush from the Mediterranean and Middle East. The **smallest** capers, **French nonpareils**, are considered to be the **finest**.

CRUNCHY SALMON CAKES WITH GREEK YOGURT SAUCE

Crunchy Salmon Cakes with Greek Yogurt Sauce

Whether you start with fresh salmon or use leftover cooked salmon, you can serve these versatile fish cakes as a main dish, as appetizers, or over greens as a main-dish salad.

—**CINDY FAN** ALHAMBRA, CA

PREP: 30 MIN. + CHILLING • **BAKE:** 15 MIN.
MAKES: 4 SERVINGS

- 1¼ **pounds salmon fillet**
- ⅛ **teaspoon plus ¼ teaspoon pepper, divided**
- 1 **teaspoon olive oil**
- 1 **small onion, finely chopped**
- 2 **tablespoons minced fresh parsley**
- 1½ **cups panko (Japanese) bread crumbs, divided**
- ½ **cup reduced-fat mayonnaise**
- 1 **tablespoon lemon juice**
- ¼ **teaspoon salt**
- 1 **teaspoon hot pepper sauce, optional**
- 2 **egg whites, lightly beaten**
  Cooking spray

SAUCE

- ¼ **cup reduced-fat plain Greek yogurt**
- 1 **teaspoon snipped fresh dill**
- ¾ **teaspoon lemon juice**
- ¼ **teaspoon capers, drained and chopped**

1. Place salmon on a baking sheet coated with cooking spray; sprinkle with ⅛ teaspoon pepper. Bake, uncovered, at 350° for 14-17 minutes or until fish flakes easily with a fork. Cool slightly; remove the skin, if necessary. Transfer salmon to a shallow dish; refrigerate, covered, for 2 hours or until chilled.

2. In a large skillet, heat oil over medium-high heat. Add onion; cook and stir onion until tender. Stir in the parsley.

3. In a large bowl, combine ½ cup bread crumbs, mayonnaise, lemon juice, salt, remaining pepper and the onion mixture; if desired, add pepper sauce. Flake salmon; add to bread crumb mixture, mixing lightly. Shape into eight 2½-in. patties.

4. Place egg whites and remaining bread crumbs in separate shallow bowls. Dip salmon patties in egg whites, then roll in crumbs to coat. Place on a baking sheet coated with cooking spray. Spritz tops with cooking spray. Bake at 425° for 14-17 minutes or until golden brown.

5. In a small bowl, mix sauce ingredients; serve with salmon cakes.

PER SERVING *2 salmon cakes with 1 tablespoon sauce equals 422 cal., 25 g fat (4 g sat. fat), 82 mg chol., 541 mg sodium, 17 g carb., 1 g fiber, 29 g pro.*

CAJUN POPCORN SHRIMP SANDWICHES

Cajun Popcorn Shrimp Sandwiches

Cajun mayo is what sets these quick pitas apart. I often double the batch and spice it all up with extra hot sauce to create a tasty sandwich dipper.
—KENT WHITAKER ROSSVILLE, GA

START TO FINISH: 30 MIN.
MAKES: 4 SERVINGS

- 2 **tablespoons butter, melted**
- 1 **teaspoon garlic powder**
- ¼ **to ½ teaspoon Cajun seasoning**
- 3½ **cups frozen breaded popcorn shrimp**
- ½ **cup mayonnaise**
- 1 **tablespoon hot pepper sauce**
- 1 **teaspoon sweet pickle relish**
- ½ **teaspoon prepared mustard**
- 8 **pita pocket halves, warmed**
- 1 **cup shredded lettuce**
- 8 **thin slices tomato**

1. In a bowl, combine butter, garlic powder and Cajun seasoning. Toss with shrimp. Prepare the shrimp according to package directions for baking.
2. Combine the mayonnaise, pepper sauce, relish and mustard. Spread into warmed pitas. Fill pitas with shrimp, lettuce and sliced tomato.

Tuna Salad Biscuit Cups

I fill easy biscuit cups with tuna salad that gets a nice crunch from water chestnuts. The cups are ideal for buffets and meals on the go.
—SUSAN JAMES COKATO, MN

START TO FINISH: 25 MIN.
MAKES: 5 SERVINGS

- 1 **tube (12 ounces) refrigerated buttermilk biscuits**
- ½ **cup mayonnaise**
- 2 **tablespoons sweet pickle relish**
- 1 **tablespoon soy sauce**
- ¼ **teaspoon dill weed**
- 1 **can (12 ounces) tuna, drained and flaked**
- 1 **can (8 ounces) water chestnuts, drained and finely chopped**

1. Flatten each biscuit into a 3-in. circle and press into a greased muffin cup. Bake at 400° for 10-12 minutes or until golden brown. Cool 5 minutes on a wire rack.
2. Meanwhile, in a small bowl, combine the mayonnaise, relish, soy sauce and dill. Stir in tuna and water chestnuts. Spoon into biscuit cups. Serve immediately.

Northwest Salmon Salad

I love that I can use my favorite Northwest ingredients—fresh salmon, blueberries and hazelnuts—all in one recipe. The salmon and the sour cream dressing are just as scrumptious in a sandwich.
—ELDA CLEVENGER DEXTER, OR

PREP: 45 MIN. • **MAKES:** 4 SERVINGS

- 1 **salmon fillet (1 pound)**
- ½ **teaspoon salt**
- ½ **teaspoon plus ⅛ teaspoon coarsely ground pepper, divided**
- 2 **tablespoons lemon juice, divided**
- 4 **fresh dill sprigs**
- 1 **cup chopped peeled cucumber**
- ½ **cup reduced-fat sour cream**
- ¼ **cup finely chopped sweet red pepper**
- ¼ **cup snipped fresh dill**
- 3 **tablespoons capers, drained**
- 8 **cups torn Bibb lettuce**
- 1 **medium peach, peeled and sliced**
- ¼ **cup chopped hazelnuts**
- ¼ **cup fresh blueberries**
- 4 **thin slices red onion, separated into rings**

1. Place salmon on a greased baking sheet; sprinkle with the salt and ½ teaspoon pepper. Drizzle with 1 tablespoon lemon juice; top with dill sprigs.
2. Bake, uncovered, at 425° for 15-18 minutes or until fish flakes easily with a fork. Flake salmon into large pieces.
3. In a small bowl, combine the cucumber, sour cream, red pepper, snipped dill, capers and remaining pepper and lemon juice.
4. Divide lettuce among four plates. Top with peach slices, hazelnuts, blueberries, onion and salmon. Serve with dressing.
PER SERVING *1 serving equals 305 cal., 18 g fat (4 g sat. fat), 67 mg chol., 571 mg sodium, 13 g carb., 3 g fiber, 25 g pro.* **Diabetic Exchanges:** *3 lean meat, 2 fat, 1 starch.*

Coquilles St. Jacques for One

Buttery scallops in rich, creamy sauce would be tough to share. Good thing you don't have to!

—**BETSY ESLEY** LAKE ALFRED, FL

START TO FINISH: 30 MIN.
MAKES: 1 SERVING

- 6 ounces bay scallops
- 3 tablespoons white wine or chicken broth
- 2 teaspoons butter
- ¼ teaspoon dried minced onion
- 1½ teaspoons all-purpose flour
- ¼ cup heavy whipping cream
- 3 tablespoons shredded cheddar cheese

TOPPING
- 4 teaspoons dry bread crumbs
- 1 teaspoon butter, melted
  Paprika

1. In a small skillet, combine the scallops, wine, butter and onion. Bring to a boil. Reduce the heat; cover and simmer for 1-2 minutes or until the scallops are firm and opaque. Using a slotted spoon, remove scallops and keep warm.

2. Bring liquid in pan to a boil; cook until the liquid is reduced to about 2 tablespoons, about 3 minutes. Stir in flour until smooth; gradually add cream. Bring to a boil; cook and stir for 1 minute or until thickened. Remove from the heat. Stir in cheese until melted. Return scallops to the skillet. Pour into a greased 6-oz. ramekin or custard cup.

3. In a small bowl, combine bread crumbs and butter; sprinkle over the top. Sprinkle with paprika. Bake, uncovered, at 400° for 4-5 minutes or until golden brown.

EAT SMART
Phyllo-Wrapped Halibut

I created these packets to convince my husband that seafood doesn't have to taste fishy. He likes the flaky phyllo wrapping with mild fish and vegetables tucked inside.

—**CARRIE VAZZANO** ROLLING MEADOWS, IL

PREP: 20 MIN. • **BAKE:** 20 MIN.
MAKES: 2 SERVINGS

- 4 cups fresh baby spinach
- ¾ cup chopped sweet red pepper
- ¾ teaspoon salt-free lemon-pepper seasoning, divided
- ½ teaspoon lemon juice
- 6 sheets phyllo dough (14 inches x 9 inches)
- 2 tablespoons reduced-fat butter, melted
- 2 halibut fillets (4 ounces each)
- ¼ teaspoon salt
- ⅛ teaspoon pepper
- ¼ cup shredded part-skim mozzarella cheese

1. In a large nonstick skillet lightly coated with cooking spray, saute spinach and red pepper until tender. Add ½ teaspoon lemon pepper and the lemon juice. Remove from the heat; cool.

2. Line a baking sheet with foil and coat the foil with cooking spray; set aside. Place one sheet of phyllo dough on a work surface; brush with butter. (Until ready to use, keep phyllo dough covered with plastic wrap and a damp towel to prevent it from drying out.) Layer the remaining phyllo over the first sheet, brushing each sheet with butter. Cut stack in half widthwise.

3. Place a halibut fillet in the center of each square; sprinkle with salt and pepper. Top with cheese and spinach mixture. Fold sides and bottom edge over fillet and roll up to enclose it; trim end of phyllo if necessary. Brush with remaining butter; sprinkle with remaining lemon pepper.

4. Place seam side down on prepared baking sheet. Bake fish at 375° for 20-25 minutes or until golden brown.

NOTE *This recipe was tested with Land O'Lakes light stick butter.*

PER SERVING *1 serving equals 330 cal., 12 g fat (6 g sat. fat), 64 mg chol., 676 mg sodium, 26 g carb., 4 g fiber, 33 g pro.* **Diabetic Exchanges:** *4 lean meat, 2 vegetable, 1 starch, 1 fat.*

PHYLLO-WRAPPED HALIBUT

QUICK CRAB MELTS

Seafood Potpies

If you're a fan of crab and shrimp, you'll really like this recipe. It's an old family favorite, and it tastes gourmet even though it's easy to make. All my friends love it!

—**CAROL HICKEY** LAKE ST. LOUIS, MO

PREP: 15 MIN. • **BAKE:** 30 MIN.
MAKES: 2 SERVINGS

- 1   sheet refrigerated pie pastry
- 1   can (6 ounces) crabmeat, drained, flaked and cartilage removed
- 1   can (4 ounces) tiny shrimp, rinsed and drained
- ½ cup chopped celery
- ½ cup mayonnaise
- ¼ cup chopped green pepper
- 2   tablespoons diced pimientos
- 1   tablespoon lemon juice
- 1½ teaspoons chopped onion
- ¼ teaspoon seafood seasoning
- ¼ cup shredded cheddar cheese

1. On a lightly floured surface, roll out pastry to ⅛-in. thickness. Cut out two 7-in. circles (discard scraps or save for another use). Press pastry circles onto the bottom and up the sides of two ungreased 10-oz. custard cups.
2. Place on a baking sheet. Bake at 425° for 7-10 minutes or until golden brown. Reduce heat to 375°.
3. In a small bowl, combine the crab, shrimp, celery, mayonnaise, green pepper, pimientos, lemon juice, onion and seafood seasoning. Spoon into hot shells. Sprinkle with cheese. Bake for 20-25 minutes or until bubbly and cheese is melted.

For an **oniony variation**, mix the cheese into the potpie filling and top the **potpies** with **French-fried onions** instead.

Quick Crab Melts

Two types of cheese melted over a savory crab mixture make these sandwiches amazing. I usually serve them for dinner, but they make terrific appetizers when you cut them in half.

—**DONNA BENNETT** BRAMALEA, ON

START TO FINISH: 15 MIN.
MAKES: 2 SERVINGS

- 1   can (6 ounces) crabmeat, drained, flaked and cartilage removed
- 3   tablespoons mayonnaise
- 5   teaspoons finely chopped celery
- 1   tablespoon minced green onion
- 2   English muffins, split
- 4   slices tomato
- 4   thin slices cheddar cheese
- 4   thin slices Monterey Jack cheese
     Paprika

1. Preheat broiler. In a small bowl, mix crab, mayonnaise, celery and green onion until blended. Place muffin halves on an ungreased baking sheet.
2. Broil 4-6 in. from the heat until toasted. Spread with crab mixture. Top with the tomato and cheeses; sprinkle with the paprika. Broil until bubbly.

Wild Rice Shrimp Bake

Shrimp lends a special touch to meals, and this recipe comes together in a flash. Don't skip the croutons on top—they're a nice contrast to the creamy casserole.

—**LEE STEARNS** MOBILE, AL

PREP: 20 MIN. • **BAKE:** 20 MIN.
MAKES: 6 SERVINGS

- 1   package (6 ounces) long grain and wild rice mix
- 1   pound uncooked medium shrimp, peeled and deveined
- 1   medium green pepper, chopped
- 1   medium onion, chopped
- 1   can (4 ounces) mushroom stems and pieces, drained
- ¼ cup butter
- 1   can (10¾ ounces) condensed cream of chicken soup, undiluted
- ½ cup seasoned stuffing croutons

1. Prepare rice according to the package directions.
2. Meanwhile, in a large skillet, saute the shrimp, green pepper, onion and mushrooms in butter until shrimp turn pink. Add the soup to the rice; stir into the shrimp mixture.
3. Transfer to a greased 2-qt. baking dish. Sprinkle with croutons. Bake, uncovered, at 350° for 20-25 minutes or until heated through.

"Enjoy moist, flavorful fish with a coating that's as crunchy and golden as deep-fried. And you can easily bake up crisp, irresistible fries to serve on the side."

—JANICE MITCHELL AURORA, CO

OVEN FISH AND CHIPS

Oven Fish and Chips

PREP: 10 MIN. • **BAKE:** 35 MIN.
MAKES: 4 SERVINGS

- 1 **pound potatoes (about 2 medium)**
- 2 **tablespoons olive oil**
- ¼ **teaspoon pepper**

FISH
- ⅓ **cup all-purpose flour**
- ¼ **teaspoon pepper**
- 1 **egg**
- 2 **tablespoons water**
- ⅔ **cup crushed cornflakes**
- 1 **tablespoon grated Parmesan cheese**
- ⅛ **teaspoon cayenne pepper**
- 1 **pound haddock or cod fillets**
  Tartar sauce, optional

1. Preheat oven to 425°. Peel and cut the potatoes lengthwise into ½-in.-thick slices; cut slices into ½-in.-thick sticks.
2. In a large bowl, toss the potatoes with oil and pepper. Transfer to a 15x10x1-in. baking pan coated with cooking spray. Bake 25-30 minutes or until golden brown and crisp, stirring once.
3. Meanwhile, in a shallow bowl, mix flour and pepper. In another shallow bowl, whisk egg with water. In a third bowl, toss cornflakes with cheese and cayenne.
4. Dip fish in the flour mixture to coat both sides; shake off excess. Dip in egg mixture, then in cornflake mixture, patting to help the coating adhere.
5. Place on a baking sheet coated with cooking spray. Bake 10-12 minutes or until fish just begins to flake easily with a fork. Serve with potatoes and, if desired, tartar sauce.

PER SERVING *1 serving equals 376 cal., 9 g fat (2 g sat. fat), 120 mg chol., 228 mg sodium, 44 g carb., 2 g fiber, 28 g pro.* **Diabetic Exchanges:** *3 starch, 3 lean meat, 1½ fat.*

SALMON WITH GINGERED RHUBARB COMPOTE

Salmon with Gingered Rhubarb Compote

Rhubarb plays the role of lemon in this recipe, brightening and accenting the rich taste of fish. I like to double the amount of compote and save half for another quick and healthy meal.

—SUSAN ASANOVIC WILTON, CT

PREP: 30 MIN. • **BAKE:** 20 MIN.
MAKES: 4 SERVINGS

- 1 **medium onion, thinly sliced**
- 4 **green onions, sliced**
- 2 **tablespoons butter**
- 4 **cups sliced fresh or frozen rhubarb**
- ¼ **cup packed brown sugar**
- ½ **cup sweet white wine or white grape juice**
- 1 **tablespoon minced fresh gingerroot**
- ½ **teaspoon salt**
- ¼ **teaspoon pepper**
- 4 **salmon fillets (6 ounces each)**
  Additional sliced green onions, optional

1. In a large ovenproof skillet, cook onions in butter over medium heat for 15-20 minutes or until golden brown, stirring frequently.
2. Add rhubarb and brown sugar; cook 3 minutes longer. Stir in the wine, ginger, salt and pepper. Bring to a boil. Reduce the heat; simmer, uncovered, for 5-10 minutes or until the rhubarb is tender, stirring occasionally.
3. Place salmon over rhubarb mixture. Bake, uncovered, at 350° for 20-25 minutes or until fish flakes easily with a fork. Sprinkle with additional green onions if desired.

Crunchy Tuna Surprise

This recipe comes from my Grandma Mollie's kitchen. With my busy lifestyle, I appreciate quick and easy family-pleasers like this.

—LISA LE SAGE WAUWATOSA, WI

START TO FINISH: 30 MIN.
MAKES: 4 SERVINGS

- 1 **can (12 ounces) tuna, drained and flaked**
- 1½ **cups cooked rice**
- 1 **can (10¾ ounces) condensed cream of mushroom soup, undiluted**
- ½ **cup 2% milk**
- ¼ **cup minced fresh parsley**
- ¾ **cup crushed cornflakes**
- 2 **tablespoons butter, melted**

1. In a large bowl, combine the first five ingredients. Transfer to a greased shallow 1½-qt. baking dish.
2. Combine the cornflake crumbs and butter; sprinkle over the top. Bake, uncovered, at 350° for 25-30 minutes or until bubbly.

Bonus: Desserts

From **old-fashioned dumplings** to bite-size **cheesecake candies**, from a fancy **hot cocoa souffle** to **fast oatmeal bars** made in the **microwave**, you'll discover a bounty of **sweet specialties** guaranteed to **delight** in this beautiful **bonus chapter**.

HOT COCOA SOUFFLE

Poppy Seed Citrus Cake

My youngest daughter loves anything with lemon, and this is her favorite cake. It's a refreshing delight all year round, but we especially like it for Easter and picnics.
—**CHAROLETTE WESTFALL** HOUSTON, TX

PREP: 15 MIN. • **BAKE:** 40 MIN. + COOLING
MAKES: 12 SERVINGS

- 1 package lemon cake mix (regular size)
- 3 eggs
- 1⅓ cups orange juice
- ½ cup canola oil
- 1 to 2 tablespoons poppy seeds
- 1 teaspoon grated lemon peel
- 1 teaspoon grated orange peel

GLAZE

- 2 cups confectioners' sugar
- 3 to 4 tablespoons orange juice
- ½ teaspoon grated lemon peel
- ½ teaspoon grated orange peel

1. In a large bowl, combine the cake mix, eggs, orange juice and oil; beat on low speed for 30 seconds. Beat on medium for 2 minutes. Fold in the poppy seeds, lemon and orange peel.
2. Pour into a well-greased and floured 10-in. fluted tube pan. Bake at 350° for 40-45 minutes or until a toothpick inserted near the center comes out clean. Cool for 10 minutes before removing from pan to a wire rack to cool completely.
3. In a small bowl, combine the confectioners' sugar and orange juice until smooth. Drizzle over warm cake. Sprinkle with lemon and orange peels.

Hot Cocoa Souffle

A friend invited me to attend a cooking demo at her church years ago, and one of the recipes prepared there was this luscious, chocolaty souffle. It tastes absolutely delicious.
—**JOAN HALLFORD** FORT WORTH, TX

PREP: 20 MIN. • **BAKE:** 40 MIN.
MAKES: 6 SERVINGS

- 5 eggs
- 4 teaspoons plus ¾ cup sugar, divided
- ½ cup baking cocoa
- 6 tablespoons all-purpose flour
- ¼ teaspoon salt
- 1½ cups fat-free milk
- 2 tablespoons butter
- 1½ teaspoons vanilla extract

1. Separate eggs; let stand at room temperature for 30 minutes. Coat a 2-qt. souffle dish with cooking spray and lightly sprinkle with 4 teaspoons sugar; set aside.
2. In a small saucepan, combine the cocoa, flour, salt and remaining sugar. Gradually whisk in milk. Bring to a boil, stirring constantly. Cook and stir 1-2 minutes longer or until thickened. Stir in butter. Transfer to a large bowl.
3. Stir a small amount of hot mixture into egg yolks; return all to the bowl, stirring constantly. Add the vanilla; cool slightly.
4. In another large bowl with clean beaters, beat egg whites until stiff peaks form. With a spatula, stir a fourth of the egg whites into chocolate mixture until no white streaks remain. Fold in remaining egg whites until combined.
5. Transfer to prepared dish. Bake at 350° for 40-45 minutes or until the top is puffed and center appears set. Serve immediately.
PER SERVING *1 serving equals 272 cal., 9 g fat (4 g sat. fat), 188 mg chol., 209 mg sodium, 41 g carb., 2 g fiber, 9 g pro.*

BILTMORE'S
BREAD PUDDING

Biltmore's Bread Pudding

Here's one of our classic dessert recipes. A golden caramel sauce enhances the rich bread pudding.
—BILTMORE ESTATE ASHEVILLE, NC

PREP: 30 MIN. • **BAKE:** 40 MIN.
MAKES: 12 SERVINGS

- 8 cups cubed day-old bread
- 9 eggs
- 2¼ cups milk
- 1¾ cups heavy whipping cream
- 1 cup sugar
- ¾ cup butter, melted
- 3 teaspoons vanilla extract
- 1½ teaspoons ground cinnamon

CARAMEL SAUCE

- 1 cup sugar
- ¼ cup water
- 1 tablespoon lemon juice
- 2 tablespoons butter
- 1 cup heavy whipping cream

1. Place bread cubes in a greased 13x9-in. baking dish. In a large bowl, whisk the eggs, milk, cream, sugar, butter, vanilla and cinnamon. Pour evenly over bread.

2. Bake, uncovered, at 350° for 40-45 minutes or until a knife inserted near center comes out clean. Let stand for 5 minutes before cutting.

3. Meanwhile, in a small saucepan, bring the sugar, water and lemon juice to a boil. Reduce heat to medium; cook until sugar is dissolved and mixture turns a golden amber color. Stir in butter until melted. Gradually stir in cream. Serve with bread pudding.

Almond Chocolate Biscotti

PREP: 20 MIN. • **BAKE:** 40 MIN. + COOLING
MAKES: ABOUT 3½ DOZEN

- 1 package chocolate cake mix (regular size)
- 1 cup all-purpose flour
- ½ cup butter, melted
- 2 eggs
- ¼ cup chocolate syrup
- 1 teaspoon vanilla extract
- ½ teaspoon almond extract
- ½ cup slivered almonds
- ½ cup miniature semisweet chocolate chips
- 1 cup white baking chips
- 1 tablespoon shortening

1. Preheat oven to 350°. In a large bowl, beat cake mix, flour, butter, eggs, chocolate syrup and extracts until well blended. Stir in almonds and chocolate chips. Divide dough in half. On ungreased baking sheets, shape each portion into a 12x2-in. log.

2. Bake 30-35 minutes or until firm to the touch. Carefully remove to wire racks; cool 20 minutes.

3. Transfer baked logs to a cutting board. Using a serrated knife, cut diagonally into ½-in. slices. Place on ungreased baking sheets, cut side down. Bake 10-15 minutes or until firm. Remove from pans to wire racks to cool completely.

4. In a microwave, melt baking chips and shortening; stir until smooth. Drizzle over biscotti; let stand until set. Store between pieces of waxed paper in airtight containers.

FREEZE OPTION *Freeze undrizzled cookies in freezer containers. To use, thaw in covered containers. Drizzle with baking chips as directed.*

Dress up a **holiday gift tin** by including a **recipe** card for the **sweet treats** the recipient will find inside. Secure the recipe with a **festive magnet**.

ALMOND CHOCOLATE BISCOTTI

**GLUTEN-FREE
RHUBARB BARS**

Gluten-Free Rhubarb Bars

Rhubarb and strawberry bring spring to your table any month of the year. The crust and crumb topping are so tasty, no one will guess these bars are gluten-free.
—**LISA WILSON** VIRGINIA, MN

PREP: 20 MIN. • **BAKE:** 35 MIN. + COOLING
MAKES: 3 DOZEN

- 2 **cups gluten-free all-purpose baking flour**
- 1 **teaspoon baking powder**
- ½ **cup cold butter**
- 2 **eggs, beaten**
- 3 **tablespoons 2% milk**
- 5 **cups sliced fresh or frozen rhubarb, thawed**
- 1 **package (3 ounces) strawberry gelatin**

TOPPING

- 1 **cup sugar**
- 1 **cup gluten-free all-purpose baking flour**
- ½ **cup cold butter**

1. In a large bowl, combine flour and baking powder. Cut in butter until mixture resembles coarse crumbs. Stir in the eggs and milk just until moistened. Press onto the bottom of a 15x10x1-in. baking pan coated with cooking spray. Top with rhubarb; sprinkle with gelatin.

2. For topping, in a small bowl, combine the sugar and flour. Cut in butter until mixture resembles coarse crumbs. Sprinkle over top. Bake at 375° for 35-40 minutes or until lightly browned. Cool on a wire rack. Cut into bars.

NOTES *Read all ingredient labels for possible gluten content prior to use. Ingredient formulas can change, and production facilities vary among brands. If you're concerned that your brand may contain gluten, contact the company. If using frozen rhubarb, measure rhubarb while still frozen, then thaw completely. Drain in a colander, but do not press liquid out.*

Molded Margaritas

With refreshing lime flavor and a festive look, these cool margaritas are perfect for parties. To make a no-alcohol version, simply replace the tequila with an equal amount of water.
—**BARBARA GERSITZ** PHILADELPHIA, PA

PREP: 15 MIN. + CHILLING
MAKES: 4 SERVINGS

- 2 **packages (3 ounces each) lime gelatin**
- 2 **cups boiling water**
- ½ **cup thawed nonalcoholic margarita mix or limeade concentrate**
- ½ **cup tequila**

In a small bowl, dissolve gelatin in boiling water. Stir in margarita mix and tequila. Pour into four margarita glasses. Refrigerate for 4 hours or until set. Gently stir with a fork before serving if desired.

Chocolate-Covered Cheesecake Squares

Satisfy your cheesecake craving with these bite-size delights! The party favorites are perfect for the holidays, showers and other special occasions.

—ESTHER NEUSTAETER LA CRETE, AB

PREP: 1½ HOURS + FREEZING
MAKES: 49 SQUARES

- 1 cup graham cracker crumbs
- ¼ cup finely chopped pecans
- ¼ cup butter, melted

FILLING

- 2 packages (8 ounces each) cream cheese, softened
- ½ cup sugar
- ¼ cup sour cream
- 2 eggs, lightly beaten
- ½ teaspoon vanilla extract

COATING

- 24 ounces semisweet chocolate, chopped
- 3 tablespoons shortening

1. Line a 9-in.-square baking pan with foil and grease the foil. In a small bowl, combine the graham cracker crumbs, pecans and butter. Press into prepared pan; set aside.

2. In a large bowl, beat the cream cheese, sugar and sour cream until smooth. Add the eggs and vanilla; beat on low speed just until combined. Pour over the crust. Bake at 325° for 35-40 minutes or until the center is almost set. Cool on a wire rack. Freeze overnight.

3. In a microwave, melt chocolate and shortening; stir until smooth. Cool mixture slightly.

4. Using foil, lift cheesecake out of the pan. Gently peel off foil; cut cheesecake into 1¼-in. squares. Work with a few pieces at a time for dipping; keep remaining squares refrigerated until ready to dip.

5. Using a toothpick, completely dip squares, one at a time, in melted chocolate; allow excess to drip off. Place on waxed paper-lined baking sheets. Spoon additional chocolate over the tops if necessary to coat. (Reheat chocolate if needed to finish dipping.) Let stand for 20 minutes or until set. Store in an airtight container in the refrigerator or freezer.

Grilled Peaches with Brandy Sauce

Fresh peaches get amazing flavor from grilling on a maple plank. Then, brandy sauce and ice cream take them over the top.

—TASTE OF HOME TEST KITCHEN

PREP: 25 MIN. • **GRILL:** 20 MIN.
MAKES: 6 SERVINGS

- Maple grilling plank
- ¼ cup butter, cubed
- ½ cup packed brown sugar
- 2 tablespoons brandy
- 3 medium peaches, peeled and halved
- 1 pint vanilla ice cream

1. Soak grilling plank in water for 1 hour.

2. In a small heavy saucepan, melt butter. Stir in brown sugar until dissolved; remove from the heat. Stir in brandy; set aside.

3. Place plank on grill over direct medium heat. Cover and heat for 3 minutes or until light to medium smoke comes from the plank and the wood begins to crackle. (This indicates the plank is ready.)

4. Place peaches on plank. Grill, covered, over medium heat for 20-23 minutes or until tender, brushing occasionally with brandy sauce. Top each peach half with a scoop of ice cream; drizzle with remaining brandy sauce.

GRILLED PEACHES WITH BRANDY SAUCE

RASPBERRY
CUSTARD KUCHEN

Raspberry Custard Kuchen

Back where I grew up in Wisconsin, people have been baking this German treat for generations. We love it for breakfast or as a special dessert. It's no fuss to fix and impressive to serve.

—**VIRGINIA ARNDT** SEQUIM, WA

PREP: 20 MIN. • **BAKE:** 40 MIN.
MAKES: 10-12 SERVINGS

- 1½ **cups all-purpose flour, divided**
- ½ **teaspoon salt**
- ½ **cup cold butter**
- 2 **tablespoons heavy whipping cream**
- ½ **cup sugar**

FILLING
- 3 **cups fresh raspberries**
- 1 **cup sugar**
- 1 **tablespoon all-purpose flour**
- 2 **eggs, beaten**
- 1 **cup heavy whipping cream**
- 1 **teaspoon vanilla extract**

1. In a bowl, combine 1 cup flour and salt; cut in butter until mixture resembles coarse crumbs. Stir in the cream; pat onto the bottom of a greased 13x9-in. baking dish. Combine the sugar and remaining flour; sprinkle over crust.
2. Arrange raspberries over crust. In a large bowl, combine sugar and flour. Stir in eggs, cream and vanilla; pour over the berries. Bake at 375° for 40-45 minutes or until lightly browned. Serve warm or cold.

Raspberries are at their best from **May** to **November**. For a pretty look, bake the **kuchen** with a mix of **golden, black and red raspberries.**

MICROWAVE MARSHMALLOW FUDGE

Microwave Marshmallow Fudge

This foolproof fudge takes just four ingredients and 15 minutes, so it's super when time is short. It's so easy, you can fix it anytime you're craving a sweet treat. Use different flavors of frosting and chips for variety.

—**SUE ROSS** CASA GRANDE, AZ

PREP: 15 MIN. + CHILLING
MAKES: ABOUT 2 POUNDS

- 1 **teaspoon butter**
- 1 **can (16 ounces) chocolate frosting**
- 2 **cups (12 ounces) semisweet chocolate chips**
- ½ **cup chopped walnuts**
- ½ **cup miniature marshmallows**

1. Line a 9-in.-square pan with foil and grease the foil with butter; set aside. In a microwave, melt frosting and chocolate chips; stir until smooth. Stir in walnuts; cool for 10 minutes. Stir in marshmallows. Transfer to prepared pan. Cover and refrigerate until firm.
2. Using foil, lift fudge out of pan. Discard foil; cut fudge into 1-in. squares. Store in an airtight container in the refrigerator.

Salted Nut Squares

A favorite of young and old, this recipe came from my sister-in-law. It's simple to prepare and delicious. Because there's no need to keep it warm or cold, it's perfect for the potluck that has you traveling longer distances.

—**KATHY TREMEL** EARLING, IA

PREP: 15 MIN. + CHILLING
MAKES: 4½ DOZEN

- 3 **cups salted peanuts without skins, divided**
- 2½ **tablespoons butter**
- 2 **cups peanut butter chips**
- 1 **can (14 ounces) sweetened condensed milk**
- 2 **cups miniature marshmallows**

1. Place half of the peanuts in an ungreased 11x7-in. dish; set aside. In a large saucepan, melt butter and peanut butter chips over low heat; stir until smooth. Remove from the heat. Add milk and marshmallows; stir until melted.
2. Pour over peanuts. Sprinkle with the remaining peanuts. Cover and refrigerate until chilled. Cut into scant 1¼-in. squares.

LEMON GELATO

Lemon Gelato

On a recent trip to Italy, I became addicted to gelato. My favorite choice was lemon because Italian lemons have an intense flavor. This recipe brings back memories of our vacation.

—**GAIL WANG** TROY, MI

PREP: 30 MIN.
PROCESS: 20 MIN. + FREEZING
MAKES: 1½ QUARTS

- 1 **cup milk**
- 1 **cup sugar**
- 5 **egg yolks, lightly beaten**
- 3 **tablespoons grated lemon peel**
- ¾ **cup lemon juice**
- 2 **cups heavy whipping cream**

1. In a small heavy saucepan, heat the milk to 175°; stir in sugar until dissolved. Whisk a small amount of hot mixture into egg yolks. Return all to the pan, whisking constantly. Add lemon peel. Cook over low heat until mixture is just thick enough to coat a metal spoon and a thermometer reads at least 160°, stirring constantly. Do not allow to boil. Remove from heat immediately. Stir in lemon juice.

2. Remove immediately from heat; stir in lemon juice and cream. Place in a bowl. Press plastic wrap onto the surface of the custard; refrigerate several hours or overnight.

3. Fill cylinder of ice cream freezer two-thirds full; freeze according to the manufacturer's directions. (Refrigerate remaining mixture until ready to freeze.) Transfer to freezer containers, allowing headspace for expansion. Freeze 2-4 hours or until firm. Repeat with remaining mixture.

Cranberry Bog Bars

These easy bars combine the flavors of oats, cranberries, brown sugar and pecans. I like to sprinkle the bars with confectioners' sugar before serving.

—**SALLY WAKEFIELD** BRUCETON MILLS, WV

PREP: 25 MIN. • **BAKE:** 25 MIN. + COOLING
MAKES: 3 DOZEN

- 1¼ **cups butter, softened, divided**
- 1½ **cups packed brown sugar, divided**
- 3½ **cups old-fashioned oats, divided**
- 1 **cup all-purpose flour**
- 1 **can (14 ounces) whole-berry cranberry sauce**
- ½ **cup finely chopped pecans**

1. In a large bowl, cream 1 cup butter and 1 cup brown sugar until light and fluffy. Combine 2½ cups oats and flour. Gradually add to creamed mixture until crumbly. Press into a greased 13x9-in. baking pan. Spread with cranberry sauce.

2. In a microwave-safe bowl, melt remaining butter; stir in the pecans and the remaining brown sugar and oats. Sprinkle over cranberry sauce. Bake at 375° for 25-30 minutes or until lightly browned. Cool on a wire rack. Cut into bars.

Frozen Mud Pie

Here's one of those "looks like you fussed" desserts that is so easy, it's become a standard for me. The cookie crust is a snap to make.

—**DEBBIE TERENZINI-WILKERSON** LUSBY, MD

PREP: 40 MIN. + FREEZING
MAKES: 8 SERVINGS

- 1½ **cups Oreo cookie crumbs**
- 1½ **teaspoons sugar, optional**
- ¼ **cup butter, melted**
- 4 **cups chocolate chip or coffee ice cream, softened**
- ¼ **cup chocolate syrup**
  Additional Oreo cookies, optional

1. In a small bowl, combine cookie crumbs and, if desired, sugar. Stir in butter. Press onto the bottom and up the sides of an ungreased 9-in. pie plate. Refrigerate for 30 minutes.

2. Spoon 2 cups ice cream into crust. Drizzle with half of the chocolate syrup; swirl with a knife. Gently top with remaining ice cream. Drizzle with remaining syrup; swirl with a knife. Freeze until firm.

3. Remove pie from the freezer 10-15 minutes before serving. Garnish with whole cookies if desired.

FROZEN MUD PIE

Cinnamon Apple Dumplings

When Mom made pies to feed the crew during wheat harvest, she always had plenty of dough left over, so she treated us kids to apple dumplings. I've carried on this tradition in my own family. Now my husband and I enjoy this special dessert even when I'm not baking pies.

—MARIE HATTRUP SONOMA, CA

PREP: 20 MIN. • **BAKE:** 35 MIN.
MAKES: 2 SERVINGS

- 1 cup all-purpose flour
- ¼ teaspoon salt
- ⅓ cup shortening
- 3 tablespoons ice water
- 2 medium baking apples
- 3 tablespoons sugar
- ½ teaspoon ground cinnamon
  Half-and-half cream

SAUCE
- ⅓ cup sugar
- 2 tablespoons Red Hots or
  ¼ teaspoon ground cinnamon
- ½ teaspoon cornstarch
- ⅔ cup water
- 1 tablespoon butter
  Additional half-and-half cream, optional

1. In a bowl, combine flour and salt. Cut in shortening until the mixture resembles coarse crumbs. With a fork, stir in water until dough forms a ball. Roll out on a floured surface to a 14x7-in. rectangle; cut pastry in half.
2. Peel and core apples; place one on each square of pastry. Combine sugar and cinnamon; spoon into apples. Moisten edges of pastry with water and gather around apples; pinch seams to seal.
3. Place dumplings in an ungreased 9x5-in. loaf pan or a shallow 1½-qt. baking dish. Brush with cream.
4. In a small saucepan, combine the sugar, Red Hots, cornstarch, water and butter. Bring to a boil over medium-low heat, stirring frequently; boil for 2 minutes. Pour between dumplings.
5. Bake at 400° for 35-45 minutes or until pastry is golden brown and apples are tender. Serve warm, with cream if desired.

WHITE CHOCOLATE MACADAMIA COOKIES

FREEZE IT

White Chocolate Macadamia Cookies

White baking chips and macadamia nuts become a fantastic duo in these buttery cookies that are a nice change from the classic chocolate chip ones.

—CATHY LENNON NEWPORT, TN

PREP: 15 MIN. • **BAKE:** 10 MIN./BATCH
MAKES: 4½ DOZEN

- ½ cup butter, softened
- ⅔ cup sugar
- 1 egg
- 1 teaspoon vanilla extract
- 1 cup plus 2 tablespoons all-purpose flour
- ½ teaspoon baking soda
- 1 cup macadamia nuts, chopped
- 1 cup white baking chips

1. Preheat oven to 350°. In a large bowl, cream butter and sugar until light and fluffy. Beat in egg and vanilla. In another bowl, whisk flour and baking soda; gradually beat into creamed mixture. Stir in nuts and baking chips.
2. Drop by heaping teaspoonfuls 2 in. apart onto ungreased baking sheets. Bake 10-12 minutes or until golden brown. Cool on pans for 1 minute. Remove cookies to wire racks to cool completely.
FREEZE OPTION *Freeze cookies, layered between waxed paper, in freezer containers. To use, thaw before serving or, if desired, reheat on a baking sheet in a preheated 350° oven for 3-4 minutes.*

Greek Honey Nut Pie

I love baklava, so I thought, "Why not use phyllo, honey and nuts to make a pie? Then you can have a bigger piece!" Fans of the Greek pastry will enjoy this twist.
—**ROSALIND JACKSON** STUART, FL

PREP: 30 MIN. • **BAKE:** 40 MIN. + COOLING
MAKES: 8 SERVINGS

- 4 cups chopped walnuts
- ¼ cup packed brown sugar
- 1 teaspoon ground cinnamon
- 1 cup butter, melted
- 1 package (16 ounces, 14x9-inch sheet size) frozen phyllo dough, thawed

SYRUP
- ¾ cup sugar
- ½ cup water
- ½ cup honey
- 1 teaspoon vanilla extract

1. In a large bowl, combine the walnuts, brown sugar and cinnamon; set aside. Brush a 9-in. pie plate with some of the butter; set aside.
2. Unroll phyllo dough; keep covered with plastic wrap and a damp towel to prevent it from drying out. Layer eight sheets of phyllo in prepared pan, brushing each layer with butter and rotating sheets to cover the pie plate. Let edges of dough hang over sides. Sprinkle a third of the nut mixture onto the bottom.
3. Layer four sheets of phyllo over nut mixture in the same manner; sprinkle with a third of the nut mixture. Repeat these last two steps. Top with an additional eight sheets of phyllo, again brushing with butter and rotating sheets. Fold ends of phyllo up over top of pie; brush with butter.
4. Using a sharp knife, cut pie into eight wedges. Cut 1-2 additional sheets of phyllo into thin strips, rolling into rose shapes if desired; arrange decoratively over top. (Save remaining phyllo for another use.) Bake at 350° for 40-45 minutes or until golden brown.
5. Meanwhile, in a saucepan, combine the sugar, water and honey; bring to a boil. Reduce heat; simmer, uncovered, for 10 minutes. Add the vanilla. Pour over warm pie. Cool on a wire rack. Refrigerate leftovers.

> "A cookie mix allows family and friends to easily bake a batch of homemade treats when they have time. No one can resist the combination of chocolate and peanut butter!"
> —**JUDY CRAWFORD** AUXVASSE, MO

EAT SMART
Peanut Butter Cup Cookie Mix

PREP: 25 MIN. • **BAKE:** 15 MIN./BATCH
MAKES: 4 DOZEN

- 1¾ cups all-purpose flour
- 1 teaspoon baking powder
- ½ teaspoon baking soda
- ¾ cup sugar
- ½ cup packed brown sugar
- 18 miniature peanut butter cups, quartered

ADDITIONAL INGREDIENTS
- ⅔ cup butter, softened
- 1 egg

In a small bowl, combine the flour, baking powder and baking soda. In a 1-qt. glass jar, layer the sugar, brown sugar and flour mixture; top with peanut butter cups. Cover and store in a cool dry place for up to 1 month.
TO PREPARE COOKIES *In a large bowl, beat butter and egg until well blended. Add contents of jar and stir until combined. Shape dough into 1-in. balls. Place 2 in. apart on greased baking sheets (do not flatten). Bake at 375° for 12-14 minutes or until lightly browned. Remove to wire racks. Store in an airtight container.*
PER SERVING *1 cookie equals 75 cal., 3 g fat (2 g sat. fat), 11 mg chol., 50 mg sodium, 10 g carb., trace fiber, 1 g pro.*
Diabetic Exchanges: *1 starch, ½ fat.*

GREEK HONEY NUT PIE

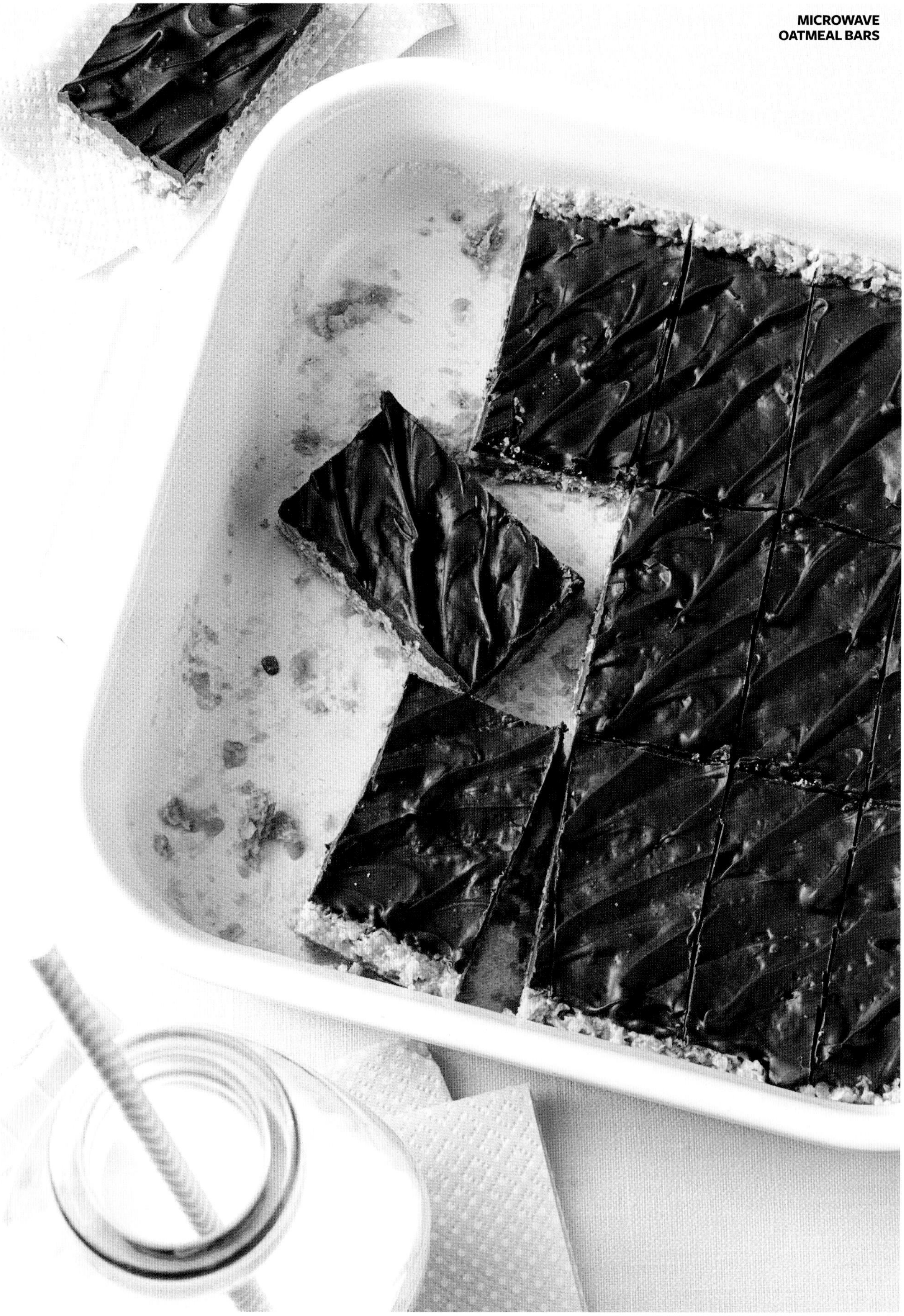

MICROWAVE OATMEAL BARS

Microwave Oatmeal Bars

My mother shared this speedy recipe with me. There are not a lot of ingredients, making these microwave treats easy enough for kids to whip up.

—ANNETTE SELF JUNCTION CITY, OH

PREP: 20 MIN. + CHILLING
MAKES: 8-10 SERVINGS

- 2 cups quick-cooking oats
- ½ cup packed brown sugar
- ½ cup butter, melted
- ¼ cup corn syrup
- 1 cup (6 ounces) semisweet chocolate chips

1. In a large bowl, combine oats and brown sugar. Stir in butter and corn syrup. Press into a greased 9-in.-square microwave-safe dish.

2. Microwave, uncovered, on high for 1½ minutes. Rotate a half turn; microwave for 1½ minutes longer. Sprinkle with the chocolate chips. Microwave at 30% power for 4½ minutes or until chips are glossy; spread chocolate evenly over top.

3. Refrigerate bars for 15-20 minutes before cutting.

NOTE *This recipe was tested in a 1,100-watt microwave.*

Corn syrup is an **invert** sugar, meaning it is **liquid** in its natural state. This quality helps it stop sugar **crystals** from forming in **frostings**, candies and other **sweet** recipes.

Rustic Autumn Fruit Tart

This beautiful dessert, featuring rich, buttery pastry with slices of apple and pear, is surprisingly simple.

—JENNIFER WICKES PINE BEACH, NJ

PREP: 25 MIN. + CHILLING
BAKE: 40 MIN. + COOLING
MAKES: 6 SERVINGS

- ½ cup butter, softened
- 4 ounces cream cheese, softened
- 1½ cups all-purpose flour
- 2 large apples, peeled and thinly sliced
- 1 medium pear, peeled and thinly sliced
- 4½ teaspoons cornstarch
- ½ teaspoon ground cinnamon
- ¼ teaspoon ground cardamom
- ¼ teaspoon ground nutmeg
- ¼ cup orange juice
- ⅓ cup packed brown sugar
- ½ cup apricot jam, warmed

1. In a small bowl, beat butter and cream cheese until smooth. Gradually add flour, beating just until mixture forms a ball. Cover and refrigerate for 1 hour.

2. Preheat oven to 375°. In a large bowl, combine apples and pear. In a small bowl, combine the cornstarch and spices; stir in orange juice until smooth. Stir in brown sugar until blended. Add to apple mixture and stir gently to coat.

3. On a lightly floured surface, roll out dough into a 14-in. circle. Transfer to a parchment paper-lined baking sheet. Spoon filling over the pastry to within 2 in. of edges. Fold up edges of pastry over filling, leaving center uncovered.

4. Bake 40-45 minutes or until the crust is golden and filling is bubbly. Spread with apricot jam. Using the parchment paper, slide tart onto a wire rack to cool.

RUSTIC AUTUMN FRUIT TART

NEW ORLEANS BEIGNETS

New Orleans Beignets

These sweet French doughnuts are square instead of round and have no hole in the middle. They're a traditional part of breakfast in New Orleans.

—BETH DAWSON JACKSON, LA

PREP: 25 MIN. + CHILLING
COOK: 5 MIN./BATCH
MAKES: 4 DOZEN

- 1 **package (¼ ounce) active dry yeast**
- ¼ **cup warm water (110° to 115°)**
- 1 **cup evaporated milk**
- ½ **cup canola oil**
- ¼ **cup sugar**
- 1 **egg**
- 4½ **cups self-rising flour**
  Oil for deep-fat frying
  Confectioners' sugar

1. In a large bowl, dissolve the yeast in warm water. Add the milk, oil, sugar, egg and 2 cups flour. Beat until smooth. Stir in enough remaining flour to form a soft dough (dough will be sticky). Do not knead. Cover and refrigerate overnight.
2. Punch dough down. Turn onto a floured surface; roll into a 16x12-in. rectangle. Cut into 2-in. squares.

3. In an electric skillet or a deep-fat fryer, heat the oil to 375°. Fry dough squares, a few at a time, until golden brown on both sides. Drain on paper towels. Roll warm beignets in the confectioners' sugar.
NOTE *As a substitute for each cup of self-rising flour, place 1½ teaspoons baking powder and ½ teaspoon salt in a measuring cup. Add all-purpose flour to measure 1 cup.*

Breakfast Upside-Down Cake

This golden cake quickly became my husband's morning favorite. And because it calls for boxed muffin mix and canned pineapple, I never have a problem finding the time to make it for him. Plus, it's pretty enough to serve to company.

—STACY WALKER WINSOR HEIGHTS, IA

PREP: 20 MIN. + RESTING
BAKE: 40 MIN. + COOLING
MAKES: 8 SERVINGS

- 1 **package (18¼ ounces) blueberry muffin mix**
- 1 **package (¼ ounce) quick-rise yeast**
- 1 **can (8 ounces) sliced pineapple**
- 1 **egg, lightly beaten**
- ⅓ **cup packed brown sugar**
- ¼ **cup butter, melted**
- 4 **maraschino cherries, halved**
  Fresh blueberries, optional

1. Rinse and drain blueberries from muffin mix; set aside. Combine muffin mix and yeast in a large bowl; set aside.
2. Drain pineapple, reserving juice in a measuring cup. Set pineapple aside. Add enough water to juice to measure ⅔ cup.
3. Pour into saucepan; heat to 120°-130°. Add to muffin mix; stir just until moistened. Beat in the egg. Cover and let rest for 10 minutes.
4. Combine brown sugar and butter; pour into a greased 9-in. round baking pan. Cut each pineapple slice in half; arrange over brown sugar mixture. Tuck cherries into pineapple.
5. Spoon half of batter over the pineapple. Sprinkle with reserved blueberries. Spread with the remaining batter.
6. Bake at 350° for 40-45 minutes or until a toothpick inserted into cake comes out clean. Immediately invert onto a serving plate. Cool completely. Garnish cake with fresh blueberries if desired.

Chocolate Lover's Pudding

I first made this dish when my husband asked me, "Why don't you ever make chocolate pudding?" It's not too rich, but it has an amazing chocolate flavor. Let's just say he doesn't have to ask me anymore—I love preparing this easy homemade treat.

—CHARIS O'CONNELL MOHNTON, PA

START TO FINISH: 30 MIN.
MAKES: 6 SERVINGS

- ½ cup sugar, divided
- 3 cups 2% milk
- 3 tablespoons cornstarch
- ¼ teaspoon salt
- 2 egg yolks, beaten
- ⅓ cup baking cocoa
- 2 ounces semisweet chocolate, chopped
- 1 tablespoon butter
- 2 teaspoons vanilla extract
  Fresh raspberries, optional

1. In a large heavy saucepan, combine ¼ cup sugar and milk. Bring just to a boil, stirring occasionally. Meanwhile, in a large bowl, combine cornstarch, salt and remaining sugar; whisk in egg yolks until smooth.

2. Slowly pour hot milk mixture in a thin stream into egg yolk mixture, whisking constantly. Whisk in cocoa. Return mixture to the saucepan and bring to a boil, stirring constantly until thickened, about 1 minute. Immediately remove from the heat.

3. Stir in the chocolate, butter and vanilla until melted. Whisk until completely smooth. Cool 15 minutes, stirring occasionally. Transfer to dessert dishes. Serve pudding warm or refrigerate, covered, 1 hour. Just before serving, top with raspberries if desired.

CHOCOLATE LOVER'S PUDDING

Butterscotch Cookies

This old-fashioned recipe has been in my family for years. It's one of my go-to cookies when I want something sweet.

—BEVERLY DUNCAN LAKEVILLE, OH

PREP: 20 MIN. + CHILLING
BAKE: 10 MIN./BATCH
MAKES: ABOUT 1½ DOZEN

- 2 tablespoons butter, softened
- 2 tablespoons shortening
- 1 cup packed brown sugar
- 1 egg
- 1 teaspoon vanilla extract
- 1½ cups all-purpose flour
- ¾ teaspoon baking soda
- ¾ teaspoon cream of tartar
- ¼ teaspoon salt
- ¼ cup English toffee bits or almond brickle chips
- ¼ cup finely chopped pecans

1. In a large bowl, cream butter, shortening and brown sugar until light and fluffy. Beat in egg and vanilla. Combine flour, baking soda, cream of tartar and salt; gradually add to creamed mixture and mix well. Stir in toffee bits and pecans. Shape into a 10-in. roll; wrap in plastic wrap. Refrigerate 4 hours or until firm.

2. Preheat oven to 375°. Unwrap dough and cut into ½-in. slices. Place 2 in. apart on baking sheets coated with cooking spray. Bake 9-11 minutes or until lightly browned. Cool cookies for 1-2 minutes before removing from pans to wire racks.

FREEZE OPTION *Place wrapped logs in a resealable plastic freezer bag; freeze. To use, unwrap frozen logs and cut into slices. If necessary, let dough stand a few minutes at room temperature before cutting. Bake as directed.*

CHERRY
CANNOLI CUPS

Sugar and Spice Pear Pie

My family loves pear pie because it's a little less tart than apple pie. This recipe's buttery crust complements the tender spiced fruit and crunchy pecans.

—**KRISTINA PONTIER** HILLSBORO, OR

PREP: 30 MIN. + STANDING
BAKE: 40 MIN. + COOLING
MAKES: 8 SERVINGS

- 5 **large pears, peeled and sliced**
- ¾ **cup sugar**
- ¼ **cup orange juice**
- 4½ **teaspoons quick-cooking tapioca**
- 1 **tablespoon grated lemon peel**
- 1 **teaspoon lemon juice**
- ½ **teaspoon ground nutmeg**
- ¼ **teaspoon salt**
- ¼ **teaspoon minced fresh gingerroot**
  Pastry for double-crust pie (9 inches)
- ½ **cup chopped pecans**
- ¼ **cup packed brown sugar**
- 3 **tablespoons butter**

1. Preheat oven to 400°. In a large bowl, combine first nine ingredients. Let stand 15 minutes.
2. Line a 9-in. pie plate with bottom crust; trim pastry even with edge. Sprinkle with pecans and brown sugar; fill with pear mixture. Dot with butter. Roll out remaining pastry to fit top of pie; place over filling. Trim, seal and flute edges. Cut slits in pastry.
3. Bake 40-45 minutes or until crust is golden brown and filling is bubbly. Cover edges with foil during the last 15 minutes to prevent overbrowning if necessary. Cool on a wire rack.
NOTE *To create a top crust similar to the one in the photo, roll out top crust on parchment paper. Using a 1-in. cutter (a leaf cutter was used for the photo), cut out dough, leaving about 1 in. of dough around each cutout. Reserve cutouts. Slide parchment paper onto a baking sheet. Freeze for 10-15 minutes. Carefully flip top crust onto pie. Trim, seal and flute edges. Score veins into reserved leaf cutouts. Moisten bottoms of cutouts with water and place along edge of pie crust.*

Cherry Cannoli Cups

Here's a sweet taste of Italy without a lot of fuss. The cute little cups, filled with a rich cherry-cheese filling, are cleverly made with wonton wrappers.

—**MARIE SHEPPARD** CHICAGO, IL

PREP: 40 MIN. • **MAKES:** 4 DOZEN

- 48 **wonton wrappers**
- ¼ **cup butter, melted**
- ¼ **cup sugar**
- 2 **cups chopped hazelnuts, divided**
- 1 **carton (15 ounces) part-skim ricotta cheese**
- 4 **ounces cream cheese, softened**
- 3 **tablespoons confectioners' sugar**
- 1 **tablespoon hazelnut liqueur, optional**
- 1 **teaspoon vanilla extract**
- 2 **jars (one 16 ounces, one 10 ounces) maraschino cherries, drained**

1. Place wonton wrappers on a work surface; brush with melted butter. Sprinkle with sugar. Press into greased miniature muffin cups. Sprinkle each wonton cup with 1 teaspoon hazelnuts.
2. Bake at 350° for 5-7 minutes or until lightly browned. Remove to a wire rack to cool completely.
3. In a large bowl, beat the ricotta, cream cheese, confectioners' sugar, liqueur if desired and vanilla until smooth. Cut 24 cherries in half and set aside. Chop remaining cherries; fold into cheese mixture.
4. Spoon 1 tablespoon filling into each wonton cup. Sprinkle with the remaining hazelnuts. Top with a reserved cherry half.
PER SERVING *1 cannoli cup equals 109 cal., 6 g fat (2 g sat. fat), 9 mg chol., 71 mg sodium, 13 g carb., 1 g fiber, 3 g pro.* **Diabetic Exchanges:** *1 starch, 1 fat.*

SUGAR AND SPICE
PEAR PIE

General Recipe Index

Alphabetical Recipe Index